"His writings are landmarks of the managerial profession."
—*Harvard Business Review*

Peter Drucker is the most influential and widely read thinker and writer on modern organizations and their management. His books have been bestsellers in the United States and in many of the more than twenty languages into which they have been translated. Among them are: *The End of Economic Man* (1939); *Concept of the Corporation* (1946); *The Practice of Management* (1954); *Managing for Results* (1964); *The Effective Executive* (1967); *The Age of Discontinuity (1969); Management: Tasks, Responsibilities, Practices* (1974); *Managing in Turbulent Times* (1980); and *Innovation and Entrepreneurship* (1985). He has also been a frequent contributor to magazines and is an editorial columnist for the *Wall Street Journal*.

Drucker has had a distinguished career as a teacher and for more than twenty years has been professor of management at the Graduate Business School of New York University. Since 1971 he has been Clark Professor of Social Science at Claremont Graduate School, California.

Books by Peter F. Drucker

MANAGEMENT

The Frontiers of Management
Innovation and Entrepreneurship
The Changing World of the Executive
Managing in Turbulent Times
Management: Tasks, Responsibilities, Practices
Technology, Management and Society
The Effective Executive
Managing for Results
The Practice of Management
Concept of the Corporation

ECONOMICS, POLITICS, SOCIETY

Toward the Next Economics
The Invisible Revolution
Men, Ideas and Politics
The Age of Discontinuity
The Landmarks of Tomorrow
America's Next Twenty Years
The New Society
The Future of Industrial Man
The End of Economic Man

FICTION

The Temptation to Do Good
The Last of All Possible Worlds

AUTOBIOGRAPHY

Adventures of a Bystander

THE FRONTIERS
OF MANAGEMENT

Where Tomorrow's Decisions
Are Being Shaped Today

Peter F. Drucker

PERENNIAL LIBRARY

Harper & Row, Publishers, New York
Cambridge, Philadelphia, San Francisco, Washington
London, Mexico City, São Paulo, Singapore, Sydney

Much of the material in this book has been published elsewhere in slightly different form; see Acknowledgment, page 355.

Chapter 18, "Paying the Professional Schools" (originally titled "Professional Schools Ought to Reap Some of Their Graduates' Earnings"), copyright © 1982 by *The Chronicle of Higher Education*. Reprinted with permission.

A hardcover edition of this book is published by Truman Talley Books, E. P. Dutton. It is hereby reprinted by arrangement with E. P. Dutton, a division of NAL Penguin, Inc.

Library of Congress Cataloging-in-Publication Data

Drucker, Peter Ferdinand, 1909–
    The frontiers of management.

    Reprint. Originally published: New York : Truman
Talley Books, c1986.
    Includes index.
    1. Management. 2. Industrial management.   I. Title.
[HD31.D7713   1987]   658   87-45043
ISBN 0-06-097111-8 (pbk.)

87 88 89 90 91 mpc 10 9 8 7 6 5 4 3 2 1

CONTENTS

PART III. MANAGEMENT

PART IV. THE ORGANIZATION

PREFACE

The Future Is
Being Shaped Today

The thirty-seven chapters in this volume: an Interview, an Afterword, and thirty-five essays and articles, cover a broad range of subjects. Yet they were planned from the beginning to be published eventually in one volume and as variations on one unifying theme: the challenges of tomorrow that face the executive today. If there is one single postulate underlying these pieces, it is that the future is being made by totally anonymous people, a CEO here, a marketing manager there, a training director or a comptroller yonder doing mundane jobs: building a management team; developing a new pricing strategy; changing a training program so that it matches people with different educational backgrounds to new technologies; or working out a new cost-accounting analysis to find out whether automating the welding line will pay off.

This, after all, is the lesson of this century. It has been a century of unprecedented disasters and cataclysms: two world wars, a Stalin, a Hitler, a Mao, and scores of lesser but no less murderous villains. Indeed we packed into every decade as much "history" as one usually finds in a century; and little of it was benign. Yet most of this world, and especially the developed world, somehow managed not only to recover from the catastrophes again and again but to regain direction and momentum —economic, social, even political. The main reason was that ordinary people, people running the everyday concerns of everyday businesses and institutions, took responsibility and kept on building for tomorrow while all around them the world came crashing down. Thus tomorrow is being shaped today.

And what kind of tomorrow it will be thus depends heavily on the knowledge, insight, foresight, and competence of the decision makers of today, and especially of the decision makers in our institutions, that is, on executives. Yet these executives are busy people. Every one of them is already fully occupied with the daily crisis—and the daily crisis is indeed the one absolutely predictable event in the working day of the executive. To enable these busy people to see and to understand the long-range implications and impacts of their immediate, everyday, urgent actions and decisions is thus the purpose to which every one of the pieces in this volume addresses itself.

There is a second theme that runs through these thirty-seven diverse and different articles and essays: Change is opportunity. Every one of the pieces in this volume looks at changes. Some are profound and major ones, such as the impact of information on organization, the meaning of the U.S. entrepreneurial surge in the last decade, or the problems created by the success of management. Other changes are perhaps ephemeral and transitory—though for that matter no less important—for example, the mismatch between traditional jobs and the expectations and qualifications of a new, young, and educated work force. Every one of these changes might be seen as a threat and is indeed seen as such by a good many executives. Every one needs to be seen and exploited as an opportunity—for doing something different, for doing something new, and, above all, for doing something better, something more productive, something more profitable. This volume therefore aims not only at providing knowledge, insight, foresight, and competence; it aims at creating vision.

PETER F. DRUCKER
Claremont, California
Summer 1986

THE FRONTIERS OF MANAGEMENT

INTERVIEW

A Talk with a Wide-Ranging Mind

Q: *The last book of yours was the one in which you wrote about the deliberateness of the innovation process. Has there been any deliberateness in your own life? Was there a plan for Peter Drucker?*

A: In retrospect, my life makes sense, but not in prospect, no. I was probably thirty before I had the foggiest notion where I belonged. For ten or twelve years before that I had experimented, not by design but by accident. I knew, even as a little boy, that I didn't want to stay in Austria, and I knew that I didn't want to waste four years going to a university. So I had my father get me a job as far away as one could go and as far away from anything that I was eventually headed for. I was an apprentice clerk in an export house. Then I worked in a small bank in Frankfurt. It's a job I got because I was bilingual in English and German. That was October 1929. The stock market crashed, and I was the last in and the first out. I needed a job and got one at the local newspaper. It was a good education, I must say.

In retrospect, the one thing I was good at was looking at phenomena and asking what they meant. I knew in 1933 how Hitler would end, and I then began my first book, *The End of Economic Man,* which could not be published until 1939, because no publisher was willing to accept such horrible insights. It was very clear to me that Hitler would end up killing the Jews. And it was also very clear that he would end up with a treaty with Stalin.

I had been quite active in German conservative politics even though I had a foreign passport, and so I knew that Hitler was not for me. I left and went first to England and then, four years later, to this country. I worked in London for an insurance company as a securities analyst and as an investment banker. If I had wanted to be a rich man I would have stayed there, but it bored me to tears.

Q: *Would you define* entrepreneur?

A: The definition is very old. It is somebody who endows resources with new wealth-producing capacity. That's all.

Q: *You make the point that small business and entrepreneurial business are not necessarily the same thing.*

A: The great majority of small businesses are incapable of innovation, partly because they don't have the resources, but a lot more because they don't have the time and they don't have the ambition. I'm not even talking of the corner cigar store. Look at the typical small business. It's grotesquely understaffed. It doesn't have the resources and the cash flow. Maybe the boss doesn't sweep the store anymore, but he's not that far away. He's basically fighting the daily battle. He doesn't have, by and large, the discipline. He doesn't have the background. The most successful of the young entrepreneurs today are people who have spent five to eight years in a big organization.

Q: *What does that do for them?*

A: They learn. They get tools. They learn how to do a cash-flow analysis and how one trains people and how one delegates and how one builds a team. The ones without that background are the entrepreneurs who, no matter how great their success, are being pushed out. For example, if you ask me what's wrong with [Apple Computer Inc. cofounders] Wozniak and Jobs . . .

Q: *That's exactly what I was going to ask.*

A: They don't have the discipline. They don't have the tools, the knowledge.

Q: *But that's the company that we've looked to for the past five or six years as being prototypical of entrepreneurial success.*

A: I am on record as saying that those two young men would not survive. The Lord was singularly unkind to them.

Q: *Really?*

A: By giving them too much success too soon. If the Lord wants to destroy, He does what He did to those two. They never got their noses rubbed in the dirt. They never had to dig. It came too easy. Success made them arrogant. They don't know the simple elements. They're like an architect who doesn't know how one drives a nail or what a stud is. A great strength is to have five to ten years of, call it management, under your belt before you start. If you don't have it, then you make these elementary mistakes.

Q: *People who haven't had this big-company experience you prescribe: would you tell them that they shouldn't attempt their own enterprise?*

A: No, I would say read my entrepreneurial book, because that's what it's written for. We have reached the point [in entrepreneurial management] where we know what the practice is, and it's not waiting around for the muse to kiss you. The muse is very, very choosy, not only in whom she kisses but in where she kisses them. And so one can't wait.

In high tech, we have the old casualty rate among young companies, eight out of ten, or seven out of ten. But outside of high tech, the rate is so much lower.

Q: *Because?*

A: Because they have the competence to manage their enterprises and to manage themselves. That's the most difficult thing for the person who starts his own business, to redefine his own role in the business.

Q: *You make it sound so easy in the book.*

A: It is simple, but not easy. What you have to do and how you do it are incredibly simple. Are you willing to do it? That is another matter. You have to ask the question.

There is a young man I know who starts businesses. He is on his fifth. He develops them to the point that they are past the baby diseases and then sells out. He's a nanny. You know, when I grew up there were still nannies around, and most of them used to give notice on the day their child spoke its first word. Then it was no longer a baby. That's what this particular fellow is, a baby nurse. When his companies reach twenty-nine employees he says, "Out!" I ask why and he says, "Once I get to thirty people, including myself, then I have to manage them, and I'm simply not going to do anything that stupid."

Q: *That example would tend to confirm the conventional wisdom, which holds that there are entrepreneurs and there are managers, but that the two are not the same.*

A: Yes and no. You see, there is entrepreneurial work and there is managerial work, and the two are not the same. But you can't be a successful entrepreneur unless you manage, and if you try to manage without some entrepreneurship, you are in danger of becoming a bureaucrat. Yes, the work is different, but that's not so unusual.

Look at entrepreneurial businesses today. A lot of them are built around somebody in his fifties who came straight out of college, engineering school, and went to work for GE. Thirty years later, he is in charge of market research for the small condenser department and is very nicely paid. His mortgage is paid up and his pension is vested, the kids are grown, and he enjoys the work and likes GE, but he knows he's never going to be general manager of the department, let alone of the division. And that's when he takes early retirement, and three weeks later, he's working for one of the companies around Route 128 in Boston. This morning I talked to one of those men. He had been in market planning and market research for a du Pont division—specialty chemicals—and he said, "You know, I was in my early fifties, and I enjoyed it, but they wanted to transfer me. . . ." Do I have to finish the story?

So now he's a vice-president for marketing on Route 128 in a company where he is badly needed, an eight-year-old company of engineers that has grown very fast and has outgrown its marketing. But he knows how one does it. At du Pont, was he an entrepreneur or was he a manager? He knows more about how one finds new markets than the boys at his new company do. He's been doing it for thirty years. It's routine. You come out with something, and it works fine in the market, but then you see what other markets there are that you never heard of. There are lots of markets that have nothing to do with the treatment of effluents, or whatever that company does, but they didn't know how to find them until this fellow came along.

There is entrepreneurial work and there is managerial work, and most people can do both. But not everybody is attracted to them equally. The young man I told you about who starts companies, he asked himself the question, and his answer was, "I don't want to run a business."

Q: *Isn't there some irony in the fact that you who study organizations aren't part of one?*

A: I couldn't work in a large organization. They bore me to tears.

Q: *Aren't you being very hard on the Route 128 and Silicon Valley people? You've called them arrogant, immature.*

A: High tech is living in the nineteenth century, the premanagement world. They believe that people pay for technology. They have a romance with technology. But people don't pay for technology: they pay for what they get out of technology.

If you look at the successful companies, they are the ones who either learn management or bring it in. In the really successful high-tech companies, the originator isn't usually there five years later. He may be on the board; he may be honorary chairman; but he is out, and usually with bitterness. The Apple story is different only in its dimensions. Steve Jobs lacked the discipline. I don't mean the self-discipline. I mean the basic knowledge and the willingness to apply it.

High tech, precisely because it has all the glamour, is

prone to arrogance far more than any other. But it's not confined to high tech.

Q: *Where else?*

A: Finance. There's a different kind of egomaniac there, but still an egomaniac. Partly for the same reason. They make too much money too soon. It spoils you, you know, to get $450,000 in stock options at age twenty-three. It's a very dangerous thing. It's too much excitement.

Q: *This* entrepreneurial society *that you write about in the book, how did it develop? And are you absolutely persuaded that it's not just a fad?*

A: Certainly, demographics have had a lot to do with it. You go back thirty years, twenty-five years, and the able graduates of, let's say, Harvard Business School all wanted to go into big business. And it was a rational, intelligent thing to do because the career opportunities were there. But now, you see, because of the baby boom, the pipelines are full.

Another reason we have an entrepreneurial society, and it's an important reason, is that high tech has made it respectable. The great role of high tech is in creating the climate for entrepreneurs, the vision. And it has also created the sources of capital. When you go to the venture capitalists, you know, most of them are no longer emphasizing high tech. But all of them began in high tech. It was high tech that created the capital flow. And how recent this is is very hard to imagine. In 1976, I published a book on pension funds in which I said that one of the great problems in making capital formation institutional is that there won't be any money for new businesses. That was only ten years ago and at that time what I said was obvious. Today it would be silly.

The third thing promoting the entrepreneurial society perhaps is the most important, although I'm not sure whether I'm talking chicken or egg. There's been a fundamental change in basic perception over the past, make it, fifty years. The trend was toward centralization—in business, in government, and in health care. At the same time, when we came out of World War II we had discovered management. But management was something that we thought could work only in large, centralized institutions. In the early 1950s, I helped start what became the Presidents' Course given by the American Management Associations. In the first years, until 1970, for every hundred people they invited, eighty wrote back and said: "This is very interesting, but I'm not GE. What would I need management for?" And the same was true when I first started to work with the American College of Hospital Administrators, which gave a seminar in management. Hospital administrators needed it, but invariably we got the answer, "We have only ninety beds; we can't afford management." This has all changed now. Don't ask me how and when. But nowadays, the only place left where you still have the cult of bigness is in Japan. There, bigger is better and biggest is best.

So, in part, the entrepreneurial society came about because we all "learned" how to manage. It's become part of the general culture. Look, Harper & Row—who is the publisher for [Tom] Peters and [Bob] Waterman—half of the 2 or 3 million books they sold were graduation presents for high school graduates.

Q: *Your book or* In Search of Excellence?

A: Oh, no, no. Not my book. My book would be hopeless. They couldn't read it, much less master it. The great virtue of the Peters and Waterman book is its extreme simplicity, maybe oversimplification. But when Aunt Mary has to give that nephew of hers a high school graduation present and she gives him *In Search of Excellence,* you know that management has become part of the general culture.

Q: *Does the arrival of the entrepreneurial society mean that we should be rejoicing now because our national economic future is assured?*

A: No. It's bringing tremendous change to a lot of vast institutions, and if they can't learn, the changes will be socially unbearable.

Q: *Has any of them started to change?*

A: My God, yes. The new companies are the least of it, historically. The more important part is what goes on in existing institutions. What is far more important is that the American railroad has become innovative with a vengeance in the last thirty years. When I first knew the railroads in the late 1940s, there was no hope for them. I was quite sure that they would all have to be nationalized. Now, even Conrail, the government-owned railroad, makes money.

What has happened in finance is even more dramatic. In, make it, 1960, some smart cookies at General Electric Credit Corporation realized that commercial paper is a commercial loan, not legally, but economically. Legally, in this country, it's a security, so the commercial banks have a hard time using it. Our number-two bank is not Chase and not Bank of America. It's General Electric Credit.

The most robotized plant in the world is probably the GE locomotive plant in Erie, Pennsylvania. Twenty years ago, GE didn't make a single locomotive in this country. It was much too expensive. They were all made by GE Brazil. Now, the U.S. plant is far more automated than anything you could possibly find in Japan or Korea.

That's where the innovation has been, and that's where we need it, because if we don't get the changes in there we will have one corpse after another, with enormous social danger.

Q: *Is that why you wrote* Innovation and Entrepreneurship?

A: I wrote the book because I felt the time had come to be a little more serious about the topic than most of the prevailing work was and also in part because, bluntly, most of the things you read or hear seem to me, on the basis of thirty years of work and experience, to be misunderstandings. The entrepreneur—the person with George Gilder's entrepreneurial personality—yes, there are such people, but they are rarely successful. On the other hand, people whom Gilder would never accept as entrepreneurs are often very successful. Entrepreneurship is not a romantic subject. It's hard work. I wanted to dislodge the nineteenth-century folklore that holds that entrepreneurship is all about small business and new business. Entrepreneurs range from the likes of Citibank, whom nobody has accused of being new or small—or General Electric Credit

—to Edward D. Jones & Co. in St. Louis, the fastest-growing American financial-services company.

But there's another reason. When I published *Practice of Management* thirty years ago, that book made it possible for people to learn how to manage, something that up to then only a few geniuses seemed able to do, and nobody could replicate it. I sat down and made a discipline of it. This book does the same with innovation and entrepreneurship.

Q: *Well, you didn't invent the stuff.*

A: In a large part, yes.

Q: *You didn't invent the strategies. They were around before you wrote them down.*

A: Not really.

Q: *No? What I'm trying to say is that people were doing these things—finding market niches, promoting entrepreneurial behavior in their employees—before your book came out.*

A: Yes, and everybody thought it required genius and that it could not be replicated. Look, if you can't replicate something because you don't understand it, then it really hasn't been invented; it's only been done.

When I came into management, a lot of it had come out of engineering. And a lot of it came out of accounting. And some of it came out of psychology. And some more came out of labor relations. Each of those was considered separate, and each of them, by itself, was ineffectual. You can't do carpentry, you know, if you have only a saw, or only a hammer, or you never heard of a pair of pliers. It's when you put all those tools into one kit that you invent. That's what I did in large part in this book.

Q: *You're certainly one of the most accessible of the serious writers on management topics.*

A: Well, I'm a professional writer, and I do not believe that obscurity is a virtue.

Q: *Why do you work alone? No staff?*

A: I don't enjoy having to do work to keep other people busy. I want to do the work I want to do and not the work I have to do because I have to pay them or they have to eat. I'm a solo performer. I've never been interested in building a firm. I'm also not interested in managing people. It bores me stiff.

Q: *Do clients come to you now?*

A: With one exception I don't do any consulting elsewhere.

Q: *Why are you interested in business? If your overarching interest is in organizations, why not study other kinds? Why not political organizations?*

A: My consulting practice is now fifty / fifty profit-nonprofit. But I didn't come out of business. I came out of political journalism. In my second book, *The Future of Industrial Man*, I came to the conclusion that the integrating principle of modern society had become the large organization. At that time, however, there was only the business organization around. In this country, the business enterprise was the first of the modern institutions to emerge. I decided that I needed to be inside, to really study a big company from the inside: as a human, social, political organization—as an integrating mechanism. I tried to get inside, and I had met quite a few people as a journalist and as an investment banker. They all turned me down. The chairman of Westinghouse was very nice to me when I came to see him, but when I told him what I wanted he not only threw me out, he gave instructions to his staff not to allow me near the building because I was a Bolshevik. This was 1940.

By 1942, I was doing quite a bit of work for the government. I had given up looking for a company to study when one day the telephone rang and the fellow said, "My name is Paul Garrett, and I am vice-president of public relations for General Motors Corp. My vice-chairman has asked me to call you to ask whether you would be willing and available to make a study of our top management structure." Since then, nobody at General Motors has ever admitted to having been responsible for this, but that is how I got into business.

Q: *You look at business from a position that is unique. You're neither an academic . . .*

A: Though I've been teaching for fifty years.

Q: *But you don't consider yourself an academic. And you certainly don't write like an academic.*

A: That is, you know, a slur on academics. It is only in the last twenty or thirty years that being incomprehensible has become a virtue in academia.

Q: *Nor are you an operations person.*

A: No, I'm no good at operations.

Q: *So you don't get down there in the mud with your clients.*

A: Oh yes, a little. Look, whatever problem a client has is my problem. Here is that mutual fund company that sees that the market is shifting from sales commissions to no front-end loads. A terrific problem, they said. I said, no, it's an opportunity. The salesman has to get his commission right away, and the customer has to pay it over five years. That's a tax shelter. Make it into something that, if you hold it for five years, you pay not income tax but capital gains tax on it. Then you'll have a new product. It's been the greatest success in the mutual fund industry. That's nitty-gritty enough, isn't it? I let him do all the work, and he consults the lawyers. I could do it, too, but he doesn't need me to sit down with his lawyers and write out the prospectus for the SEC.

Q: *Do you read the new management books that come out?*

A: I look at a great deal of them. Once in a while you get a book by a practitioner, like [Intel Corp. president] Andy Grove's book, *High Output Management,* on how one maintains the entrepreneurial spirit in a very big and rapidly growing company. I think that's a beautiful book and very important. But in order to get a book like that, I plow through a lot of zeros. Fortunately, the body processes cellulose very rapidly.

Q: *It doesn't bother you that Tom Peters and Bob Waterman got rich and famous for a book built on ideas, Peters has said, that you had already written about?*

A: No. The strength of the Peters book is that it forces you to look at the fundamentals. The book's great weakness—which is a strength from the point of view of its success—is that it makes managing sound so incredibly easy. All you have to do is put that book under your pillow, and it'll get done.

Q: *What do you do with your leisure time?*

A: What leisure time?

Q: *Maybe I should have asked if you have any?*

A: On my seventieth birthday, I gave myself two presents. One was finishing my first novel and the other was a second professorship, this one in Japanese art. For fifty years, I've been interested in Oriental art, and now I've reached a point where I'm considered, especially in Japan, to be the expert in certain narrow areas—advising museums, helping collectors. That takes a fair amount of time.

Also, I don't know how many hundreds or thousands of people there are now all over the world who were either clients of mine or students and who take the telephone and call to hear themselves talk and for advice.

I swim a great deal and I walk a great deal. But leisure time in the sense of going bowling, no.

Q: *How do you write?*

A: Unsystematically. It's a compulsion neurosis. There's no pattern.

Q: *Do you use a typewriter?*

A: Sometimes. It depends. And I never know in advance how it's going to work.

Q: *How long, for example, does it take you to write a* Wall Street Journal *column?*

A: To write it, not very long—a day. To do it, much longer. They're only fourteen hundred, fifteen hundred words. I recently did a huge piece on the hostile takeover wave—six thousand, seven thousand words—for *The Public Interest.* I had to change quite a bit. It suddenly hit me that I know what a hostile takeover is, but how many readers do? That had to be explained. I totally changed the structure, and *that* takes a long time for me. Once I understand it, though, I can do it very fast. See, I've made my living as a journalist since I was twenty. My first job was on a paper that published almost as much copy as *The Boston Globe. The Globe* has 350 editorial employees; we were 14 employees fifty years ago, which is much healthier.

On my first day—I was barely twenty—I was expected to write two editorials.

Q: *If the business of America is business, and all that sort of thing, why don't businesspeople have a better popular image than they do?*

A: The nice thing about this country is that nobody's popular except people who don't matter. This is very safe. Rock stars are popular, because no rock star has ever lasted for more than a few years. Rock stars are therefore harmless. The wonderful thing about this country is the universal persecution mania. Every group feels that it is being despised and persecuted. Have you ever heard the doctors talk about how nobody appreciates how much they bleed for the good of humanity? Everybody is persecuted. Everybody feels terribly sorry for himself. You sit down with university professors, and it is unbelievable how terrible their lot is. The businessman feels unloved, misunderstood, and neglected. And have you ever sat down with labor leaders?

They are all of them right. It's all true. This is not a country that has great respect, and this is one of its great safeguards against tyranny. We save our adulation for people who will never become a menace—for baseball players and rock stars and movie idols who are completely innocuous. We have respect for accomplishment, but not for status. There is no status in this country. There's respect for the office of the president, but no respect for the president. As a consequence, here, everybody feels persecuted and misunderstood, not appreciated, which I think is wonderful.

Q: *Would you like to say something disrespectful about economists?*

A: Yes. Economists never know anything until twenty years later. There are no slower learners than economists. There is no greater obstacle to learning than to be the prisoner of totally invalid but dogmatic theories. The economists are where the theologians were in 1300: prematurely dogmatic.

Until fifty years ago, economists had been becomingly humble and said all the time, "We don't know." Before 1929, nobody believed that government had any responsibility for the economy. Economists said, "Since we don't know, the only policy with a chance for success is no policy. Keep expenditures low, productivity high, and pray."

But after 1929, government took charge of the economy and economists were forced to become dogmatic, because suddenly they were policymakers. They began asserting, Keynes first, that they had the answers, and what's more the answers were pleasant. It was like a doctor telling you that you have inoperable liver cancer, but it will be cured if you go to bed with a beautiful seventeen-year-old. Keynes said there's no problem that can't be cured if only you keep purchasing power high. What could be nicer? The monetarist treatment is even easier: There's nothing that won't be cured if you just increase the money supply by 3 percent per year, which is also increasing incomes. The supply-siders are more pleasant still: There's no disease that can't be cured by cutting taxes.

We have no economic theory today. But we have as many economists as the year 1300 had theologians. Not one of them, however, will ever be sainted. By 1300, the age of saints was over, more or less, and there is nothing worse than the theologian who no longer has faith. That's what our economists are today.

Q: *What about government? Do you see any signs that the entrepreneurial society has penetrated government as an organization?*

A: The basic problem of American government today is that it no longer attracts good people. They know that nothing can be done; government is a dead-end street. Partly it's because, as in business, all the pipelines are full, but also because nobody has belief in government. Fifty years ago, even twenty years ago, government was the place where the ideas were, the innovation, the new things. Japan is the only country where government is still respected and where government service still attracts the top people.

Q: *So there's nothing for government to do, in your view?*
A: Oh, no, no. The days of the welfare state are over, but

we are not going to abolish it. We have to find its limits. What are the limits? At what point does welfare do damage? This is the real question, and it's brought up by the success of the welfare state. The problems of success, I think, are the basic issues ahead of us, and the only thing I can tell you is that they don't fit the political alignments of the nineteenth and early twentieth centuries. They do not fit liberal and conservative and socialist. The traditional parties make absolutely no sense whatever to anybody of age thirty. And yet, what else is there?

Q: *Is Ronald Reagan's administration promoting or inhibiting this entrepreneurial society of yours?*

A: It's a very interesting administration: totally schizophrenic. When you look at its deeds, it hasn't done one darn thing Mr. Carter wouldn't have done. And probably he wouldn't have done it any worse either, or any better. The words, however, are different.

This is a very clear symptom, I think, that there has been an irrevocable shift in the last ten years. No matter who is in power, he would no longer believe in big government and would preach cutting expenses and would end up doing nothing about it. This is because we, the American people, are at that interesting point where we are all in favor of cutting the deficit—at somebody else's expense. It's a very typical stage in alcoholism, you know, where you know you have to stop— tomorrow.

Q: *Do you think we will?*

A: Alcoholics usually don't reform until they're in the gutter. Maybe we won't wait that long. Three years ago, to do anything about Social Security would have been unspeakable. Now it's speakable. It's not doable yet, but I think we're inching toward solutions.

Q: *You're not too worried about the future then?*

A: Well, one can get awfully pessimistic about the world. It's clearly not in good shape, but it probably never has been, not in my lifetime. One of my very early childhood memories is the outbreak of World War I. My father and his brother-in-law, who was a very famous lawyer, jurist, and philosopher, and my father's close friend at the time, who was Tomás Masaryk, the founder of Czechoslovakia, a great historian and much older of course. . . . I still remember our house. Hot-air heating pipes carry sound beautifully. Our bathroom was above my father's study. I was not quite five, and I listened at the hot-air register to my father and my uncle Hans and Masaryk saying, "This is the end not just of Austria, but of civilization." That is the first thing that I can remember clearly. And then I remember the endless obituaries in the newspaper. That's the world I grew up in and was very conscious of, the last days of anything that had any value. And it hasn't changed since. So it's awfully easy for me to be pessimistic, but what's the use of it? Lots of things worry me. On the other hand, we have survived against all odds.

Q: *It's hard to place you, politically . . .*

A: I'm an old—not a neo—conservative. The neoconservatives started out on the Left, and now they are basically old-fashioned liberals, which is respectable, but I've never been one. For instance, although I believe in the free market, I have serious reservations about capitalism. Any system that makes one value absolute is wrong. Basically, the question is not what are our rights, but what are our responsibilities. These are very old conservative approaches, and I raised them in the first book I wrote, *The End of Economic Man*, when I was in my twenties, so I have not changed.

Q: *Were you ever tempted to go into politics?*

A: No, I realized very early that I was apolitical, in the sense that I hadn't the slightest interest in power for myself. And if you have no interest in power, you are basically a misfit in politics. On the other hand, give me a piece of paper and pencil, and I start to enjoy myself.

Q: *What other things cheer you?*

A: I am very much impressed by the young people. First, that most of the things you hear about them are nonsense, for example, complaints that they don't work. I think that basically they're workaholics. And there is a sense of achievement there. But I'm glad that I'm not twenty-five years old. It's a very harsh world, a terribly harsh world for young people.

[1985]

This interview was conducted by senior writer Tom Richman and appeared in the October 1985 issue of Inc.

Part I

ECONOMICS

1

The Changed World Economy

There is a lot of talk today of the changing world economy. But
—and this is the point of this chapter—the world economy is
not *changing*. It has already *changed* in its foundations and in
its structure, and irreversibly so in all probability.

Within the last ten or fifteen years, three fundamental
changes have occurred in the very fabric of the world's economy:

1. The primary-products economy has come "uncoupled"
from the industrial economy;

2. In the industrial economy itself, production has come
uncoupled from employment;

3. Capital movements rather than trade in goods and services have become the engines and driving force of the world
economy. The two have not, perhaps, become uncoupled. But
the link has become quite loose, and worse, quite unpredictable.

These changes are permanent rather than cyclical. We
may never understand what caused them—the causes of eco-

nomic change are rarely simple. It may be a long time before economic theorists accept that there have been fundamental changes, and longer still before they adapt their theories to account for them. They will surely be most reluctant, above all, to accept that the world economy is in control rather than the macroeconomics of the national state, on which most economic theory still exclusively focuses. Yet this is the clear lesson of the success stories of the last twenty years: of Japan and South Korea; of West Germany, actually a more impressive though far less flamboyant performance than Japan; and of the one great success within the United States, the turnaround and rapid rise of an industrial New England that, only twenty years ago, was widely considered moribund.

But practitioners, whether in government or in business, cannot wait till there is a new theory, however badly needed. They have to act. And then their actions will be the more likely to succeed the more they are being based on the new realities of a changed world economy.

≫ *The Primary-Products Economy*

The collapse in nonoil commodity prices began in 1977 and has continued, interrupted only once, right after the 1979 petroleum panic, by a speculative burst that lasted less than six months and was followed by the fastest drop in commodity prices ever recorded.

In early 1986, overall, raw-materials prices (other than petroleum*) were at the lowest level in recorded history in relation to the prices of manufactured goods and services—as low as in 1932, and in some cases (lead and copper) lower than at the depths of the Great Depression.

The collapse of raw-materials prices and the slowdown of raw-materials demand is in startling contrast to what was confidently predicted. Ten years ago *The Report of the Club of*

---

*And when its price dropped in early 1986 below $15 per barrel, oil too sold for no more than it did in 1933 in relation to the prices of manufactured goods and services.

Rome predicted that desperate shortages for *all* raw materials were an absolute certainty by the year 1985. Even more recently, in 1980 the *Global 2000 Report* of President Carter's administration concluded that world demand for food would increase steadily for at least twenty years; that food production worldwide would go down except in developed countries; and that real food prices would double. This forecast largely explains why American farmers bought up whatever farmland was available, thus loading on themselves the debt burden that now threatens so many of them.

But contrary to all these predictions, agricultural output in the world actually rose almost a full third between 1972 and 1985 to reach an all-time high. And it rose the fastest in less developed countries. Similarly, production of practically all forest products, metals, and minerals has been going up between 20 and 35 percent in these last ten years, again with production rising the fastest in less developed countries. And there is not the slightest reason to believe that the growth rates will be slackening, despite the collapse of prices. Indeed, as far as farm products are concerned, the biggest increase, at an almost exponential rate of growth, may still be ahead.*

But perhaps even more amazing than the contrast between what everybody expected and what happened is that the collapse in the raw-materials economy seems to have had almost no impact on the industrial economy of the world. Yet, if there was one thing that was "known" and considered "proved" without doubt in business cycle theory, it was that a sharp and prolonged drop in raw-materials prices *inevitably,* and within eighteen months to two and a half years, brings on a worldwide depression in the industrial economy. The industrial economy of the world is surely not normal by any definition of the term. But it is also surely not in a worldwide depression. Indeed,

*On this, see two quite different discussions, one by Dennis Avery, senior agricultural analyst, of the U.S. Department of State, "U.S. Farm Dilemma; the Global Bad News Is Wrong," *Science* 230, 24 (October 1985); and Barbara Insel, International Affairs Fellow at the Council on Foreign Relations in New York, "A World Awash in Grain," *Foreign Affairs* (Fall 1985).

industrial production in the developed noncommunist countries has continued to grow steadily, albeit at a somewhat slower rate, especially in Western Europe.

Of course the depression in the industrial economy may only have been postponed and may still be triggered, for instance, by a banking crisis caused by massive defaults on the part of commodity-producing debtors, whether in the Third World or in Iowa. But for almost ten years, the industrial world has run as though there were no raw-materials crisis at all.

The only explanation is that for the developed countries —excepting only the Soviet Union—the primary-products sector has become marginal where it had always been central before.

In the late 1920s, before the Great Depression, farmers still constituted nearly one-third of the U.S. population, and farm income accounted for almost a quarter of the gross national product (GNP). Today they account for one-twentieth of the population and GNP, respectively. Even adding the contribution that foreign raw-materials and farm producers make to the American economy through their purchases of American industrial goods, the total contribution of the raw-materials and food-producing economies of the world to the American GNP is, at most, one-eighth. In most other developed countries, the share of the raw-materials sector is even lower than in the United States. Only in the Soviet Union is the farm still a major employer, with almost a quarter of the labor force working on the land.

The raw-materials economy has thus come uncoupled from the industrial economy. This is a major structural change in the world economy, with tremendous implications for economic and social policy and economic theory, in developed and developing countries alike.

For example, if the ratio between the prices of manufactured goods and the prices of primary products (other than petroleum)—that is, of foods, forest products, metals, and minerals—had been the same in 1985 as it had been in 1973, or even in 1979, the U.S. trade deficit in 1985 might have been a full third less, $100 billion as against an actual $150 billion. Even the U.S. trade deficit with Japan might have been almost a third lower, some $35 billion as against $50 billion. American farm exports would have brought almost twice as much. And our industrial exports to one of our major customers, Latin America, would have held; their near-collapse alone accounts for a full one-sixth of the deterioration in U.S. foreign trade. If primary-products prices had not collapsed, America's balance of payments might even have shown a substantial surplus.

Conversely, Japan's trade surplus with the world might have been a full one-fifth lower. And Brazil in the last few years would have had an export surplus almost 50 percent higher than its actual one. Brazil would then have had little difficulty meeting the interest on its foreign debt and would not have had to endanger its economic growth by drastically curtailing imports as it did. Altogether, if raw-materials prices in relationship to manufactured goods prices had remained at the 1973 or even the 1979 level, there would be no crisis for most debtor countries, especially in Latin America.

What has happened? And what is the outlook?

Demand for *food* has actually grown almost as fast as the Club of Rome and the *Global 2000 Report* anticipated. But the supply has been growing much faster. It not only has kept pace with population growth; it steadily outran it. One cause of this, paradoxically, is surely the fear of worldwide food shortages, if not of world famine. It resulted in tremendous efforts to increase food output. The United States led the parade with a farm policy successfully aiming (except in one year: 1983) at subsidizing increased food production. The European Common Market followed suit, and even more successfully. The greatest increases, both in absolute and in relative terms, have, however, been in developing countries: in India, in post-Mao China, and in the rice-growing countries of Southeast Asia.

And then there is also the tremendous cut in waste. Twenty-five years ago, up to 80 percent of the grain harvest of India fed rats and insects rather than human beings. Today in most parts of India the wastage is down to 20 percent, the result of such unspectacular but effective infrastructure innovations as small concrete storage bins, insecticides, or three-wheeled motorized carts that take the harvest straight to a processing plant instead of letting it sit in the open for weeks on end.

And it is not too fanciful to expect that the true revolution on the farm is still ahead. Vast tracts of land that hitherto were practically barren are being made fertile, either through new methods of cultivation or through adding trace minerals to the soil: the sour clays in the Brazilian highlands, for instance, or aluminum-contaminated soils in neighboring Peru, which never produced anything before and which now produce substantial quantities of high-quality rice. Even greater advances are registered in biotechnology, both in preventing diseases of plants and animals and in increasing yields.

In other words, just as the population growth of the world is slowing down, and in many parts quite dramatically, food production is likely to increase sharply.

But import markets for food have all but disappeared. As a result of its agricultural drive, Western Europe has become a substantial food exporter plagued increasingly by unsalable surpluses of all kinds of foods, from dairy products to wine and from wheat to beef. China, some observers now predict, will have become a food exporter by the year 2000. India has already reached that stage, especially in respect to wheat and coarse grains. Of all major noncommunist countries only Japan is still a substantial food importer, buying abroad about one-third of her food needs. Today most of this comes from the United States. Within five or ten years, however, South Korea, Thailand, and Indonesia—low-cost producers that are increasing food output fast—will compete with the United States to become Japan's major suppliers. The only remaining major world-market food buyer may then be the Soviet Union, and Russia's food needs are likely to grow. However, the food surpluses in the world are so large, maybe five to eight times what Russia would ever need to buy, that the Russian food needs are not by themselves enough to put upward pressure on world prices. On the contrary, the competition for access to the

Russian market among the surplus producers—the United States, Europe, Argentina, Australia, New Zealand (and, probably within a few years, India as well)—is already so intense as to knock down world food prices.

For practically all *nonfarm commodities,* whether forest products, minerals, or metals, world demand itself—in sharp contrast to what the Club of Rome so confidently predicted— is shrinking. Indeed, the amount of raw materials needed for a given unit of economic output has been dropping for the entire century, except in wartime. A recent study by the International Monetary Fund* calculates the decline as being at the rate of one and a quarter percent a year (compound) ever since 1900. That would mean that the amount of industrial raw materials needed for one unit of industrial production is now no more than two-fifths of what it was in 1900, and the decline is accelerating. Even more startling are recent Japanese developments. In 1984, Japan, for every unit of industrial production, consumed only 60 percent of the raw materials she had consumed for the same amount of industrial production in 1973, only eleven years earlier.

Why this decline? It is not that industrial production is becoming less important, a common myth for which, as we shall see shortly, there is not the slightest evidence. What is happening is much more important. Industrial production is steadily switching from heavily material-intensive to far less material-intensive products and processes. One reason for this is the emergence of the new and especially the high-tech industries. The raw materials in a semiconductor microchip account for 1 to 3 percent; in an automobile their share is 40 percent; and in pots and pans, 60 percent. But the same scaling down of raw-material needs goes on in old industries, and with respect to old products as well as new ones. Fifty to one hundred pounds of fiberglass cable transmits as many telephone messages as does one ton of copper wire, if not more.

This steady drop in the raw-material intensity of manufac-

Real Primary Commodity Prices by David Sapsford, IMF Internal Memorandum, May 17, 1985.

turing processes and manufacturing products extends to energy as well, and especially to petroleum. To produce one hundred pounds of fiberglass cable requires no more than one-twentieth of the energy needed to mine and smelt enough copper ore to produce one ton of copper and then to draw it out into copper wire. Similarly plastics, which are increasingly replacing steel in automobile bodies, represent a raw-materials cost, including energy, of less than half that of steel.

And if copper prices were to double—and that would still mean a fairly low price by historical standards—we would soon start to "mine" the world's largest copper deposits, which are not the mines of Chile or of Utah, but the millions of tons of telephone cable under the streets of our large cities. It would then pay us to replace the underground copper cables with fiberglass.

Thus it is quite unlikely that raw-materials prices will rise substantially compared to the prices of manufactured goods (or of high-knowledge services such as information, education, or health care) except in the event of a major prolonged war.

One implication of this sharp shift in the terms of trade of primary products concerns the developed countries, whether major raw-materials exporters like the United States or major raw-materials importers such as Japan. The United States for two centuries has seen maintenance of open markets for its farm products and raw materials as central to its international trade policy. This is in effect what is meant in the United States by an "open world economy" and by "free trade." Does this still make sense? Or does the United States instead have to accept that foreign markets for its foodstuffs and raw materials are in long-term and irreversible decline? But also, does it still make sense for Japan to base its international economic policy on the need to earn enough foreign exchange to pay for imports of raw materials and foodstuffs? Since Japan opened herself to the outside world 120 years ago, preoccupation, amounting almost to a national obsession, with this dependence on raw-materials and food imports has been the driving force of

Japan's policy, and not in economics alone. But now Japan might well start out with the assumption, a far more realistic one in today's world, that foodstuffs and raw materials are in permanent oversupply.

Taken to their logical conclusion, these developments might mean that some variant of the traditional Japanese policy—highly "mercantilist" with strong deemphasis of domestic consumption and equally strong emphasis on capital formation, and with protection of "infant" industries—might suit the United States better than its own traditions. Conversely the Japanese might be better served by some variant of America's traditional policies, and especially by shifting from favoring savings and capital formation to favoring consumption. But is such a radical break with a hundred years and more of political convictions and commitments likely? Still, from now on the fundamentals of economic policy are certain to come under increasing criticism in these two countries, and in all other developed countries as well.

They will also, however, come under increasing scrutiny in major Third World nations. For if primary products are becoming of marginal importance to the economics of the developed world, traditional development theories and traditional development policies are losing their foundations. All of them are based on the assumption, historically a perfectly valid one, that developing countries pay for imports of capital goods by exporting primary materials—farm and forest products, minerals, metals. All development theories, however much they differ otherwise, further assume that raw-materials purchases on the part of the industrially developed countries must rise at least as fast as industrial production in these countries. This then implies that, over any extended period of time, any raw-materials producer becomes a better credit risk and shows a more favorable balance of trade. But this has become highly doubtful. On what foundation, then, can economic development be based, especially in countries that do not have a large enough population to develop an industrial economy based on the home market? And, as we shall presently see, economic development of these countries can also no longer be based on low labor costs.

≫ What "De-Industrialization" Means

The second major change in the world economy is the uncoupling of manufacturing production from manufacturing employment. To increase manufacturing production in developed countries has actually come to mean *decreasing* blue-collar employment. As a consequence, labor costs are becoming less and less important as a "comparative cost" and as a factor in competition.

There is a great deal of talk these days about the "de-industrialization" of America. But in fact, manufacturing production has gone up steadily in absolute volume and has not gone down at all as a percentage of the total economy. Ever since the end of the Korean War, that is, for more than thirty years, it has held steady at around 23 to 24 percent of America's total GNP. It has similarly remained at its traditional level in all of the major industrial countries.

It is not even true that American industry is doing poorly as an exporter. To be sure, this country is importing far more manufactured goods than it ever did from both Japan and Germany. But it is also exporting more than ever before—despite the heavy disadvantage in 1983, 1984, and most of 1985 of a very expensive dollar, of wage increases larger than our main competitors had, and of the near-collapse of one of our main industrial markets, Latin America. In 1984, the year the dollar soared, exports of American manufactured goods rose by 8.3 percent, and they went up again in 1985. The share of U.S.–manufactured exports in world exports was 17 percent in 1978. By 1985 it had risen to 20 percent, with West Germany accounting for 18 percent and Japan for 16 (the three countries together thus accounting for more than half of the total).

Thus it is not the American economy that is being "de-industrialized." It is the American labor force.

Between 1973 and 1985, manufacturing production in the United States actually *rose* by almost 40 percent. Yet manufacturing employment during that period went down steadily. There are now 5 million fewer people employed in blue-collar work in the American manufacturing industry than there were in 1975.

Yet in the last twelve years total employment in the United States grew faster than at any time in the peacetime history of any country—from 82 to 110 million between 1973 and 1985, that is, by a full third. The entire growth, however, was in nonmanufacturing, and especially in non–blue-collar jobs.

The trend itself is not new. In the 1920s, one out of every three Americans in the labor force was a blue-collar worker in manufacturing. In the 1950s, the figure was still one in every four. It now is down to one in every six—and dropping.

But although the trend has been running for a long time, it has lately accelerated to the point where, in peacetime at least, no increase in manufacturing production, no matter how large, is likely to reverse the long-term decline in the number of blue-collar jobs in manufacturing or in their proportion of the labor force.

And the trend is the same in all developed countries and is, indeed, even more pronounced in Japan. It is therefore highly probable that developed countries such as the United States or Japan will, by the year 2010, employ no larger a proportion of the labor force in manufacturing than developed countries now employ in farming—at most, one-tenth. Today the United States employs around 18 million people in blue-collar jobs in the manufacturing industry. Twenty-five years hence the number is likely to be 10—at most, 12—million. In some major industries the drop will be even sharper. It is quite unrealistic, for instance, to expect the American automobile industry to employ, twenty-five years hence, more than one-third of its present blue-collar force, even though production might be 50 percent higher.

If a company, an industry, or a country does not succeed

in the next quarter century in sharply increasing manufacturing production, while sharply reducing the blue-collar work force, it cannot hope to remain competitive, or even to remain "developed." It would decline fairly fast. Great Britain has been in industrial decline these last twenty-five years, largely because the number of blue-collar workers per unit of manufacturing production went down far more slowly than in all other noncommunist developed countries. Yet Britain has the highest unemployment rate among noncommunist developed countries: more than 13 percent.

The British example indicates a new but critical economic equation: A country, an industry, or a company that puts the preservation of blue-collar manufacturing jobs ahead of being internationally competitive (and that implies steady shrinkage of such jobs) will soon have neither production nor steady jobs. The attempt to preserve industrial blue-collar jobs is actually a prescription for unemployment.

On the national level, this is accepted only in Japan so far. Indeed, Japanese planners, whether those of the government or those of private business, start out with the assumption of a doubling of production within fifteen or twenty years based on a cut in blue-collar employment of 25 to 40 percent. And a good many large American companies such as IBM, General Electric, or the big automobile companies forecast parallel development. Implicit in this is also the paradoxical fact that a country will have the less *general* unemployment the faster it shrinks blue-collar employment in manufacturing.

But this is not a conclusion that politicians, labor leaders, or indeed the general public can easily understand or accept.

What will confuse the issue even more is that we are experiencing several separate and different shifts in the manufacturing economy.

One is the acceleration of the substitution of knowledge and capital for manual labor. Where we spoke of *mechanization* a few decades ago, we now speak of *robotization* or *automation*. This is actually more a change in terminology than a change in reality. When Henry Ford introduced the assembly line in 1909, he cut the number of man-hours required to produce a motorcar by some 80 percent in two or three years: far more than anybody expects to happen as a result even of the most complete robotization. But there is no doubt that we are facing a new, sharp acceleration in the replacement of manual workers by machines, that is, by the products of knowledge.

A second development—and in the long run it may be fully as important if not more important—is the shift from industries that are primarily labor-intensive to industries that, from the beginning, are primarily knowledge-intensive. The costs of the semiconductor microchip are about 70 percent knowledge and no more than 12 percent labor. Similarly, of the manufacturing costs of prescription drugs, "labor" represents no more than 10 or 15 percent, with knowledge—research, development, and clinical testing—representing almost 50 percent. By contrast, in the most fully robotized automobile plant labor would still account for 20 or 25 percent of the costs.

Another, and highly confusing, development in manufacturing is the reversal of the dynamics of size. Since the early years of this century, the trend in all developed countries has been toward larger and ever larger manufacturing plants. The "economies of scale" greatly favored them. Perhaps equally important, what one might call the economies of management favored them. Up until recently, modern management seemed to be applicable only to fairly large units.

This has been reversed with a vengeance the last fifteen to twenty years. The entire shrinkage in manufacturing jobs in the United States has been in large companies, beginning with the giants in steel and automobiles. Small and especially medium-size manufacturers have either held their own or actually added people. In respect to market standing, exports, and profitability too, smaller and especially middle-size businesses have done remarkably better than the big ones. The same reversal of the dynamics of size is occurring in the other developed countries as well, even in Japan, where bigger was always better and biggest meant best! The trend has reversed itself even in old industries. The most profitable automobile company these last years has not been one of the giants, but a medium-size manufacturer in Germany: BMW. The only profitable steel companies worldwide have been medium-size makers of specialty products, such as oil-drilling pipe, whether in the United States, in Sweden, or in Japan.

In part, especially in the United States,* this is a result of a resurgence of entrepreneurship. But perhaps equally important, we have learned in the last thirty years how to manage the small and medium-size enterprise—to the point that the advantages of smaller size, for example, ease of communications and nearness to market and customer, increasingly outweigh what had been forbidding management limitations. Thus in the United States, but increasingly in the other leading manufacturing nations such as Japan and West Germany, the dynamism in the economy has shifted from the very big companies that dominated the world's industrial economy for thirty years after World War II to companies that, while much smaller, are still professionally managed and, largely, publicly financed.

But also there are emerging *two distinct* kinds of "manufacturing industry": one group that is materials-based, the industries that provided economic growth in the first three-quarters of this century; and another group that is information- and knowledge-based, pharmaceuticals, telecommunications, analytical instruments, information processing such as computers, and so on. And increasingly it is in the information-based manufacturing industries in which growth has come to center.

These two groups differ in their economic characteristics and especially in respect to their position in the international economy. The products of materials-based industries have to be exported or imported as products. They appear in the balance of trade. The products of information-based industries can be exported or imported both as products and as services.

An old example is the printed book. For one major scien-

*On this, see my book *Innovation and Entrepreneurship* (New York: Harper & Row, 1985).

tific publishing company, "foreign earnings" account for two-thirds of total revenues. Yet the company exports few books, if any; books are heavy. It sells "rights." Similarly, the most profitable computer "export sale" may actually show up in the statistics as an "import." It is the fee some of the world's leading banks, some of the big multinationals, and some Japanese trading companies get for processing in their home offices data sent in electronically from their branches or their customers anywhere in the world.

In all developed countries, knowledge workers have already become the center of gravity of the labor force, even in numbers. Even in manufacturing they will outnumber blue-collar workers within fewer than ten years. And then, exporting knowledge so that it produces license income, service fees, and royalties may actually create substantially more jobs than exporting goods.

This then requires, as official Washington has apparently already realized, far greater emphasis in trade policy on "invisible trade" and on abolishing the barriers, mostly of the non-tariff kind, to the trade in services, such as information, finance and insurance, retailing, patents, and even health care. Indeed, within twenty years the income from invisible trade might easily be larger, for major developed countries, than the income from the export of goods. Traditionally, invisible trade has been treated as a stepchild, if it received any attention at all. Increasingly, it will become central.

Another implication of the uncoupling of manufacturing production from manufacturing employment is, however, that the choice between an industrial policy that favors industrial *production* and one that favors industrial *employment* is going to be a singularly contentious political issue for the rest of this century. Historically these have always been considered two sides of the same coin. From now on, however, the two will increasingly pull in different directions and are indeed becoming alternatives, if not incompatible.

"Benevolent neglect"—the policy of the Reagan administration these last few years—may be the best policy one can hope for, and the only one with a chance of success. It is not an accident, perhaps, that the United States has, next to Japan, by far the lowest unemployment rate of any industrially developed country. Still, there is surely need also for systematic efforts to retrain and to replace redundant blue-collar workers—something that no one as yet knows how to do successfully.

Finally, low labor costs are likely to become less and less of an advantage in international trade, simply because in the developed countries they are going to account for less and less of total costs. But also, the *total* costs of automated processes are lower than even those of traditional plants with low labor costs, mainly because automation eliminates the hidden but very high costs of "not working," such as the costs of poor quality and of rejects, and the costs of shutting down the machinery to change from one model of a product to another.

Examples are two automated U.S. producers of television receivers, Motorola and RCA. Both were almost driven out of the market by imports from countries with much lower labor costs. Both then automated, with the result that their American-made products successfully compete with foreign imports. Similarly, some highly automated textile mills in the Carolinas can underbid imports from countries with very low labor costs, for example, Thailand. Conversely, in producing semiconductors, some American companies have low labor costs because they do the labor-intensive work offshore, for instance, in West Africa. Yet they are the high-cost producers, with the heavily automated Japanese easily underbidding them, despite much higher labor costs.

The cost of capital will thus become increasingly important in international competition. And it is the cost in respect to which the United States has become, in the last ten years, the highest-cost country—and Japan the lowest-cost one. A reversal of the U.S. policy of high interest rates and of high cost of equity capital should thus be a priority of American policymakers, the direct opposite of what has been U.S. policy for the past five years. But this, of course, demands that cutting the government deficit rather than high interest rates becomes our defense against inflation.

For developed countries, and especially for the United States, the steady downgrading of labor costs as a major competitive factor could be a positive development. For the Third World, and especially for the *rapidly industrializing countries* —Brazil, for instance, or South Korea or Mexico—it is, however, bad news. Of the rapidly industrializing countries of the nineteenth century, one, Japan, developed herself by exporting raw materials, mainly silk and tea, at steadily rising prices. One, Germany, developed by "leapfrogging" into the "high-tech" industries of its time, mainly electricity, chemicals, and optics. The third rapidly industrializing country of the nineteenth century, the United States, did both. Both ways are blocked for the present rapidly industrializing countries: the first one because of the deterioration of the terms of trade for primary products, the second one because it requires an "infrastructure" of knowledge and education far beyond the reach of a poor country (although South Korea is reaching for it!). Competition based on lower labor costs seemed to be the way out. Is this way going to be blocked too?

≫ *From* "Real" *to* "Symbol" *Economy*

The third major change is the emergence of the *symbol economy*—capital movements, exchange rates and credit flow —as the flywheel of the world economy, in the place of the *real economy*: the flow of goods and services—and largely independent of the latter. It is both the most visible and yet the least understood of the changes.

World trade in goods is larger, much larger, than it has ever been before. And so is the invisible trade, the trade in services. Together, the two amount to around $2.5 to $3 trillion a year. But the London Eurodollar market, in which the world's financial institutions borrow from and lend to each other, turns over $300 billion each working day, or $75 trillion a year, that is, at least twenty-five times the volume of world trade.

In addition, there are the (largely separate) foreign-exchange transactions in the world's main money centers, in which one currency is traded against another (for example, U.S. dollars against the Japanese yen). These run around $150 billion a day, or about $35 trillion a year: twelve times the worldwide trade in goods and services.

No matter how many of these Eurodollars, or yen, or Swiss francs are just being moved from one pocket into another and thus counted more than once, there is only one explanation for the discrepancy between the volume of international money transactions and the trade in goods and services: capital movements unconnected to, and indeed largely independent of, trade greatly exceed trade finance.

There is no one explanation for this explosion of international—or more accurately, transnational—money flows. The shift from fixed to "floating" exchange rates in 1971 may have given the initial impetus (though, ironically, it was meant to do the exact opposite). It invited currency speculation. The surge in liquid funds flowing to Arab petroleum producers after the two "oil shocks" of 1973 and 1979 was surely a major factor. But there can be little doubt that the American government deficit also plays a big role. It sucks in liquid funds from all over into the "Black Hole" that the American budget has become* and thus has already made the United States into the world's major debtor country. Indeed, it can be argued that it is the budget deficit which underlies the American trade and payments deficit. A trade and payments deficit is, in effect, a loan from the seller of goods and services to the buyer, that is, to the United States. Without it the administration could not possibly finance its budget deficit, or at least not without the risk of explosive inflation.

*This is cogently argued by Stephen Marris, for almost thirty years economic adviser to the Organization for Economic Cooperation and Development (OECD), in his *Deficits and the Dollar: The World Economy at Risk* (Washington, D.C.: Institute of International Economics, December 1985).

Altogether, the extent to which major countries have learned to use the international economy to avoid tackling disagreeable domestic problems is unprecedented: the United States, for example, by using high interest rates to attract foreign capital and thus avoiding facing up to its domestic deficit, or the Japanese through pushing exports to maintain employment despite a sluggish domestic economy. And this "politicization" of the international economy is surely also a factor in the extreme volatility and instability of capital flows and exchange rates.

Whatever the causes, they have produced a basic change: In the world economy, the real economy of goods and services and the symbol economy of money, credit and capital are no longer tightly bound to each other, and are, indeed, moving further and further apart.

Traditional international economic theory is still neoclassical and holds that trade in goods and services determines international capital flows and foreign-exchange rates. Capital flows and foreign-exchange rates these last ten or fifteen years have, however, moved quite independently of foreign trade and indeed (for instance, in the rise of the dollar in 1984/85) have run counter to it.

But the world economy also does not fit the Keynesian model in which the symbol economy determines the real economy. And the relationship between the turbulences in the world economy and the domestic economies has become quite obscure. Despite its unprecedented trade deficit, the United States has, for instance, had no deflation and has barely been able to keep inflation in check. Despite its trade deficit, the United States also has the lowest unemployment rate of any major industrial country, next to Japan. The U.S. rate is lower, for instance, than that of West Germany, whose exports of manufactured goods and trade surpluses have been growing as fast as those of Japan. Conversely, despite the exponential growth of Japanese exports and an unprecedented Japanese trade surplus, the Japanese domestic economy is not booming but has remained remarkably sluggish and is not generating any new jobs.

What is the outcome likely to be? Economists take it for granted that the two, the real economy and the symbol economy, must come together again. They do disagree, however—and quite sharply—about whether they will do so in a "soft landing" or in a head-on collision.

The soft-landing scenario—the Reagan administration is committed to it, as are the governments of most of the other developed countries—expects the U.S. government deficit and the U.S. trade deficit to go down together until both attain surplus, or at least balance, sometime in the early 1990s. And then capital flows and exchange rates would both stabilize, with production and employment high and inflation low in major developed countries.

In sharp contrast to this is the "hard-landing" scenario. With every deficit year the indebtedness of the U.S. government goes up, and with it the interest charges on the U.S. budget, which in turn raises the deficit even further. Sooner or later, the argument goes, this then must undermine foreign confidence in America and the American dollar: some authorities consider this practically imminent. Then foreigners stop lending money to the United States. Indeed, they try to convert the dollars they hold into other currencies. The resulting "flight from the dollar" brings the dollar's exchange rates crashing down. It also creates an extreme credit crunch, if not a "liquidity crisis," in the United States. The only question is whether the result will be a deflationary depression in the United States, a renewed outbreak of severe inflation, or, the most dreaded affliction, *stagflation,* that is, both a deflationary, stagnant economy and an inflationary currency.

There is, however, also a totally different "hard-landing" scenario, one in which it is Japan rather than the United States that faces a hard—a very hard—landing. For the first time in peacetime history the major debtor, the United States, owes its foreign debt in its own currency. To get out of its debt it does not need to repudiate, to declare a moratorium, or to negotiate a rollover. All it has to do is to devalue its currency, and the foreign creditor has effectively been expropriated.

For *foreign creditor* read Japan. The Japanese by now hold about half of the dollars the United States owes foreigners. In addition, practically all their other claims on the outside world are in dollars, largely because the Japanese have so far resisted all attempts to make the yen an international trading currency lest the government lose control over it. Altogether, the Japanese banks now hold *more* international assets than do the banks of any other country, including the United States. And practically all these assets are in U.S. dollars—640 *billions* of them! A devaluation of the U.S. dollar thus falls most heavily on the Japanese and immediately expropriates them.

But also, the Japanese might be the main sufferers of a hard landing in their trade and their domestic economy. By far the largest part of Japan's exports go to the United States. If there is a hard landing, the United States might well turn protectionist almost overnight; it is unlikely that we would let in large volumes of imported goods were our unemployment rate to soar. But this would immediately cause severe unemployment in Tokyo and Nagoya and Hiroshima and might indeed set off a true depression in Japan.

There is still another hard-landing scenario. In it neither the United States nor Japan—nor the industrial economies altogether—experiences the hard landing; this will be suffered by the already depressed primary-products producers. Practically all primary materials are traded in dollars; thus, their prices may not go up at all should the dollar be devalued. They actually went down when the dollar plunged by 30 percent between June 1985 and January 1986. Japan may thus be practically unaffected by a dollar devaluation; all she needs her dollar balances for, after all, is to pay for primary-products imports, as she buys little else on the outside and has no foreign debt. The United States, too, may not suffer, and may even benefit as American industrial exports become more competitive. But while the primary producers sell mainly in dollars, they have to pay in other developed-nations currencies for a large part of their industrial imports. The United States, after all, although the world's leading exporter of industrial goods, still accounts for one-fifth only of the industrial goods on the world market. Four-fifths are furnished by others—the Germans, the Japanese, the French, the British, and so on. Their prices in U.S. dollars are likely to go up. This then might bring on a further deterioration in the terms of trade of the already depressed primary producers. Some estimates of the possible drop go as high as 10 percent, which would entail considerable hardship for metal mines in South America and Rhodesia, and also for farmers in Canada, Kansas, or Brazil.

There is, however, one more possible scenario. And it involves no "landings," whether soft or hard. What if the economists were wrong and both American budget deficit and American trade deficit could go on and on, albeit perhaps at lower levels than in recent years? This would happen if the outside world's willingness to put its money into the United States were based on other than purely economic considerations—on their own internal domestic politics, for instance, or simply on escaping political risks at home that appear to be far worse than a U.S. devaluation.

Actually, this is the only scenario that is so far supported by hard facts rather than by theory. Indeed, it is already playing.

The U.S. government forced down the dollar by a full third (from a rate of 250 to a rate of 180 yen to the dollar) between June 1985 and February 1986—one of the most massive devaluations ever of a major currency, though called a readjustment. America's creditors unanimously supported this devaluation and indeed demanded it. More amazing still, they have since increased their loans to the United States, and substantially so. There is agreement, apparently, among international bankers that the United States is the more creditworthy the more the lender stands to lose by lending to it!

And a major reason for this Alice in Wonderland attitude is that our biggest creditors, the Japanese, clearly prefer even very heavy losses on their dollar holdings to domestic unemployment. For without the exports to the United States, Japan might have unemployment close to that of Western Europe, that is at a rate of 9 to 11 percent, and concentrated in the politically most sensitive smokestack industries in which Japan is becoming increasingly vulnerable to competition by newcomers, such as South Korea.

Similarly, economic conditions alone will not induce the Hong Kong Chinese to withdraw the money they have transferred to American banks in anticipation of Hong Kong's "return" to Red China in 1997—and these deposits amount to billions. The even larger amounts, at least several hundred billions, of "flight capital" from Latin America that have found refuge in the U.S. dollar, will also not be lured away by purely economic incentives, such as higher interest rates.

The sum needed from the outside to keep going both a huge U.S. budget deficit and a huge U.S. trade deficit would be far too big to make this scenario more than a possibility. Still, if political factors are in control, then the symbol economy is indeed truly uncoupled from the real economy, at least in the international sphere.

And whichever scenario proves right, none promises a return to "normality" of any kind.

One implication of the drifting apart of symbol and real economy is that from now on the exchange rates between major currencies will have to be treated in economic theory and business policy alike as a "comparative-advantage" factor, and as a major one to boot.

Economic theory teaches that the *comparative-advantage* factors of the real economy—comparative labor costs and labor productivity, raw-materials costs, energy costs, transportation costs, and the like—determine exchange rates. And practically all businesses base their policies on this theorem. Increasingly, however, exchange rates decide how labor costs in country A compare to labor costs in country B. Increasingly, exchange rates are a major comparative cost and one totally beyond business control. And then, any firm at all exposed to the international economy has to realize that it is in two businesses at the same time. It is both a maker of goods (or a supplier of services) and a financial business. It cannot disregard either.

Specifically, the business that sells abroad—whether as an exporter or through subsidiaries in foreign countries—will have to protect itself against foreign-exchange exposure in respect to all three: proceeds from sales, working capital devoted to manufacturing for overseas markets, and investments abroad. This will have to be done whether the business expects the value of its own currency to go up or to go down. Businesses that buy abroad will have to do the same. Indeed, even purely domestic businesses that face foreign competition in their home market will have to learn to hedge against the currency in which their main competitors produce. If American businesses had been run that way during the years of the overvalued dollar, that is, from 1982 through 1985, most of the losses in market standing abroad and in foreign earnings might have been prevented. These were *management failures* rather than acts of God. Surely stockholders, but also the public in general, have every right to expect managements to do better the next time around.

In respect to government policy there is one conclusion: Don't be clever. It is tempting to exploit the ambiguity, instability, and uncertainty of the world economy to gain short-term advantages and to duck unpopular political decisions. But it does not work. Indeed—and this is the lesson of all three of the attempts made so far—disaster is a more likely outcome than success.

The Carter administration pushed down the U.S. dollar to artificial lows to stimulate the American economy through the promotion of American exports. American exports did indeed go up—spectacularly so. But far from stimulating the domestic economy, this depressed it and resulted in simultaneous record unemployment and accelerated inflation, the worst of all possible outcomes.

Mr. Reagan then, a few years later, pushed up interest rates to stop inflation and also pushed up the dollar. This did indeed stop inflation. It also triggered massive inflows of capital. But it so overvalued the dollar as to create a surge of foreign imports. As a result, the Reagan policy exposed the most vulnerable of the old smokestack industries, such as steel and automotive, to competition they could not possibly meet with a dollar exchange rate of 250 yen to the dollar (or a D Mark rate of three to the dollar). And it deprived them of the earnings they needed to modernize themselves. Also, the policy seriously damaged, perhaps irreversibly, the competitive position of American farm products in the world markets, and at the worst possible time. Worse still, his "cleverness" defeated Mr. Reagan's major purpose: the reduction of the U.S. government deficit. Because of the losses to foreign competition, domestic industry did not grow enough to produce higher tax revenues. Yet the easy and almost unlimited availability of foreign money enabled the Congress (and the administration) to postpone again and again action to cut the deficit.

The Japanese, too, may have been too clever in their attempt to exploit the disjunction between the international symbol economy and the international real economy. Exploiting an undervalued yen, the Japanese have been pushing exports, a policy quite reminiscent of America under the Carter administration. But, as earlier in America, the Japanese policy failed to stimulate the domestic economy; it has been barely growing these last few years, despite the export boom. As a result, the Japanese, as mentioned earlier, have become dangerously overdependent on one customer, the United States. And this has forced them to invest huge sums in American dollars, even though every thoughtful Japanese (including, of course, the Japanese government and the Japanese Central Bank) knew all along that these claims would end up being severely devalued.

Surely these three lessons should have taught us that government policies in the world economy will succeed to the extent to which they try to harmonize the needs of the two economies, rather than to the extent to which they try to exploit the disharmony between them. Or to repeat very old wisdom: "In finance don't be clever; be simple and conscientious." But, I am afraid, this is advice that governments are not likely to heed soon.

≫ *Conclusion*

It is much too early even to guess what the world economy of tomorrow will look like. Will major countries, for instance, succumb to the traditional fear reaction—that is, retreat into protectionism—or will they see a changed world economy as an opportunity?

Some of the main *agenda* are however pretty clear by now.

High among them will be the formulation of new *development concepts* and new development policies, especially on the part of the rapidly industrializing countries such as Mexico or Brazil. They can no longer hope to finance their development by raw-materials exports, for example, Mexican petroleum. But it is also becoming unrealistic for them to believe that their low labor costs will enable them to export large quantities of finished goods to the developed countries—which is what the Brazilians, for instance, still expect. They would do much better to go into *production sharing,* that is, to use their labor advantage to become subcontractors to developed-country manufacturers for highly labor-intensive work that cannot be automated—some assembly operation, for instance, or parts and components needed in relatively small quantities only. Developed countries simply do not have the labor anymore to do such work. Yet even with the most thorough automation it will still account for 15 or 20 percent of manufacturing work.

Such production sharing is, of course, how the noncommunist Chinese of Southeast Asia—Singapore, Hong Kong, Taiwan—bootstrapped their development. Yet in Latin America production sharing is still politically quite unacceptable and, indeed, anathema. Mexico, for instance, has been deeply committed—since its beginnings as a modern nation in the early years of this century—to making her economy less dependent on, and less integrated with, that of its big neighbor to the north. That this policy has been a total failure for eighty years has only strengthened its emotional and political appeal.

But even if production sharing is used to the fullest, it would not by itself provide enough income to fuel development, especially of countries so much larger than Chinese city-states. We thus need a new model and new policies. Can we, for instance, learn something from India? Everyone knows, of course, of India's problems—and they are legion. Few people seem to know, however, that India, since independence, has done a better development job than almost any other Third World country: the fastest increase in farm production and farm yields; a growth rate in manufacturing production equal to that of Brazil, and perhaps even of South Korea (India now has a bigger industrial economy than any but a handful of *developed* countries!); the emergence of a large and highly entrepreneurial middle class; and, arguably the greatest achievement, progress in providing both schooling and health care in the villages. Yet the Indians followed none of the established models. They did not, like Stalin, Mao, and so many of the Africans, despoil the peasants to produce capital for industrial development. They did not export raw materials. And they did not export the products of cheap labor. But ever since Nehru's death in 1964 India has encouraged and rewarded farm productivity and sponsored consumer-goods production and local entrepreneurs. India and her achievement are bound to get far more attention from now on than they have received.

The developed countries, too, need to think through their policies in respect to the Third World—and especially in respect to the hopes of the Third World, the rapidly industrializing countries. There are some beginnings: the new U.S. proposals for the debts of the primary-products countries that U.S. Treasury Secretary Baker recently put forth, or the new lending criteria which the World Bank recently announced and under which loans to Third World countries from now on will be made conditional on a country's overall development policies rather than based mainly on the soundness of individual projects. But these proposals are so far aimed more at correcting past mistakes than at developing new policies.

The other major agenda item is, inevitably, going to be the international monetary system. Since the Bretton Woods Conference at the end of World War II, it has been based on the U.S. dollar as the "reserve currency." This clearly does not work anymore. The reserve currency's country must be willing to subordinate its domestic policies to the needs of the international economy, for instance, risk domestic unemployment to keep currency rates stable. And when it came to the crunch, the United States refused to do so, as Keynes, by the way, predicted forty years ago.

The stability the reserve currency was supposed to supply could be established today only if the major trading countries —at a minimum the United States, West Germany, and Japan —agreed to coordinate their economic, fiscal, and monetary policies, if not to subordinate them to joint, and that would mean supranational, decision making. Is such a development even conceivable, except perhaps in the event of worldwide financial collapse? The European experience with the far more modest *European Currency Unit* (ECU) is not encouraging; so far, no European government has been willing to yield an inch for the sake of the ECU. But what else could be done? Or have we come to the end of the 300-year-old attempt to regulate and stabilize money on which, in the last analysis, both the modern national state and the international system are largely based?

Finally, there is one *conclusion*: Economic dynamics have decisively shifted to the world economy.

Prevailing economic theory—whether Keynesian, monetarist, or supply-side—considers the national economy, especially that of the large developed countries, to be autonomous and the unit of both economic analysis and economic policy. The international economy may be a restraint and a limitation, but it is not central, let alone determining. This "macroeconomic axiom" of the modern economist has become increasingly shaky. The two major developed countries that fully subscribe to it in their economic policies, Great Britain and the

United States, have done least well economically in the last thirty years and have also had the most economic instability. West Germany and Japan never accepted the macroeconomic axiom. Their universities teach it, of course. But their policy-makers, both in government and in business, reject it. Instead, both have all along based their economic policies on the world economy, have systematically tried to anticipate its trends, and to exploit its changes as opportunities. Above all, both make the country's competitive position in the world economy the first priority in their policies—economic, fiscal, monetary, and largely even social—to which domestic considerations are normally subordinated. And these two countries have, of course, done far better, both economically and socially, than Great Britain and the United States these last thirty years. In fact, their focus on the world economy and the priority they give it may be the real "secret" of their success.

Similarly the secret of successful businesses in the developed world—the Japanese, the German carmakers like Mercedes and BMW, ASEA and Ericsson in Sweden, IBM and Citibank in the United States, but equally of a host of medium-size specialists in manufacturing and in all kinds of services—has been that they base their plans and their policies on exploiting the world economy's changes as opportunities.

From now on any country—but also any business, especially a large one—that wants to do well economically will have to accept that it is the world economy that leads and that domestic economic policies will succeed only if they strengthen, or at least not impair, the country's international competitive position.

This may be the most important—it surely is the most striking—feature of the changed world economy.

[1986]

2

America's Entrepreneurial Job Machine

"Where have all the jobs gone?" has been the constant question in all industrial Western countries these past few years. But for the United States, another question is at least as important—perhaps much more so—and yet it is never asked: Where have all the jobs come from? All developed industrial countries are losing jobs in the smokestack industries—even Japan. But only the U.S. economy is creating new jobs at a much faster rate than the smokestack industries are losing old ones, indeed at a rate that is almost unprecedented in our peacetime history.

Between 1965 and 1984, America's population aged sixteen to sixty-five grew 38 percent, to 178 million people from 129 million. But jobs during that period increased 45 percent to 103 million from 71 million. By this fall (1984) they are likely to reach 105 million, or 106 million, which would mean a rise of almost 50 percent since 1965. And more than half this growth occurred since the energy crisis in the fall of 1973—years of "oil shocks," of two recessions, and of the near-collapse of the smokestack industries. Indeed the 1981–82 recession, for all its trauma, barely slowed the rapid pace of new-job creation. At its bottom, in fall 1982, there still were 15 million more jobs than there had been in 1973, despite record unemployment.

In Japan, jobs these past ten years have grown about 10 percent, only half the U.S. rate, to 56 million from 51 million. Western Europe has had job *shrinkage*. In Western Europe, there were 3 million fewer jobs in 1984—after full allowance for cyclical unemployment—than there were in 1974.

And the U.S. economy in 1984 had about 10 million more jobs than even optimists predicted fifteen years ago. Such a careful and authoritative expert as Columbia University's Eli Ginzberg then thought that during the late 1970s and early 1980s the federal government would have to become the "employer of first resort" to provide jobs for the children of the "baby boom." But without any government help we have provided half as many again as needed to absorb the members of the baby boom. This was in order to accommodate what nobody foresaw fifteen years ago: the rush of married women into jobs. Where have all these jobs come from?

They didn't come from the sectors that for almost forty years through the 1960s provided virtually all the new jobs in the U.S. economy: government and big business. Government stopped expanding its employment in the early 1970s and has barely maintained it since. Big business has been losing jobs since the early 1970s. In the past five years alone, the Fortune 500—the country's biggest manufacturing companies—have permanently lost around 3 million jobs. Nearly all job creation has been in small and medium-size businesses, and practically all of it in entrepreneurial and innovative businesses.

"Aha," everyone will say, "high tech." But everyone will be wrong. High technology is tremendously important: as vision setter, pace setter, excitement maker, maker of the future. But as a maker of the present it is still almost marginal, accounting for no more than 10 percent of the jobs created in the past ten years. And it is reasonably certain that its job-creation rate won't increase significantly until after 1990.

New-job creation mainly is in "low-tech" or "no-tech" businesses. One indication is *Inc.* magazine's annual list of the fastest-growing publicly owned businesses more than five years and fewer than fifteen years old. Being confined to publicly owned companies, the list has a strong high-tech bias. Yet 80 of the 100 companies on the 1982 list were decidedly low tech or no tech: women's wear makers, restaurant chains, and the like. And *Inc.*'s list of the five-hundred fastest-growing closely held companies is headed by a maker of exercise equipment for the home.

The most illuminating analysis, however, is a study of *mid-size growth companies*—those with annual sales of $25 million to $1 billion a year—made by the consulting firm McKinsey & Co. A majority of these concerns aren't high tech; a majority are manufacturers rather than service companies. These mid-size growth companies grew three times as fast as the Fortune 250, the economy's big companies, in sales, profits, and employment during 1975–1980. Even during the worst of the 1981–1982 recession, when the Fortune 250 cut employment nearly 2 percent in one year, the mid-size growth companies added 1 million jobs—or 1 percent of the country's employed labor force. And all that these companies have in common is that they are organized for systematic entrepreneurship and purposeful innovation.

For about ten years now, the U.S. economy's dynamics have been shifting to entrepreneurial and innovative businesses—mostly low tech or no tech. In economics ten years is a long time, long enough to talk of a "structural change." What explains this shift isn't clear yet. Surely there has been a sharp shift in values, attitudes, and aspirations of a lot of educated young people, a shift totally different from the "Greening of America" we were promised fifteen years ago, when the real change actually began. There are many young people around now who are risk takers and who want material success badly enough to impose on themselves the grueling discipline and endless hours of the entrepreneur.

But where does the money come from? A decade ago, we worried that there would be no capital available for new ventures; now it seems there is more venture capital than there are ventures. The biggest factor in the entrepreneurial explosion—and the one truly new technology—is probably a managerial breakthrough: the development since World War II of a body of organized knowledge of entrepreneurship and innovation.

The American development clearly disproves the most widely held and most serious explanation of the economic crisis of the past ten years and the most widely held and most serious prediction for the decades to come: the *no-growth* theory based on the "Kondratieff long wave" (named after the Russian Nikolai Kondratieff, born in 1892 and executed sometime in the 1930s on Stalin's orders because his economic model accurately predicted that collectivization would cut rather than multiply farm output).

According to the *long-wave theory,* developed economies enter a long period of inexorable stagnation every fifty years. The technologies that carried the growth in the earlier ascending stages of the Kondratieff cycle still seem to do very well during the last twenty years before the "Kondratieff bust." Indeed, they show record profits and can pay record wages; being "mature," they no longer need to invest heavily.

But what looks like blooming health is, in effect, wasting sickness; the "record profits" and "record wages" are already capital liquidation. And then when the tide turns with the Kondratieff bust, these mature industries all but collapse overnight. The new technologies are already around, but for another twenty years they can't generate enough jobs or absorb enough capital to fuel a new period of economic growth. For twenty years there is thus a "Kondratieff stagnation" and "no growth," and there is nothing anybody—least of all government—can do about it but wait it out.

The smokestack industries in the United States and Western Europe do seem to conform to the Kondratieff cycle. In Japan, too, they seem to be headed the same way and to be only a few years behind. High tech also conforms: it doesn't generate enough new jobs or absorb enough new capital yet to offset the shrinkage in the smokestack industries.

But the job creation by entrepreneurial and innovative businesses in the United States simply isn't compatible with Kondratieff. Or, rather, it bears a remarkable resemblance to the "atypical Kondratieff wave" of Germany and the United States after 1873—twenty-five years of great turbulence in these countries and of economic and social change, but also twenty-five years of rapid economic growth.

This atypical Kondratieff wave was discovered and described by Joseph Schumpeter (1883–1950) in his classic *Business Cycles* (1939). This book introduced Kondratieff to the West; but it also pointed out that the Kondratieff stagnation occurred only in England and France after 1873, the period on which Kondratieff based his long wave. Germany and the United States also had a "crash." But recovery began almost at once, and five years later both countries were expanding rapidly and continued to do so up to World War I. And what made these two countries atypical and made them the growth economies of the late nineteenth century was their shift to an entrepreneurial economy.

There are massive threats in the world economy. There is the crisis of the welfare state with its uncontrolled and seemingly uncontrollable government deficits and the resulting inflationary cancer. There is the crisis of the commodity producers everywhere, in the Third World as much as on the Iowa farm. Commodity prices for several years have been lower in relation to the prices of manufactured goods than at any time since the Great Depression, and in all economic history, there has never been a prolonged period of very low commodity prices that wasn't followed by depression in the industrial economy. And surely the shrinkage of jobs in the smokestack industries and their conversion to being capital-intensive rather than labor-intensive, that is, to automation, will put severe strains —economic, social, political—on the system.

But at least for the United States, the Kondratieff no-growth prediction is practically ruled out by what has already happened in the American economy and by the near-50 percent increase in jobs since the smokestack industries reached their Kondratieff peak fifteen or twenty years ago.

[1984]

3

Why OPEC
Had to Fail

When they meet in December 1982, the members of the Organization of Petroleum Exporting Countries will decide whether they can hold their cartel together for another year, or whether their attempt to keep both prices high and all production going has failed. The OPEC countries produced in 1982 only about 60 percent of the oil they pumped before the quadrupling of prices in 1973, and by 1982 even prices were beginning to be under pressure. Indeed, a strong case can be made that OPEC is declining just the way cartels have always declined.

To understand what is happening to OPEC, it is helpful to review the rules of cartel theory, first formulated in 1905 by a young German economist, Robert Liefmann, in his book *Die Kartelle*, and validated by all subsequent experience.

The first of these rules is that a cartel is always the product of weakness. Growing industries don't form cartels: only declining ones do.

At first, it was assumed this rule did not apply to OPEC. It was assumed that OPEC could raise prices so astronomically because oil consumption had been growing exponentially and was slated to grow even faster.

But study after study since the price explosion of 1973 shows that the developed countries had previously been growing *less* dependent on petroleum. From 1950 to 1973, the energy required to produce an additional unit of manufacturing output in developed countries declined by 1.5 percent per year; since then the decline has been much more rapid.

The story is the same in transportation. Since 1960 the energy needed for each additional passenger mile or revenue freight mile has fallen as the result of the switch to jet airplanes, to compact and subcompact cars, and to diesel bus and truck engines. Even in heating and air-conditioning, the third major consumer of energy, there has been no increase in the incremental input unit of energy since 1960.

Perhaps most important, energy use in developed countries rose faster than GNP during the first half of the century, but since 1950 it has been growing slower than GNP. In the industrial countries, to produce one unit of GNP, it took 26 percent less oil in 1982 than it had taken nine years earlier.

The relative decline in oil consumption suggests that during economic downturns the industry will drop more sharply than the overall economy but will recover less than the economy in every upturn cycle.

According to the second basic rule of cartel theory, if a cartel succeeds in raising the price of a commodity, it will depress the prices for all other commodities of the same general class.

When OPEC raised oil prices in 1973, it was generally believed that the prices of all other primary commodities—agricultural products, metals, and minerals—would rise in parallel with the petroleum price. But a year later, the prices of all other primary products began to go down. They have been going down ever since.

Indeed, the share of disposable income that developed countries spend on all primary products, including oil, is lower today than in 1973. And the terms of trade are more adverse to primary producers than they were ten years ago. They are as unfavorable as they were in the great raw materials depression of the early 1930s.

One surprising consequence of this is that Japan, the country most panicked by OPEC and the "oil shock," has actually been a beneficiary of OPEC, while the United States has been OPEC's chief victim. Japan imports all its oil. But this amounts to less than 10 percent of its total imports, with the rest consisting mostly of other primary products such as foodstuffs, cotton, timber, metals, and minerals. Their prices have come down.

Conversely, the United States is the world's largest exporter of nonpetroleum primary commodities, particularly agricultural products, whose prices are much lower than they would be were it not for OPEC.

A cartel, according to the third rule, will begin to unravel as soon as its strongest member, the largest and lowest-cost producer, must cut production by 40 percent to support the smaller and weaker members. Even a very strong producer will not and usually cannot cut further. The weaker members will then be forced to maintain their production by undercutting the cartel price. In the end, the cartel will collapse into a free-for-all. Or the strongest member will use its cost advantage to drive the weaker and smaller members out of the market. OPEC has been singularly lucky. Its second strongest member, Iran, has been forced to cut output by more than 50 percent as a result of revolution and war. Even so, the largest producer, Saudi Arabia, has had to cut its output by more than 40 percent to prevent a collapse of the cartel price. The other, weaker members, as predicted by the theory, have begun to bootleg petroleum at substantial discounts of as much as 15 percent below the posted price.

In the meantime, as the fourth of the cartel rules predicts, OPEC has lost its dominance of the oil market. "Any cartel undermines the market shares of its members within ten years or so," Mr. Liefmann concluded in 1905. In 1973, the OPEC countries accounted for almost 60 percent of the oil supply of the industrialized countries. Their share nine years later had fallen to about 45 percent (and by 1985 to a third). As predicted by cartel theory, OPEC is losing market position to newcomers outside it, such as Mexico, the North Sea, and Gabon.

The fifth and final rule is that in the end a cartel permanently impairs the position of its product, unless it cuts prices steadily and systematically, as did the only long-lived monopolists on record, the explosives cartel before World War I and the Bell Telephone System from 1910 through 1970. However, the experience of most past cartels, for example, the European steel cartel between the wars, suggests that for a long time to come, petroleum will lose markets fast when it becomes more expensive but will not regain markets by becoming cheaper.

It would be foolish to dismiss the features that distinguish OPEC from other cartels. The most important is surely geopolitics: Much of the world's petroleum, and particularly so much of the oil with low exploration and production costs, comes from areas of political instability. The developed countries might well decide to maintain costlier but politically safer sources of hydrocarbons; for example, Soviet natural gas for Western Europe or Mexican oil for the U.S. strategic petroleum reserve. But a decision to pay a premium price as political insurance could only speed the decline in consumption and in dependence on petroleum.

One cannot yet rule out what all the energy specialists predict: that the oil market is different, and OPEC will behave differently from other cartels. The test will come with the first sustained economic upturn in the developed countries. We will then know whether petroleum consumption will go up as fast as the economy, or whether, as cartel theory predicts, it will rise much more slowly or perhaps not at all.

[1982]

1986 Note: The test did indeed come with the 1983 upturn in the American economy. And as cartel theory predicted, consumption did not go up as fast as the economy, indeed hardly went up at all. What then delayed the cartel's collapse for two years, until the fall of 1985, was Saudi Arabia's willingness— possible only for a country that has very few mouths to feed —to cut production another 15 percent to below one-quarter of capacity output. But even this did not reverse the downward slide of both oil consumption and oil prices. And when the collapse came—in the fall of 1985—it went faster and further than any earlier major cartel had collapsed.

4

The Changing
Multinational

Most multinationals are still structured and run pretty much the way the American and German inventors of the species designed them, all of 125 years ago. But this design is becoming obsolete.

In the typical multinational there is a parent company with "daughters" in foreign countries. Major decisions—what products (or services) to sell worldwide, capital appropriations, key personnel—are centralized in the parent. Research and development are done exclusively in and by the parent and in its home country. But in manufacturing, marketing, finance, and people management, the daughters have wide autonomy. They are run by nationals of their own country with, at most, one or two home-office "expatriates" in the top group. And their avowed goal is to be "a good citizen of our country." The ultimate accolade for a multinational has been that a daughter is being seen in its country as "one of us." "In Stuttgart," goes the standard boast, "no one even knows that we are an American company. Our CEO there is head of the local Chamber of Commerce this year. Of course he is a German."

But every one of these design features is becoming inappropriate and, indeed, counterproductive. In the four areas where local autonomy has been the traditional goal, the multinational increasingly has to make systems decisions rather than let each daughter make decisions for itself. Even to be a "good citizen" threatens to become an impediment.

Manufacturing economics is running into head-on conflict with the traditional design. In the typical multinational, the local daughter tries to manufacture as much as possible of the end product it sells. "Ninety percent of whatever goes into the tractor we sell in France is made in France" is a typical statement. But, increasingly, even a market as big as France (even one as big as the United States) is becoming too small for efficient production of everything. Automation in particular calls for centralization across an ever-widening spectrum of products and processes.

The world's most efficient automobile-engine plant, Fiat's fully automated factory in southern Italy, needs, to be fully economical, more than twice the volume Fiat can absorb—a major reason that Fiat has been flirting with Ford-Europe as a potential marriage partner. But many services also increasingly demand specialization and centralization to be truly competitive. "That we are number one in equipment leasing in Europe," says a U.S. banker, "we owe largely to our having one centralized operation for the entire Continent, whereas each major European bank operates in one country only."

But the decision to centralize all European manufacturing of one part—compressors, for instance—in one plant in France, however justified by economics, will immediately run afoul of the "good citizen" commitment. It means "taking away jobs" from West Germany, Italy, and Britain and will thus be fought tooth and nail by the German, Italian, and British governments and by the labor unions. It is going to be opposed even more strongly by the managements of the daughters in all these countries. They will see it, with justification, as demoting them from masters in their own house to plant managers.

Similar pressures to go transnational and thus to take decisions away from the local subsidiary are also building up in marketing. Even such large countries as West Germany and France are no longer big enough or distinct enough to be discrete markets for everything. In some products and services the market has indeed become global, with customers' values, preferences, and buying habits the same, regardless of nation or culture. In other products, markets are becoming more segmented—but by life-styles, for instance, rather than by geography. In still others, the successful way to market is to emphasize the foreignness of a product (and sometimes even of a service, as witness the success of the American-style hospital in Britain). Increasingly a marketing decision becomes a systems decision. This is particularly true in respect to service to distributors and customers, which everywhere is becoming crucial.

And when it comes to finance, the "autonomous" subsidiary becomes a menace. The splintering of financial-management decisions is responsible in large measure for the poor performance of the American multinationals in the years of the overvalued dollar, when most of them lost both market standing and profitability. We do know how to minimize the impacts of exchange-rate fluctuations on both sales and profits (see Chapter 5: "Managing Currency Exposure"). Now that fluctuating exchange rates, subject to sudden wide swings and geared primarily to capital movements and to governmental decisions, have come to be the norm, localized financial management has become a prescription for disaster for anyone operating in the international economy. Financial management now requires taking financial operations away from all operating units, including the parent, and running them as systems operations, the way old hands at the game, such as Exxon and IBM, have for many years.

But in today's world economy, capital appropriations also have to be managed as systems decisions. This is the one area of multinational management, by the way, in which the Japanese are well, and dangerously, ahead of the Western-based multinational, precisely because they treat foreign units as branches, not daughters.

In the Japanese multinational, the earnings and the cash flow of the overseas units are no more "theirs" than the earnings and cash flow of the Nagoya branch are Nagoya property. This enables the Japanese to take earnings out of one unit, for example, the United States or the German one—but also out of the Japanese parent—and to invest them in developing tomorrow's growth markets, such as Brazil or India. The Western-based multinational, conversely, expects the subsidiary in Brazil or India to finance its future market development out of its own near-term earnings, with the funds earned in more mature countries earmarked for investment there, or for dividend payments. Thus the Japanese treat the world market the way American companies treat the United States, where funds earned in New England are freely used for investment in the Northwest. As a result, the Japanese are rapidly gaining control of tomorrow's markets—which in the long run may be a greater threat to U.S. (and Western) industry than Japanese competition in its home markets.

Precisely because the subsidiary of the multinational will increasingly have to become part of a system in manufacturing, marketing, and financial management, management people will increasingly have to become transnational. Traditionally the foreign unit could offer its management people careers roughly commensurate with what domestic companies of comparable size could offer: opportunities to become top management in "their" company. This top management could then expect to have authority quite similar to that of top management in a truly domestic company.

"In all my twenty years as CEO," the former head of the Swiss subsidiary of National Cash Register once said, "there were only six decisions where I had to go to the parent company in Dayton for approval." Increasingly, however, almost every major decision will have to be made as a joint decision.

This means, on the one hand, that the local management of the subsidiary will have far less autonomy and will see itself as middle management. On the other hand, it will have to know the entire system rather than only its own company and its own country.

To attract the people of talent it needs, the multinational therefore increasingly will have to open its management jobs everywhere to wherever the talent can be found, regardless of passport. Also, it will have to expose prominent young people early and often to the whole system rather than have them spend their careers in their own native countries and in the subsidiaries located there. A few multinationals do this already, IBM and Citicorp foremost among them. A Venezuelan headquartered in North Dakota is, for instance, head of Citicorp's U.S. credit-card operations. But these are still exceptions.

Finally, research and development—the one function almost totally centralized today in the multinational's home country—will have to be transnationalized. Research increasingly will have to go where the qualified people are and want to work. It may not entirely be an accident that the companies and industries in which the United States has best maintained its leadership position, IBM, for instance, or the pharmaceutical industry, are precisely those that long ago—despite all the difficulties of language, culture, and compensation—transnationalized research.

Economic realities are thus forcing the multinational to become a transnational system. And yet the political world in which every business has to operate is becoming more nationalist, more protectionist, indeed more chauvinistic, day by day in every major country. But the multinational really has little choice: If it fails to adjust to transnational economic reality, it will fast become inefficient and uneconomical, a bureaucratic "cost center" rather than a "profit center." It must succeed in becoming a bridge between both the realities of a rapidly integrating world economy and a splintering world polity.

[1985]

5

Managing
Currency Exposure

Old and amply tested wisdom holds that unless a company's business is primarily the trading of currencies or commodities, the firm inevitably will lose, and heavily, if it speculates in either. Yet the fluctuating exchange rates of the current world economy make speculators out of the most conservative managements.

Indeed, what was "conservative" when exchange rates were predictable has become a gamble against overwhelming odds. This holds true for the multinational concern, for the company with large exports, and for the company importing parts and supplies in substantial quantities. But the purely domestic manufacturer, as many U.S. businesses have found to their sorrow in recent years, is also exposed to currency risk if, for instance, its currency is seriously overvalued, thus opening its market to foreign competition. (On this see also Chapter 1: "The Changed World Economy.")

Businesses therefore have to learn to protect themselves against several kinds of foreign-exchange dangers: losses on sales or purchases in foreign currencies; the foreign-exchange exposure of their profit margins; and loss of sales and market standing in both foreign and domestic markets. These risks cannot be eliminated. But they can be minimized or at least contained. Above all, they can be converted into a known, predictable, and controlled cost of doing business not too different from any other insurance premium.

The best-known and most widely used protection against foreign-exchange risks is *hedging,* that is, selling short against known future revenues in a foreign currency and buying long against known future foreign-exchange payment obligations. A U.S. maker of specialty chemicals, for instance, exports 50 percent of its $200 million sales, with 5 percent going to Canada and 9 percent each to Japan, Britain, West Germany, France, and Italy. *Selling short* (that is, for future delivery) Canadian dollars, Japanese yen, British pounds, German marks, French francs, and Italian lire (or buying an option to sell them) in amounts corresponding to the sales forecast for each country converts, in effect, the foreign-exchange receipts from future sales into U.S. dollars at a fixed exchange rate and eliminates the risk of currency fluctuations.

The company that has to make substantial future payments in foreign currencies—for imports of raw materials, for instance, or for parts—similarly hedges by buying *forward* (that is, for future receipt) the appropriate currencies in the appropriate amounts. And other expected revenues and payments in foreign currencies—dividends from a foreign unit, for instance—can be similarly protected by hedging.

Hedging and options are now available for all major currencies and, for most of them, at reasonable costs. But still, selling short the Italian-lire equivalent of $8 million could be quite expensive. More important, hedging only ensures against the currency risk on revenues and payments. It does not protect profit margins. Increasingly, therefore, companies are resorting to foreign-currency financing.

The specialty-chemicals company cited previously incurs

all its costs in U.S. dollars. If the dollar appreciates in the course of a year, the company's costs appreciate with it in terms of the foreign currencies in which it sells half its output. If it raises its prices in these foreign currencies, it risks losing sales, and with them profits—and, worse, permanent market standing. If it does not raise its prices in the foreign currencies, its profit margins shrink, and with them its profits.

In a world of volatile and unpredictable foreign-exchange fluctuations, businesses will have to learn to hedge their costs as well as their receipts. The specialty-chemicals company, for instance, might raise its total money requirements in the currencies in which it gets paid, that is, 50 percent in U.S. dollars and the rest in the currencies of its main foreign markets. This would bring into alignment the reality of its finances with the reality of its markets. Or an American company exporting 50 percent of its output might raise all its equity capital in dollars on the New York Stock Exchange but borrow all its other money needs short term in the "ECU," the currency of account of the European Common Market. Then if the dollar appreciates, the profit in dollars the company makes as its ECU loans mature may offset the currency loss on its export sales.

"Internationalizing" the company's finances is also the best—perhaps the only—way in which a purely domestic manufacturer can protect itself to some degree against foreign competition based on currency rates. If a currency is appreciating so fast as to give foreign competition a decided edge—the most recent example is the rapid rise of the dollar in 1983–84 vis-à-vis the yen and the mark—a domestic manufacturer may borrow in the currencies of its foreign competitors or sell those currencies short. The profit the company makes in its own currency when buying back the amount it owes in the foreign currencies then enables it to lower its domestic price and thus to meet the competition that is based on the foreign-exchange rate.

This is, however, a tricky and dangerous game. It straddles the fine line between hedging and "speculating." The amounts risked, therefore, always should be strictly limited and the exposure time kept short. The successful practitioners of this strategy never sell short or borrow for more than ninety days at any one time. Yet it was this strategy that protected many West German manufacturers against losing their home market to the Americans when the dollar was grossly undervalued during the years of the Carter inflation. And although the strategy might be speculative, the alternative, to do nothing, might be more speculative still.

With currency fluctuations a part of economic reality, business will have to learn to consider them as just another cost, faster changing and less predictable, perhaps, than costs of labor or capital but otherwise not so different.

Specifically this means that businesses, and especially businesses integrated with or exposed to the world economy, will have to learn to manage themselves as composed of two quite dissimilar parts: a *core business* permanently domiciled in one country or in a few countries, and a *peripheral business* capable of being moved, and moved fast, according to differentials in major costs—labor, capital, and exchange rates.

A business producing highly engineered products might use its plants in its home country to produce those parts on which the quality, performance, and integrity of its products depend—say 45 percent or 50 percent of the value of the finished product. And if the company has plants in more than one developed country, it might shift this core production among those plants according to exchange-rate advantages. The remaining 50 percent or 55 percent of its production would be peripheral and quite mobile, to be placed on short-term contracts wherever the costs are lowest, whether in developed countries with favorable exchange rates or in Third World countries with favorable labor rates.

The volatile foreign-exchange fluctuations of today's world economy demand that managements, even of purely domestic businesses, manage their companies as "international" companies and as ones embedded in the world economy. It might even be said that exchange-rate instability means that there are no more American or German or French businesses; there are only Americans or Germans or Frenchmen managing world-economy businesses, at least in manufacturing, banking, and finance. This is the most paradoxical result of the shift, nearly fifteen years ago, from fixed to floating exchange rates.

One of the major advantages then claimed for floating exchange rates was the strengthening of the national character of business by eliminating, or greatly lessening, differentials in comparative costs between major economies. But we also were promised then that floating exchange rates would eliminate, or greatly lessen, international short-term capital movements.

Exchange rates were supposed to adjust themselves automatically to the balance of trade between countries. And, indeed, economic theory still preaches that foreign-exchange rates are determined by the balance of trade in goods and services. Instead, with liquid short-term funds amounting to $3 trillion sloshing around the world economy, short-term flows of capital have come to determine exchange rates and, largely, the flow of goods and services.

Floating exchange rates were also expected to eliminate, or at least to curtail, government manipulation of foreign-exchange rates by imposing fiscal discipline on governments. But surely the United States would have had to face up years ago to its government deficit had the American government not been able to postpone the day of reckoning by keeping the dollar's value high. Above all, however, floating exchange rates were expected to promote currency stability and to eliminate volatile currency fluctuations: the exact opposite of what they actually have achieved.

But the fact that the economic reality of a floating-exchange-rate world economy is totally different from what it was expected to be does not change the fact that it is reality and will continue to be reality for the foreseeable future. Managements have to learn to manage currency instability and currency exposure.

[1985]

6

Export Markets
and Domestic Policies

People in Japan wouldn't believe me when, in 1982, I told them that President Reagan would cut off American equipment for the gas pipeline from Siberia to Western Europe. "That would take world leadership for heavy earth-moving equipment away from Caterpillar and the United States and hand it on a platter to Komatsu and us Japanese! But earth-moving equipment is the one heavy industry with long-term growth potential. No government would do this!" Several of the usually superpolite Japanese came close to calling me a liar when I said that the impact on the competitive position of this major American manufacturing industry wouldn't even be considered by the administration in making the decision. It wasn't—and it couldn't have been, given American political mores.

Similarly, the impact on the competitive position of U.S. manufactured goods wasn't even discussed in 1981 in the decision to fight inflation primarily by raising interest rates, even though this meant pushing up the international value of the dollar and pricing American goods out of the world market.

For 150 years, ever since Andrew Jackson, it has been a "given" of U.S. politics that American manufacturing's competitive position in export markets isn't a legitimate concern of the policymaker.

It's true that we have a long tradition of protecting our domestic market. Despite all our free-trade rhetoric, protectionism is as American as apple pie. And at least since the Civil War the competitive position of U.S. farm products in the world market has been a major policy concern.

Yet it has long been thought improper to consider the impact on manufactured exports when setting policy. Only one president in the last 150 years thought otherwise: Herbert Hoover. For all the rest, even the most "pro-business" ones, concern for manufactured exports was taboo. It meant "looking after the profits of the fat cats."

For a long time this did little harm. Manufactured exports were at most of marginal importance, accounting for no more than 5 percent to 8 percent of output—and even less in our major industries. But this has changed drastically in the last twenty years. Politicians and economists still berate U.S. manufacturers for their "neglect of export markets," and article after article implores the industry "to learn to sell abroad." But the American manufacturing industry now exports more than twice as large a proportion of its output as Japan; indeed the export share of U.S. industrial production exceeds that of any major industrial nation except West Germany.

In part this is the result of American multinationalism. The subsidiaries and affiliates of U.S. companies, far from taking away American jobs, are the best customers of the domestic manufacturing industry. Part of the tremendous expansion of American manufactured exports is, however, the result of a very real change in the attitude and the competence of American business, especially of small and medium-size high-tech companies. As a result, exports of manufactured goods accounted in 1982 for one of every five jobs in U.S. factories.

Yet 1982 was not a good year for the exporter. Part of the cause was the world recession, but the major reason was the overvalued dollar. Fred Bergsten, former assistant secretary of the Treasury for international economics and now a consultant to private industry, reckons that a 10 percent lower dollar would have raised the level of American exports a full quarter higher than they were; exports would have reached almost one-fourth of a much higher U.S. manufacturing output. According to Mr. Bergsten, the overvalued dollar cost more American manufacturing jobs and created more unemployment than the crises in the steel and auto industries combined. The world market still means more to the American farmer than it does to the industrial worker: two-fifths of farm sales against one-quarter or one-fifth of manufactured-goods sales. But even in a year of poor export sales such as 1982, the world market was the largest single customer of American factory labor.

Under these conditions the traditional separation between American domestic policy and concern for the U.S. competitive position in the export markets for manufactured goods can no longer be justified.

There are three ways of building concern for our foreign trade into the policy-making process. The first—it might be called the *internationalist* one—is to make sure that the impact of any decision is carefully considered. This is essentially what the West Germans do, and today they are the closest to genuine free traders in industrial goods. It is one of the main jobs of the West German ministry of economics to work out an economic impact statement describing the foreign-trade consequences of proposed government policies. This doesn't guarantee, of course, that other considerations are subordinated. I would guess, for instance, that the Reagan administration would have gone ahead with both its high-interest strategy and the ban on supplies to the Siberian pipeline even if it had considered an economic impact statement on each. But at least the "internationalist" position ensures that international competitiveness won't be sacrificed or damaged unthinkably and by default.

The second way to build concern for competitive strength into policy-making might be called the *nationalist* position. It holds that a political decision shouldn't weaken competitive economic strength in the world market; on the contrary, whenever possible, it should strengthen it. This is essentially the line General De Gaulle took when he ran France. Like all believers in realpolitik from Richelieu to Henry Kissinger, the general didn't put a high priority on economics. "Money," the realpolitiker has always believed, "grows out of the barrel of a gun." Yet in every major decision De Gaulle carefully searched for the solution that would enhance France's competitive position in the world economy or at least not damage it.

Third, there is the *mercantilist* position: strengthening the competitive position of the country's manufacturing in the world market is the first priority in public policy, to which other considerations are normally to be subordinated. De Gaulle's conservative successors, Pompidou and Giscard d'Estaing, held this view: it has been the traditional French position since the seventeenth century. But the real pros today are the Japanese.

Clearly these positions overlap. No country has ever followed one of the three exclusively. Also not every one is equally accessible to every country at all times. The mercantilist stance, for instance, is almost incompatible with great-power ambitions, which is why De Gaulle, with all his respect for French traditions, did not embrace it. And only the first, internationalist one fits easily with a free-market economy and fits United States needs and political realities. Even that policy would be a radical break with American political traditions; it would require substantial changes in the policy-making process and in our institutional arrangements, such as congressional committees.

However, we shall have to realize that safeguarding competitive economic strength is a legitimate concern of the policymaker and needs to be built into the policy-making process. With a fourth or a fifth of all manufacturing workers dependent on exports of manufactured goods for their livelihood, protectionism no longer protects. It only aggravates industrial decline and creates unemployment. But if a major country like the United States loses competitive strength in the world market, it is almost bound to become increasingly protectionist, however counterproductive this may be. It is high time that, breaking the habits, rhetoric, and traditions of 150 years, we build concern for our foreign position in manufactured goods into our policy-making process.

[1983]

7

Europe's
High-Tech Ambitions

High-tech entrepreneurship is all the rage in Europe these days. The French have established a high-powered ministry that will make the encouragement of high-tech entrepreneurship a top government priority. The West Germans are starting up venture-capital firms on the United States model and are talking of having their own Silicon *Tal,* or valley. They have even coined a new word—*Unternehmer-Kultur* (entrepreneurial culture)—and are busy writing learned papers and holding symposia on it. Even the British are proposing government aid to new high-tech enterprises in fields such as semiconductors, biotechnology, or telecommunications.

The Europeans are right, of course, to be concerned about the widening high-tech gap between themselves and their U.S. and Japanese competitors. Without indigenous high-tech capacity and production, no country can expect to be a leader anymore. And yet, the European belief that high-tech entrepreneurs can flourish, all by themselves and without being embedded in an entrepreneurial economy, is a total misunderstanding.

One reason is politics. High tech by itself is the maker of tomorrow's jobs rather than today's. To provide the new jobs needed to employ a growing work force a country needs "low-tech" or "no-tech" entrepreneurs in large numbers—and the Europeans do not want these. In the United States, employment in the Fortune 1,000 companies and in government agencies has fallen by 5 million people in the last fifteen to twenty years. Total employment, however, has risen to 106 million now from 71 million in 1965. Yet high tech during this period has provided only about 5 million new jobs: that is, no more than smokestack industry and government have lost. All the additional jobs in the U.S. economy—35 millions of them—have been provided by middle-tech, low-tech, and no-tech entrepreneurs: by makers of surgical instruments, of exercise equipment for use in the home, of running shoes; by financial-service firms and toy makers; by "ethnic" restaurants and low-fare airlines.

If entrepreneurial activity is confined to high tech—and this is what the Europeans are trying to do—unemployment will continue to go up as smokestack industries either cut back production or automate. No government, and certainly no democratic one, could then possibly continue to subordinate the ailing giants of yesteryear to an uncertain high-tech tomorrow. Soon, very soon, it would be forced by political realities to abandon the support of high tech and to put all its resources on defending, subsidizing, and bailing out existing employers and especially the heavily unionized smokestack companies. The pressures to do that are already building fast.

In France, the Communists pulled out of the government over this issue in 1983. President François Mitterrand's own Socialist Party, especially its powerful and vocal left wing, is also increasingly unhappy with his high-tech policies. They are also increasingly unpopular, moreover, with large employers.

Indeed the French Right, in its attempt to regain a majority in the 1986 parliamentary elections, made a reversal of Mr. Mitterrand's industrial policy its main plank and demanded that France give priority to employment in existing industries and scuttle high-tech entrepreneurship.

In West Germany, demands to shore up old businesses to maintain employment and to deny access to credit and capital to new entrepreneurs are growing steadily. Banks are already under some pressure from their main clients, the existing businesses, which expect them not to provide financing to any conceivable competitor, and in West Germany the banks are the main channel for capital and credit, if not the only one. Even in Britain, there is growing pressure on Prime Minister Margaret Thatcher—especially from back-benchers in her own Conservative Party fearful of their fate in the next election—to forget all the big plans for encouraging high-tech entrepreneurship and concentrate instead on bolstering the ailing old industries.

There is a subtler but perhaps more important reason why high-tech entrepreneurship won't work except in a much broader entrepreneurial economy. The necessary social support is lacking. High-tech entrepreneurship is the mountaintop. It must rest on a massive mountain: middle-tech, low-tech, no-tech entrepreneurship pervading the economy and society.

In the United States, 600,000 businesses are now being founded each year, about seven times as many as in the booming 1950s and 1960s. But no more than 1.5 percent of these—about 10,000 a year—are high-tech companies. The remaining 590,000 new ventures each year range from no tech—the new ethnic restaurant or a garbage pickup and disposal service—to such middle-tech concerns as a small robotized foundry for special-purpose nonferrous castings. Without these, however, the high-tech ventures would be stillborn. They would not, for instance, attract high-caliber workers.

In the absence of an entrepreneurial economy, scientists or engineers would then prefer (as they still do in Europe) the security and prestige of the "big-company" job. And a high-tech venture equally needs accountants and salespeople and managers—and none of them would want to work in small, new enterprises, high-tech or not, unless it became the accepted thing to do, if not indeed the preferred employment. Thirty years ago such people in the United States also looked to the big established company, or to government, for their job and career opportunities. That they are now available to the new venture, despite its risks and uncertainties, is what has made possible our entrepreneurial economy and the jobs it creates.

But the impetus for this did not come from glamorous high tech. It came from a multitude of quite unglamorous but challenging jobs with good career opportunities in all kinds of totally unglamorous low-tech or middle-tech businesses. They provide a massive entrepreneurial economy. High tech provides the imagination, to be sure, but other firms provide the daily bread.

And then also, no tech, low tech, and middle tech provide the profits to finance high tech. Contrary to what most people believe, high tech is distinctly unprofitable for a long time. The world's computer industry ran at a heavy overall loss every year for thirty years; it did not break even until the early 1970s. IBM, to be sure, made a lot of money; and a few other—primarily U.S.—computer makers moved into the black during the 1960s. But these profits were more than offset by the heavy losses of the big electric-apparatus makers: GE, Westinghouse, Siemens, Phillips, RCA, and others. Similarly, it will be at least another ten years before either the biogenetic industry or robot makers as a whole break even, and probably just as long before the microcomputer industry overall makes any money. During that period the no-tech, low-tech, and middle-tech ventures provide the profit stream to finance the capital needs of high tech. Without them, there is unlikely to be enough capital available.

So far, however, there is little recognition of these facts to be found in Europe, and none among European governments. Things may change. Our own entrepreneurial surge started some fifteen years ago. Western Europe is by and large some fifteen years behind the most important U.S. demographic trends—the baby boom, the baby bust, and the explosion in college education.

In the United States these very trends are surely contributing factors in the renewal of entrepreneurship. With the tremendous number of educated baby-boomers already in good jobs, opportunities in the big companies and in government are beginning to be scarce and young people entering the labor force are willing and eager to join small and new ventures. In Europe, the baby-boomers are just hitting the market.

So far, however, European governments are still hostile to entrepreneurs other than in high-tech areas (in France contemptuous to boot). European tax laws, for instance, penalize them and restrict their access to capital and credit. But European society also discourages people, and especially the educated young, from doing anything so "uncouth" as going to work for anyone but a government agency or a big, established company. Unless this changes—and so far there are few signs of this—the infatuation with high-tech entrepreneurship will neither revive the ailing European economies nor even provide much high tech. It must end the way an earlier European high-tech infatuation, Concorde, ended: a very little *gloire,* an ocean of red ink, but neither jobs nor technological leadership.

[1984]

8

What We Can Learn from the Germans

No one these days talks of a "German miracle," least of all the Germans. And there are no bestselling books about German management, and no seminars on "What We Can Learn from the Germans." Yet the German economic performance these last few years is every bit as impressive as that of the Japanese, and more solid.

A few years ago West Germany furnished 13 percent of all industrial goods in world trade; its share of a substantially expanded industrial-goods world trade in 1985 was up to 17 percent. It still trails the United States: our share in industrial exports is 20 percent. But Germany is substantially ahead of Japan's 16 percent share. Yet West Germany has no more than a quarter of the U.S. population and only half as many people as Japan. Per capita West Germany's industrial exports are thus almost four times those of the United States and twice those of Japan.

And they are better balanced than Japan's. The Japanese have one dominant customer, the United States, which accounts for almost half of the total in Japan's main export industries. There is only one West German company—and that a fairly small one: Porsche—that is as heavily dependent on the American customer as are practically all major Japanese exporters; more than half of Porsche's production is sold in the United States. No other West German company sells as much as one-tenth or one-twelfth of its exports in the U.S. market. A sharply devalued U.S. dollar is a headache for a good many German companies. But it is a calamity for many Japanese manufacturers. Altogether no one foreign customer is so dominant as to make Germany dependent on it.

Similarly, West Germany is not dependent for its export income on any one product group the way the Japanese are dependent on just four: steel, automobiles, semiconductors, and consumer electronics. No one product category—not even automobiles, despite Mercedes, BMW, and Porsche—accounts for more than one-twelfth of the German export total. By contrast, the four major Japanese export categories supply more than two-thirds of Japan's export surplus. And in every single industrial product group a West German firm, often a small or medium-size specialist, is among the world's leading suppliers. The Japanese, by contrast, are not even represented as world-market suppliers in the majority of industrial product categories.

West Germany has also been far more successful so far in using exports to lead domestic recovery. To be sure, the Japanese export drive has prevented massive unemployment at home. Without it the Japanese smokestack industries—both the badly depressed steel industry and an automobile industry that faces stagnant domestic demand—would register double-digit unemployment, that is, unemployment that even the Japanese policy of keeping redundant workers on the payroll rather than laying them off could not possibly hide. But the Japanese domestic economy and Japanese industrial employment have remained sluggish and stagnant for almost five years now despite the tremendous export boom. By contrast West Germany's domestic demand for such engineering industries as machine tools or forklift trucks almost doubled from 1983 to 1986, and industrial employment in 1985 grew by 200,000 to 300,000 jobs.

Finally West Germany is the only developed country other than the United States where there is a substantial entrepreneurial surge, especially in Germany's equivalent to the "Sunbelt," the area around Stuttgart in the country's southwest corner. Altogether about 10,000 new businesses were started in West Germany last year, still far fewer than in the United States but about four times as many as in the Germany of the 1970s.

And all this has been accomplished with almost no inflation, with interest rates kept low, and with a sharp reduction by more than a third in the budget deficit, while the trade surplus and the payments surplus are steadily going up.

Of course there are problems, and fairly serious ones. Unemployment, while lower than in most European industrial countries, and dropping, is still very high by German standards: 9 percent. However much of this is probably the result of demographics, and self-correcting. The German baby boom did not subside until the late 1960s, that is, six or seven years after it did so in the United States and more than ten years after it subsided in Japan. As a result, very large age-groups have been entering the German labor force through the mid-1980s—but that wave has crested and is going down fairly fast. Within a few years there is likely to be a shortage of young people entering the German labor force and a corresponding drop in unemployment.

Another soft spot is high tech. Only in biotechnology is West Germany a serious contender so far. It is well behind in computers, microelectronics, and telecommunications. And whether the government-sponsored venture-capital program for high-tech start-ups will have results remains to be seen. So far the German thrust is primarily in *high engineering* (for example, temperature- or corrosion-resistant pumps or automated baking ovens) rather than in high tech.

The biggest threat may be labor costs. West Germany is

far behind both the United States and Japan in factory automation. Labor costs are therefore crucial. Productivity has been doing well, as well as in Japan and far better than in the United States. But although the German unions have been conscious of their country's dependence on competitive labor costs and restrained in their wage demands, there are growing signs of upward wage pressure and union militancy now that business activity is rapidly revving up. It could not come at a worse time than in 1986 when the D Mark is rapidly rising, especially against the dollar, thus cutting sharply into German export earnings and the German competitive position. If the German economy stalls in 1987 or 1988, it will be largely because labor costs will make it uncompetitive.

Still, the West German achievement is significant enough to demand more attention than it usually gets. What explains it?

There are surely some cultural factors. Chief among them is probably the unique German system of apprentice training, going back all of 150 years. Young people entering the labor force spend three days a week at work and two and one-half to three days in school, for two years or so. They thus simultaneously receive both practical experience and theoretical learning, becoming at the same time skilled workers and trained technicians. And they can apply what they have learned in school on Saturday morning back on the job on Monday and do practically on Wednesday what will be explained in school theoretically on Thursday. This is in large measure the explanation for Germany's success in raising productivity steadily: it creates not only the right attitude but also the theoretical foundation. It also creates receptivity to change, fully as much as "quality circles" do in Japan, if not more so.

But then there is also government policy. The United States has preached supply-side economics but largely practiced Keynesianism these last few years. The German government doesn't do much preaching, but it practices unalloyed supply-side economics, albeit with great moderation. Income taxes were cut in 1985 by $8 billion—the U.S. equivalent would be almost four times that amount. The government is now contemplating even bigger cuts for 1986 and 1987. Several government-owned enterprises have actually been "privatized," though the extreme Right vetoed the "privatization" of the biggest of them, the government-owned airline *Lufthansa.* Scores of regulations have been abolished or relaxed. Capital markets have been deregulated to give small and medium-size firms access to the equity market, which formerly was virtually closed to them.

But the real secret of the Germans is probably neither culture nor government. It is business policy. Managements— with government and public opinion supporting them—have made maintenance of their firm's competitive position in the world market their first priority and the overriding goal in their planning. For almost all of them the domestic market is still the biggest single customer, as it is, of course, also for most businesses in the United States or in Japan. Yet in making a decision, West German management, even in fairly small companies, is likely to ask first: Will this strengthen or weaken us in the world markets? Is this altogether the way the world markets are going? This is also the first question a German banker is likely to ask in financing a business. It is also the one management argument to which, at least so far, the German labor unions have been willing to listen.

Germans like to accentuate the negative; they tend to dwell on all that is wrong or precarious in their economy. But it might make sense for us on the outside to ask: Is there anything *we* might conceivably learn from the German achievement?

[1986]

9

On Entering the Japanese Market

Nothing seems more obvious to the Westerner than the enormous difficulty of doing business in Japan. But nothing quite so baffles the Japanese as to hear a Westerner say this. "How can this possibly be?" they'll exclaim. "Just look at all the Western businesses that lead in their markets in Japan: IBM and Citibank, Coca-Cola and American Hospital Supply, Swiss chocolates and Mars bars, Levi's jeans and McDonald's hamburgers. And there are any number of smaller foreign companies that are leaders in their market in Japan: the Swedish maker of specialty robotics, for instance, or the midwestern manufacturer of analytical instruments. Provided the product and the service are good, all it takes to do business in Japan is to do it the Japanese way."

But that's exactly the problem. The Japanese way may indeed not be particularly difficult. But it is quite different.

The first difference—and the one most Westerners find hardest to grasp—is that you don't "do" business in Japan. Business is not an "activity"; it is a "commitment." The purchasing agent orders goods, to be sure. But first he commits himself to a supplier, and to a relationship that is presumed to be permanent or at least long-lasting. And until the newcomer, whether Japanese or foreign, proves itself committed in turn, the purchasing agent will not buy its wares no matter how good their quality or how cheap their price. American Hospital Supply, by now, enjoys leadership in the tightly regulated Japanese health-care market. But when it first opened in Japan, twenty years ago, the company spent five years knocking on doors before it wrote its first order. Indeed, quick results in Japan often mean ultimate failure: you are doing business with the wrong people.

"Lifetime employment"—the best-known in the West of the commitments—is actually becoming somewhat less of a problem for the newcomer from abroad. Temporary employment agencies are flourishing in Japan, supplying everything from salespeople to secretaries to accountants. Older women with previous work experience reenter the market as "temporaries." Blue-collar workers, who are no longer needed at large companies because of automation but cannot be dismissed because they enjoy lifetime employment, are lent out. And seasoned and well-connected middle managers and professionals are also available. Forced to retire from their Japanese firms at age fifty-five, these men then become available to foreign ones.

In all other areas, however, the emphasis on mutual commitment as the basis for doing business is increasing. This is particularly true of service. The manufacturer of a car, a pump, or a refrigerator implicitly commits itself to supplying parts as long as the article lasts.

It makes little sense, therefore, to try to enter the Japanese market through massive investment in bricks and mortar. The smart way is to invest instead in building a Japanese presence: to invest in a few people and their training, in service, in market research, in market development, and in promotion.

Above all, it pays to invest from the beginning in gaining recognition as a leader. Brand loyalty is probably no more common in Japan than anyplace else. But brand recognition is of far greater importance. When you ask why the supermarkets in Tokyo carry Swiss chocolates, the answer is always "But everybody knows they are the best." Similar brand recognition underlies the success in the Japanese market of Cross in fine writing instruments, of Massachusetts-based Millipore in water treatment, or of the London stockbrokers Vickers Da Costa (now a Citibank affiliate) in foreign-exchange trading. Every one of these successes resulted from identifying one particular market niche and then concentrating for a long time on attaining leadership in it.

There are considerable structural or cultural differences that should not be disregarded. One such difference—and the one Westerners soon become aware of—is the rule that rank must equal age within a social group, for example, managers in a company. Within such a group a younger man must not be the superior of an older one. I know of no Japanese company where the president is older than the chairman, for instance. If there are nonfamily members in the management group of a family company, even the son and heir will not, as a rule, become a member of senior management until he is forty. And a civil servant automatically retires the moment a younger man is promoted ahead of him. But the foreign company will—and quite rationally—want younger men from its headquarters in the United States or Europe to head its Japanese subsidiary or joint venture. This often condemns the venture to failure. It paralyzes the Japanese, who simply do not know how to behave. To them the congruence of rank and age is not a principle of organization; it is one of morality.

All one has to do, however, is finesse the problem the way the Japanese have for centuries. The younger man is not the "superior"—he is an "adviser," or he stays on the payroll of the parent company as "liaison" and is not even shown on the Japanese subsidiary's organization chart.

Another difference is in respect to economic structure. Here the biggest difference is the position of the manufacturer or supplier—based on differences in financial structure and on different social concepts. Grossly simplified, the manufacturer or supplier is expected both to finance the distributor and to look after him. One reason for this is that in Japan distributors, whether wholesalers or retailers, do not have easy access to credit. The banks were originally organized to siphon the public's savings into manufacturing industry—and that is still the way they see themselves and their function. Hence the manufacturer is expected to finance the distribution of his goods. And although there are large modern distributors—like department stores and supermarket chains—the bulk of distribution is still done through marginally small mom-and-pop stores or by very small local wholesalers.

This explains the importance of the "trading company" and the fact that even large manufacturers use it to distribute their goods. The *trading company* is primarily a commercial banker for the local wholesaler or retailer and secondarily the provider of management to both, supplying them with the rudiments of inventory control, accounting, and often even training. Newcomers, however, find it harder and harder as a rule to link up with a trading company. Earlier joint ventures by Americans with companies in such groups as Mitsubishi, Sumitomo, Itoh, or Mitsui worked so well because these groups could give the joint venture immediate access to distribution financing and distribution service through their trading companies. Now most of the established trading companies already handle products that compete with those of the newcomer.

This problem is easing, but only slowly. To the extent to which modern distribution systems grow, for example, supermarkets, they are becoming capable of both financing and managing themselves and therefore are becoming independent of—and in fact hostile to—the trading company. Nonetheless, the newcomer, and especially the Westerner, must realize that he will have to provide financing for his distributors. To do this was the secret of Coca-Cola's success in Japan; it made Coke, within a few years, Japan's leading soft drink. But the manufacturer will also have to organize—and often supply—the service for his products, because local dealers possess neither the necessary manpower nor the management capacity.

In addition, manufacturers are expected to care for their distributors and, often, suppliers as well. This is implicit in their commitment. It is often the manufacturer's job to help distributors or suppliers get the bank credit they need—perhaps not by legally guaranteeing their loans but by taking moral responsibility for them. And it is expected, though less and less so, to stand behind them should they get into trouble: to find a buyer for the distributor's business for instance, when the owner dies, or a chief executive for a small supplier, and so on.

The greatest cultural problem for the Westerner in doing business in Japan is, however, the need for the "go-between" and the dependence on him. To a large extent government in Japan functions through competition between different factions, each organized as a ministry, for example, Ministry of International Trade and Industry, Ministry of Finance, and Bank of Japan—the three main government agencies in the economic field. Each of these constantly strives to increase its power and the scope of its control and considers the others as rivals. And each in turn is allied with groups in the economy and society, for example, a particular industry or political faction or an aspirant to the prime minister's office.

This is the reason even very large Japanese companies do not deal directly with their own government. They use a go-between, usually a retired high government servant. He knows his way around. He has been to the same university as the men now in power and can therefore talk to them over drinks rather than in their offices. He, in turn, can be told what the score is and how his client, the business, should behave to get what it wants. The go-between can ask difficult questions and receive very frank and direct answers. But unless a foreign investor has a Japanese joint-venture partner, it is not always easy to find and identify the right go-between.

Yes, my Japanese friends are right when they say that it is easy to do business in Japan as long as you do it the way the Japanese do it. But my American friends are also right when they complain how enormously difficult it is to do business in Japan. But do they really have much choice? Although the Japanese do not buy many imports, their appetite for goods made by American firms in Japan is apparently insatiable. According to a study by McKinsey & Co., the Japanese in 1984 spent $600 each on American brands, compared with $287 spent by each American on Japanese goods.

[1985]

10

Trade with Japan: The Way It Works

Never before has a major debtor country owed its foreign creditors in its own currency as the United States does today. All other major debtor nations today—Brazil, Mexico, Zaire— owe in their creditor's currency, primarily in dollars. So, in the 1920s, did Germany and the other Continental European countries, the big debtors of those days. But the foreign debt of the United States today is owed in U.S. dollars.

The advantages to the United States are tremendous, and as unprecedented as the situation itself. For the first time a debtor nation stands to benefit both on its capital account and on its trading account from devaluing its currency. Historically a debtor country gains a competitive position for its products by devaluing its currency, though usually only for a fairly short period; its exports go up, its imports go down, and a trade deficit turns into a trade surplus—as it did in the Carter administration when American policy sharply forced the dollar down. But at the same time the country's balance of payments deteriorates, because interest and principal have to be paid in the creditor's currency. If the foreign debt is high, the balance-of-payments penalty may be greater than the balance-of-trade gain, which is, for instance, why the Germans in 1931 chose (wrongly, hindsight would say) to impose currency controls to maintain a grossly overvalued exchange rate for the mark rather than devalue it and boost exports and employment.

A sharp fall in the dollar's external value, however, should both improve the American trade balance and sharply cut the burden of the United States' foreign debt on the domestic economy and its real value to America's creditors.

Why then has the Reagan administration waited so long before taking action to correct the dollar's obvious overvaluation, especially against the yen? That the dollar's overvaluation has been a major, perhaps the major, factor in the decline in the competitiveness of both American agricultural and American manufactured products had been universally accepted at least since 1983. Yet U.S. policy—and that means both the Federal Reserve Board and the Treasury—consistently, until late in 1985, aimed at maintaining the highest possible dollar exchange rate, to the exclusion, or so it seemed to most foreign observers, of any other economic-policy consideration or goal.

The answer is, of course, that the administration has needed massive foreign borrowings. The Japanese alone in 1985 were lending the United States between $50 billion and $60 billion, which they could obtain only through their trade surplus with the United States. They thus supplied the lion's share of the money needed to finance the U.S. budget deficit. Faced as Washington was with the alternatives of sharply cutting government spending or borrowing domestically and driving up interest rates, a foreign-trade deficit with all its consequences for American jobs and America's long-range competitive position might understandably have appeared as the least evil.

But as the U.S. foreign debt is in U.S. currency, the foreign creditor can easily be expropriated. It takes no legal action, no default, no debt repudiation, and it can be done without asking the creditors, indeed without telling them. All it requires is devaluation of the dollar. Indeed between June when the dollar peaked at a rate of 250 yen and February of 1986 the United States' Japanese creditors—mainly the Bank of Japan, the major Japanese banks, and the big trading companies—lost a third of the value of their holdings of U.S. Treasury securities, the form in which most of the Japanese investment in the United States is held. (On this see also Chapter 1: "The Changed World Economy.")

No one in the United States seems to know this—at least no one comments on it. But every policymaker I know in Japan —government official, banker, businessman, academic economist—is keenly conscious of this. And every one is quite convinced that this loss is inevitable. Although some Japanese, especially among the economists, worry lest such a loss endanger the solvency of the Japanese banking system, they all see it as a lesser evil compared with each of Japan's other alternatives.

Seen from Japan there is no practical way to restore the trade balance between the two countries. For its major cause is neither the overvalued dollars, nor the weakness of American industry, aggressive Japanese exports, and least of all barriers to the imports of American goods into Japan (total elimination of which—and it is, of course, highly desirable and way overdue—would at most slice $5 billion to $6 billion off a $50-billion deficit).

The major cause is the worldwide slump in primary-products prices, and especially in the prices of farm and forest products. Measured against the prices of manufactured goods —and especially of high-value-added manufactured goods such as the autos, cameras, consumer electronics, and semiconductors that constitute the bulk of Japanese exports to the United States—primary products now sell at their lowest prices in history, lower even than during the Great Depression. Japan is the world's largest importer of primary products, and indeed the only sizable importer of foodstuffs in the world (save the Soviet Union) now that Common Market Europe has itself become an exporter and China as well as India are in food balance. And Japan is the world's largest exporter of high-value-added manufactured goods. The United States by contrast is the world's largest exporter of farm and forest products. If U.S.–Japanese trade is adjusted for this—that is, if the ratio between primary-products prices and manufactured-goods prices is assumed to have remained where it was in 1973—at least one-third, maybe two-fifths, of America's trade deficit with Japan disappears.

Yet no action either country could take will correct this imbalance: there is a worldwide surplus of primary products for the foreseeable future. Indeed, the only action that could be taken—and it might be taken were the United States to engage in a trade war against Japan—is for the Japanese to switch their primary-products buying (of cotton, tobacco, soybeans, wheat, corn, timber, and so on) away from the United States. They could do so within twelve months. They are already being offered ample quantities of all these products by other suppliers, and at prices lower than those payable to the American producers, except at much lower yen-dollar rates.

But then Japan sees no political alternative to pushing exports (and thereby financing the U.S. deficit at the risk of almost certain serious loss). Otherwise Japan faces unemployment of a magnitude—at least twice the current American 7 percent unemployment rate—that no Japanese government could risk. The domestic Japanese economy has been flat for five long years; none of the measures taken to revive it has had much effect. There is growing political pressure to reflate. Yet the Japanese government deficit is already so high that increasing it might reignite inflation. And the short but severe bout of inflation their country suffered from the mid-1970s convinced many thoughtful Japanese, especially in the Bank of Japan and the Ministry of Finance, that they have low resistance against that dangerous disease.

Export supplies something like 15 percent of Japanese jobs. Without the exports of its major customer, the auto industry, the Japanese steel industry would probably be sicker even than the American one; where Nippon Steel operated in 1985 at a low (and loss-making) 60 percent of capacity, it would fall below 40 percent. Proportionately the steel and automobile industries in Japan account for at least twice the blue-collar work force they account for in the United States. This problem is aggravated by postwar Japanese society's being based on the promise of lifetime employment, by the inability of dismissed or laid-off Japanese workers to get new jobs because of the rigidities of the Japanese wage system, and by the country's having no unemployment insurance. Small wonder, then, that the Japanese policymaker prefers the almost certain but future losses on the loans made to the U.S. government to the political and social—and immediate—risks of massive unemployment at home.

These are the economic realities of the American-Japanese relationship. They explain in large part why the Japanese so far have not been greatly impressed by U.S. short-run threats of protectionist retaliation against Japanese goods. They figure that the United States is unlikely to do anything that would both endanger its already deeply depressed farm economy and force America to take action on its government deficit. So far they have been right: the U.S. bark has been far worse than its toothless bite. But these realities would also indicate that the U.S. government fails to understand what it can do.

Action on the part of the Japanese to remove barriers to the entry of American goods and American firms would not materially affect the trade imbalance. But it might have significant psychological impact and remove a good deal of the emotion that threatens to poison relations between the two countries. Yet it is a plain misunderstanding of economic and political realities to believe, as President Reagan has been believing, that Prime Minister Nakasone, or any other Japanese political leader, can make voluntary concessions. He must have some "wicked foreigner" to blame, must be able to say "I had to yield at gunpoint"—especially as Japanese politics are so turbulent today that no one has a dependable majority.

But the real implication of the realities is that the key to the American-Japanese trade problem, and to the problem of America's competitive position in the world economy altogether, does not lie in a cheaper dollar, and not even in higher American productivity and lower comparative labor costs. Higher primary-products prices would help greatly, but there is little prospect for them in the face of the worldwide overproduction and surpluses. The root of America's problem is the U.S. government deficit and the resulting growing dependence on borrowing abroad.

[1985]

11

The Perils of
Adversarial Trade

"Why is the West obsessed with our exports"? every Japanese
visitor asks. "The Germans export even more and their trade
surpluses are also growing rapidly." But there is a difference,
though the Japanese are oblivious to it. The Germans do indeed
top the Japanese as *exporters* of manufactured goods: only the
United States exports even more of them than the Germans.
But the Germans are also the world's second-largest *importers*
of such goods—again topped only by the United States. The
Japanese, however, only sell; they do not buy. They practice
adversarial trade.

   The original eighteenth-century model of international
trade—the one Adam Smith formulated—assumes *comple-
mentary* trade: warm and dry Portugal sells wine in exchange
against wool to cool and wet England. Each side buys what it
cannot produce itself and sells what it is ideally equipped to
make. There are only winners and no losers.

   But since the middle of the nineteenth century the growth
sector in the international economy has been *competitive trade*

between developed countries. Both parties buy from each other similar goods, which both are capable of producing. Thus the United States is both the world's largest exporter and the world's largest importer of chemicals. Per capita, the Swiss are the world's largest exporters of machine tools and textile machinery, but also the world's largest importers of both. Germany exports more motor vehicles (including trucks and buses) than does Japan; but for every five German motor vehicles sold abroad, the Germans import three. In competitive trade there are losers: the United States—or German, or British, or Swiss —manufacturer of weaving looms, for instance, whose technically inferior or more expensive product is being edged out of the market by the more advanced or cheaper make of his foreign competitor. But overall everybody gains: not only the consumer but also the competing producers who are being forced to concentrate on what they do best, thus optimizing both resources and returns. In fact, in competitive trade the foreign competitor of an industry is commonly also its best customer.

But in adversarial trade both sides lose—one side, the buyer right away, the other side, the seller, within a decade or so.

In adversarial trade the seller's goods displace the goods produced by the manufacturers of the buying country without any compensating purchases from that country. No alternative markets for the foreign buyer's manufacturers are thus being created, and no purchasing power either. Because there are no compensatory sales for the domestic manufacturer in the buying country he cannot earn the resources needed to modernize his plants and processes or to acquire the production volume needed to bring down his costs. To the extent therefore to which the seller in adversarial trade succeeds, he weakens rather than strengthens the buyer's industry and productive economy. And if the seller in adversarial trade is truly successful, he eventually destroys the buyer's industry. Twelve years ago, for example, there were more than a dozen American plants manufacturing forklift trucks. Today there is none—not even an assembly operation. The same has largely happened in consumer electronics, for example, in video cassette recorders and in many categories of machine tools and semiconductors. This then also means that in the end even the consumer in the buying country loses. The drop in his income as a producer, that is, in income, will eventually more than offset his gains through lower prices as a consumer. Indeed the effects of adversarial competition—no matter how unintended—are strikingly similar to what economist and lawyer both condemn as *predatory pricing,* that is pricing so low as to destroy competitors and establish a monopoly.

Yet the seller in adversarial trade may lose in the end even more than the buyer and be totally unable to prevent it. The seller has no defense against retaliatory action on the part of the buyer. He cannot counter-act by stopping *his* purchases: he does not make any. To be sure, the Japanese are among America's best customers for agricultural and forest products. But although the American farmer's political power is still formidable, U.S. primary-products exports have become far too small a part of the total to be a decisive factor, and they are steadily going down further. And there is little doubt that the United States could manage without Japanese manufactured-goods imports, and at fairly low cost. And so could Western Europe. But Japan without industrial exports to the United States would face a major depression with double-digit unemployment.

The seller in adversarial trade is also bound in the end to lose financially. He cannot be paid at all. Buyers can, after all, pay only if they have an income, that is, if they themselves get paid as sellers. The seller in adversarial trade, the seller who does not buy, will therefore find out in the end that he has given away his wares, though he cannot expect the recipient to appreciate the gift.

Japan now has the world's largest-ever surplus of liquid funds, as large as anything OPEC ever had and soon to be even larger. Japan's banks hold $640 billion in external assets, practically all in cash or in short-term securities such as U.S. Treasury Bills. This is many times what Japan needs to finance her trade, is indeed so large that Japan could for six years pay for all her imports without having to earn a single yen through her exports. The only parallel in economic history is America's surplus in the years immediately after World War II, when the United States had the only functioning major economy in the world. Such a surplus can either be used to buy goods—something the Japanese are not willing to do. It can be given away, as the United States did in the years of the Marshall Plan. Or it will be taken away. The Japanese can, of course, continue to pile up more surplus. But this only means that they extend even more credit that will never be repaid. And eventually bad debts have to be written off.

Till now Japan has been the only practitioner of adversarial trade. It did not plan it, to be sure, though it is a logical outcome of the traditional Japanese approach to international trade—an approach, by the way, that made ample sense as long as Japan was still catching up, that is, until fairly recently, perhaps 1965 or so. Now, however, Japan's neighbor, South Korea, is deliberately embarking on adversarial trade. And if mainland China ever develops industrially, she too—at least in her present frame of mind—will surely try to be only a seller and not a buyer, that is, to practice adversarial trade.

Some small steps to correct the imbalance created by adversarial trade are being taken. We will hear a good deal in the months and years to come of "voluntary quotas" but also of "Japanese dumping." The Japanese, especially the Japanese automobile makers, are rapidly moving some production to the United States and to Western Europe to counteract anti-Japanese measures. But—something the Japanese are totally blind to, by the way—this is still seen as predatory in the buyer's country because it replaces the domestic manufacturer whom Japanese adversarial trading had first damaged or destroyed. Moving production to the buyer's country—unless accompanied by buying for export from that country—is at best half a loaf. More effective would be a "production consortium" in which manufacturers in the buying country supply the seller as subcontractors or partners—the way, for instance, in which Boeing has placed 30 or 40 percent of the development and manufacturing work on a new commercial aircraft with Japanese companies, or in which Rolls-Royce in Great Britain is brought in as the engine supplier for American-made planes sold to European airlines. So far, however, consortium deals have been resisted by the Japanese. They might also pay their share by taking over from the American banks the "problem loans" to developing countries—something that is beginning to be discussed in New York and Washington, though so far only behind closed doors.

But unless the Japanese take the initiative in such measures which somehow or other counteract the worst consequences of adversarial trade—and so far they have shown not the slightest sign of doing so or even of recognizing that a problem exists—political measures will be taken to abort, or at least to limit, adversarial trade, and pretty soon. Western Europe has already gone quite far in protecting itself against it, especially in respect to Japanese-made automobiles. And the United States is bound to follow suit. So far the president has opposed any kind of protectionism. But it would take only a small economic downturn or a small increase in unemployment for protectionist measures to be enacted by the Congress with overwhelming majorities—and with overwhelming public support; and there is no shortage of protectionist proposals.

There is need to stop, or at least to confine, adversarial trade. But there is also great danger that the measures taken to do so will do far more harm than good, and especially do harm to the U.S. economy and to U.S. manufacturing. None of the proposals being discussed today—the proposal, for instance, which is now before a subcommittee of the House of Representatives and which would ban foreign manufactured goods unless they had 30 or 40 percent "domestic content"—distinguishes between competitive and adversarial trade. They are all uniformly protectionist and penalize *all* manufactured imports. But this would seriously harm and perhaps destroy our exports to the countries that buy from us, that is, to our trading partners in competitive trade. The Europeans would immediately retaliate. And all our healthy industries—perhaps three-quarters of the country's industrial base—are dependent for their growth, if not for their very survival, on exports to Europe: from aircraft and analytical instruments; through bio-medicine, pharmaceuticals, and computers; to chemicals, robots, electrical machinery, and software. What we need is a measure that arrests the degenerative disease of adversarial trade without killing off the healthy tissue of competitive trade —perhaps by limiting whatever trade restrictions we might enact to imports from countries and industries that do not buy from other developed countries (including the United States) manufactured goods of a similar kind at least equal in value to 50 or 60 percent of their exports.

The Japanese assert that it is not their fault that we find their goods more attractive than what we produce ourselves and that their export strength is simply the result of their working harder and doing a better job, whether in design, in quality, in price, or in service. This is right on the whole— *Japan Inc.* is largely a figment of the Western imagination. But it is also irrelevant. Adversarial trade will not be tolerated very long. It was not planned as such; but it turned out to be a policy to beggar one's neighbor. And that is always self-defeating.

[1986]

12

Modern Prophets: Schumpeter or Keynes?

The two greatest economists of this century, Joseph A. Schumpeter and John Maynard Keynes, were born, only a few months apart, a hundred years ago: Schumpeter on February 8, 1883, in a provincial Austrian town; Keynes on June 5, 1883, in Cambridge, England. (And they died only four years apart—Schumpeter in Connecticut on January 8, 1950, Keynes in southern England on April 21, 1946.) The centenary of Keynes's birth is being celebrated with a host of books, articles, conferences, and speeches. If the centenary of Schumpeter's birth were noticed at all, it would be in a small doctoral seminar. And yet it is becoming increasingly clear that it is Schumpeter who will shape the thinking and inform the questions on economic theory and economic policy for the rest of this century, if not for the next thirty or fifty years.

The two men were not antagonists. Both challenged long-standing assumptions. The opponents of Keynes were the very "Austrians" Schumpeter himself had broken away from as a student, the neoclassical economists of the Austrian School. And although Schumpeter considered all of Keynes's answers wrong, or at least misleading, he was a sympathetic critic. Indeed, it was Schumpeter who established Keynes in America. When Keynes's masterpiece, *The General Theory of Employment, Interest and Money*, came out in 1936, Schumpeter, by then the senior member of the Harvard economics faculty, told his students to read the book and told them also that Keynes's work had totally superseded his own earlier writings on money.

Keynes, in turn, considered Schumpeter one of the few contemporary economists worthy of his respect. In his lectures he again and again referred to the works Schumpeter had published during World War I, and especially to Schumpeter's essay on the *Rechenpfennige* (that is, money of account) as the initial stimulus for his own thoughts on money. Keynes's most successful policy initiative, the proposal that Britain and the United States finance World War II by taxes rather than by borrowing, came directly out of Schumpeter's 1918 warning of the disastrous consequences of the debt financing of World War I.

Schumpeter and Keynes are often contrasted politically, with Schumpeter being portrayed as the "conservative" and Keynes the "radical." The opposite is more nearly right. Politically Keynes's views were quite similar to what we now call "neoconservative." His theory had its origins in his passionate attachment to the free market and in his desire to keep politicians and governments out of it. Schumpeter, by contrast, had serious doubts about the free market. He thought that an "intelligent monopoly"—the American Bell Telephone system, for instance—had a great deal to recommend itself. It could afford to take the long view instead of being driven from transaction to transaction by short-term expediency. His closest friend for many years was the most radical and most doctrinaire of Europe's left-wing socialists, the Austrian Otto Bauer, who, though staunchly anticommunist, was even more anticapitalist. And Schumpeter, although never even close to being a socialist himself, served during 1919 as minister of finance in Austria's only socialist government between the wars. Schumpeter always maintained that Marx had been dead wrong in every one of his answers. But he still considered himself a son of Marx and held him in greater esteem than any other economist. At least, so he argued, Marx asked the right questions, and to Schumpeter questions were always more important than answers.

The differences between Schumpeter and Keynes go much deeper than economic theorems or political views. The two saw a different economic reality, were concerned with different problems, and defined *economics* quite differently. These differences are highly important to an understanding of today's economic world.

Keynes, for all that he broke with classical economics, operated entirely within its framework. He was a heretic rather than an infidel. Economics, for Keynes, was the equilibrium economics of Ricardo's 1810 theories, which dominated the nineteenth century. This economics deals with a closed system and a static one. Keynes's key question was the same question the nineteenth-century economists had asked: "How can one maintain an economy in balance and stasis?"

For Keynes, the main problems of economics are the relationship between the "real economy" of goods and services and the "symbol economy" of money and credit; the relationship between individuals and businesses and the "macroeconomy" of the nation-state; and finally, whether production (that is, supply) or consumption (that is, demand) provides the driving force of the economy. In this sense Keynes was in a direct line with Ricardo, John Stuart Mill, the "Austrians," and Alfred Marshall. However much they differed otherwise, most of these nineteenth-century economists, and that includes Marx, had given the same answers to these questions: The "real economy" controls, and money is only the "veil of things," the microeconomy of individuals and businesses determines, and government can, at best, correct minor discrepancies and, at worst, create dislocations; and supply controls, with demand a function of it.

Keynes asked the same questions that Ricardo, Mill, Marx, the "Austrians," and Marshall had asked but, with unprecedented audacity, turned every one of the answers upside down. In the Keynesian system, the "symbol economy" of money and credit are "real," and goods and services dependent on it and its shadows. The macroeconomy—the economy of the nation-state—is everything, with individuals and firms having neither power to influence, let alone to direct, the economy nor the ability to make effective decisions counter to the forces of the macroeconomy. And economic phenomena, capital formation, productivity, and employment are functions of demand.

By now we know, as Schumpeter knew fifty years ago, that every one of these Keynesian answers is the wrong answer. At least they are valid only for special cases and within fairly narrow ranges. Take, for instance, Keynes's key theorem: that monetary events—government deficits, interest rates, credit volume, and volume of money in circulation—determine demand and with it economic conditions. This assumes, as Keynes himself stressed, that the turnover velocity of money is constant and not capable of being changed over the short term by individuals or firms. Schumpeter pointed out fifty years ago that all evidence negates this assumption. And indeed, whenever tried, Keynesian economic policies, whether in the original Keynesian or in the modified Friedman version, have been defeated by the microeconomy of business and individuals, unpredictably and without warning, changing the turnover velocity of money almost overnight.

When the Keynesian prescriptions were initially tried—in the United States in the early New Deal days—they seemed at first to work. But then, around 1935 or so, consumers and businesses suddenly sharply reduced the turnover velocity of money within a few short months, which aborted a recovery based on government deficit spending and brought about a second collapse of the stock market in 1937. The best example, however, is what happened in this country in 1981 and 1982. The Federal Reserve's purposeful attempt to control the economy by controlling the money supply was largely defeated by consumers and businesses who suddenly and almost violently shifted deposits from thrifts into money-market funds and from long-term investments into liquid assets—that is, from low-velocity into high-velocity money—to the point where no one could really tell anymore what the *money supply* is or even what the term means. Individuals and businesses seeking to optimize their self-interest and guided by their perception of economic reality will always find a way to beat the "system"—whether, as in the Soviet bloc, through converting the entire economy into one gigantic black market or, as in the United States in 1981 and 1982, through transforming the financial system overnight despite laws, regulations, or economists.

This does not mean that economics is likely to return to pre-Keynesian neoclassicism. Keynes's critique of the neoclassic answers is as definitive as Schumpeter's critique of Keynes. But because we now know that individuals can and will defeat the system, we have lost the certainty which Keynes imposed on economics and which has made the Keynesian system the lodestar of economic theory and economic policy for fifty years. Both Friedman's monetarism and supply-side economics are desperate attempts to patch up the Keynesian system of equilibrium economics. But it is unlikely that either can restore the self-contained, self-confident equilibrium economics, let alone an economic theory or an economic policy in which one factor, whether government spending, interest rates, money supply, or tax cuts, controls the economy predictably and with near-certainty.

That the Keynesian answers were not going to prove any more valid than the pre-Keynesian ones that they replaced was clear to Schumpeter from the beginning. But to him this was much less important than that the Keynesian questions—the questions of Keynes's predecessors as well—were not, Schum-

peter thought, the important questions at all. To him the basic
fallacy was the very assumption that the healthy, the "normal,"
economy is an economy in static equilibrium. Schumpeter,
from his student days on, held that a modern economy is
always in dynamic disequilibrium. Schumpeter's economy is
not a closed system like Newton's universe—or Keynes's
macroeconomy. It is forever growing and changing and is biological rather than mechanistic in nature. If Keynes was a
"heretic," Schumpeter was an "infidel."

Schumpeter was himself a student of the great men of
Austrian economics and at a time when Vienna was the world
capital of economic theory. He held his teachers in lifelong
affection. But his doctoral dissertation—it became the earliest
of his great books, *The Theory of Economic Development*
(which in its original German version came out in 1911, when
Schumpeter was only twenty-eight years old)—starts out with
the assertion that the central problem of economics is not
equilibrium but structural change. This then led to Schumpeter's famous theorem of the innovator as the true subject of
economics.

Classical economics considered innovation to be outside the
system, as Keynes did, too. Innovation belonged in the category of "outside catastrophes" like earthquakes, climate, or
war, which, everybody knew, have profound influence on the
economy but are not part of economics. Schumpeter insisted
that, on the contrary, *innovation*—that is, entrepreneurship
that moves resources from old and obsolescent to new and
more productive employments—is the very essence of economics and most certainly of a modern economy.

He derived this notion, as he was the first to admit, from
Marx. But he used it to disprove Marx. Schumpeter's *Economic Development* does what neither the classical economists
nor Marx nor Keynes was able to do: It makes profit fulfill an
economic function. In the economy of change and innovation,
profit, in contrast to Marx and his theory, is not a *Mehrwert,*
a "surplus value" stolen from the workers. On the contrary, it

is the only source of jobs for workers and of labor income. The theory of economic development shows that no one except the innovator makes a genuine "profit"; and the innovator's profit is always quite short-lived. But innovation in Schumpeter's famous phrase is also "creative destruction." It makes obsolete yesterday's capital equipment and capital investment. The more an economy progresses, the more capital formation will it therefore need. Thus what the classical economist—or the accountant or the stock exchange—considers "profit" is a genuine cost, the cost of staying in business, the cost of a future in which nothing is predictable except that today's profitable business will become tomorrow's white elephant. Thus, capital formation and productivity are needed to maintain the wealth-producing capacity of the economy and, above all, to maintain today's jobs and to create tomorrow's jobs.

Schumpeter's "innovator" with his "creative destruction" is the only theory so far to explain why there is something we call "profit." The classical economists very well knew that their theory did not give any rationale for profit. Indeed, in the equilibrium economics of a closed economic system there is no place for profit, no justification for it, no explanation of it. If profit is, however, a genuine cost, and especially if profit is the only way to maintain jobs and to create new ones, then capitalism becomes again a moral system.

Morality and profits: The classical economists had pointed out that profit is needed as the incentive for the risk taker. But is this not really a bribe and thus impossible to justify morally? This dilemma had driven the most brilliant of the nineteenth-century economists, John Stuart Mill, to embrace socialism in his later years. It had made it easy for Marx to fuse dispassionate analysis of the "system" with the moral revulsion of an Old Testament prophet against the exploiters. The weakness on moral grounds of the profit incentive enabled Marx at once to condemn the capitalist as wicked and immoral and assert "scientifically" that he serves no function and that his speedy demise is "inevitable." As soon, however, as one shifts from the axiom of an unchanging, self-contained, closed economy to Schumpeter's dynamic, growing, moving, changing economy, what is called profit is no longer immoral. It becomes a moral imperative. Indeed, the question then is no longer the question that agitated the classicists and still agitated Keynes: How can the economy be structured to minimize the bribe of the functionless surplus called profit that has to be handed over to the capitalist to keep the economy going? The question in Schumpeter's economics is always, Is there sufficient profit? Is there adequate capital formation to provide for the costs of the future, the costs of staying in business, the costs of "creative destruction"?

This alone makes Schumpeter's economic model the only one that can serve as the starting point for the economic policies we need. Clearly the Keynesian—or classicist—treatment of innovation as being "outside," and in fact peripheral to, the economy and with minimum impact on it, can no longer be maintained (if it ever could have been). The basic question of economic theory and economic policy, especially in highly developed countries, is clearly: How can capital formation and productivity be maintained so that rapid technological change as well as employment can be sustained? What is the minimum profit needed to defray the costs of the future? What is the minimum profit needed, above all, to maintain jobs and to create new ones?

Schumpeter gave no answer; he did not much believe in answers. But seventy years ago, as a very young man, he asked what is clearly going to be the central question of economic theory and economic policy in the years to come.

And then, during World War I, Schumpeter realized, long before anyone else—and a good ten years before Keynes did—that economic reality was changing. He realized that World War I had brought about the monetarization of the economies of all belligerents. Country after country, including his own still fairly backward Austria-Hungary, had succeeded during the war in mobilizing the entire liquid wealth of the community, partly through taxation but mainly through borrowing. Money and credit, rather than goods and services, had become the "real economy."

In a brilliant essay published in a German economic journal in July 1918—when the world Schumpeter had grown up in and had known was crashing down around his ears—he argued that, from now on, money and credit would be the lever of control. What he argued was that neither supply of goods, as the classicists had argued, nor demand for goods, as some of the earlier dissenters had maintained, was going to be controlling anymore. Monetary factors—deficits, money, credit, taxes—were going to be the determinants of economic activity and of the allocation of resources.

This is, of course, the same insight on which Keynes later built his *General Theory*. But Schumpeter's conclusions were radically different from those Keynes reached. Keynes came to the conclusion that the emergence of the symbol economy of money and credit made possible the "economist-king," the scientific economist, who by playing on a few simple monetary keys—government spending, the interest rate, the volume of credit, or the amount of money in circulation—would maintain permanent equilibrium with full employment, prosperity, and stability. But Schumpeter's conclusion was that the emergence of the symbol economy as the dominant economy opened the door to tyranny and, in fact, invited tyranny. That the economist now proclaimed himself infallible, he considered pure *hubris*. But, above all, he saw that it was not going to be economists who would exercise the power, but politicians and generals.

And then, in the same year, just before World War I ended, Schumpeter published *The Tax State* ("The Fiscal State" would be a better translation). Again, the insight is the same Keynes reached fifteen years later (and, as he often acknowledged, thanks to Schumpeter): The modern state, through the mechanisms of taxation and borrowing, has acquired the power to shift income and, through "transfer payments," to control the distribution of the national product. To

Keynes this power was a magic wand to achieve both social justice and economic progress, and both economic stability and fiscal responsibility. To Schumpeter—perhaps because he, unlike Keynes, was a student of both Marx and history—this power was an invitation to political irresponsibility, because it eliminated all economic safeguards against inflation. In the past the inability of the state to tax more than a very small proportion of the gross national product, or to borrow more than a very small part of the country's wealth, had made inflation self-limiting. Now the only safeguard against inflation would be political, that is, self-discipline. And Schumpeter was not very sanguine about the politician's capacity for self-discipline.

Schumpeter's work as an economist after World War I is of great importance to economic theory. He became one of the fathers of business cycle theory.

But Schumpeter's real contribution during the thirty-two years between the end of World War I and his death in 1950 was as a political economist. In 1942, when everyone was scared of a worldwide deflationary depression, Schumpeter published his best-known book, *Capitalism, Socialism and Democracy,* still, and deservedly, read widely. In this book he argued that capitalism would be destroyed by its own success. This would breed what we would now call the *new class*: bureaucrats, intellectuals, professors, lawyers, journalists, all of them beneficiaries of capitalism's economic fruits and, in fact, parasitical on them, and yet all of them opposed to the ethos of wealth production, of saving, and of allocating resources to economic productivity. The forty years since this book appeared have surely proved Schumpeter to be a major prophet.

And then he proceeded to argue that capitalism would be destroyed by the very democracy it had helped create and made possible. For in a democracy, to be popular, government would increasingly shift income from producer to nonproducer, would increasingly move income from where it would be saved and become capital for tomorrow to where it would be consumed. Government in a democracy would thus be under increasing inflationary pressure. Eventually, he prophesied, inflation would destroy both democracy and capitalism.

When he wrote this in 1942, almost everybody laughed. Nothing seemed less likely than an inflation based on economic success. Now, forty years later, this has emerged as the central problem of democracy and of a free-market economy alike, just as Schumpeter had prophesied.

The Keynesians in the 1940s ushered in their "promised land," in which the economist-king would guarantee the perfect equilibrium of an eternally stable economy through control of money, credit, spending, and taxes. Schumpeter, however, increasingly concerned himself with the question of how the public sector could be controlled and limited so as to maintain political freedom and an economy capable of performance, growth, and change. When death overtook him at his desk, he was revising the presidential address he had given to the American Economic Association only a few days earlier. The last sentence he wrote was "The stagnationists are wrong in their diagnosis of the reason the capitalist process should stagnate; they may still turn out to be right in their prognosis that it will stagnate—with sufficient help from the public sector."

Keynes's best-known saying is surely "In the long run we are all dead." This is one of the most fatuous remarks ever made. Of course, in the long run we are all dead. But Keynes in a wiser moment remarked that the deeds of today's politicians are usually based on the theorems of long-dead economists. And it is a total fallacy that, as Keynes implies, optimizing the short term creates the right long-term future. Keynes is in large measure responsible for the extreme short-term focus of modern politics, of modern economics, and of modern business—the short-term focus that is now, with considerable justice, considered a major weakness of American policymakers, both in government and in business.

Schumpeter also knew that policies have to fit the short term. He learned this lesson the hard way—as minister of finance in the newly formed Austrian republic in which he, totally unsuccessfully, tried to stop inflation before it got out of hand. He knew that he had failed because his measures were not acceptable in the short term—the very measures that, two years later, a noneconomist, a politician and professor of moral theology did apply to stop the inflation, but only after it had all but destroyed Austria's economy and middle class.

But Schumpeter also knew that today's short-term measures have long-term impacts. They irrevocably make the future. Not to think through the futurity of short-term decisions and their impact long after "we are all dead" is irresponsible. It also leads to the wrong decisions. It is this constant emphasis in Schumpeter on thinking through the long-term consequences of the expedient, the popular, the clever, and the brilliant that makes him a great economist and the appropriate guide for today, when short-run, clever, brilliant economics—and short-run, clever, brilliant politics—have become bankrupt.

In some ways, Keynes and Schumpeter replayed the best-known confrontation of philosophers in the Western tradition —the Platonic dialogue between Parmenides, the brilliant, clever, irresistible sophist, and the slow-moving and ugly, but wise Socrates. No one in the interwar years was more brilliant, more clever than Keynes. Schumpeter, by contrast, appeared pedestrian—but he had wisdom. Cleverness carries the day. But wisdom endureth.

[1983]

Part II

PEOPLE

13

Picking People
The Basic Rules

Executives spend more time on managing people and making people decisions than on anything else, and they should. No other decisions are so long lasting in their consequences or so difficult to unmake. And yet, by and large, executives make poor promotion and staffing decisions. By all accounts, their batting average is no better than .333: at most one-third of such decisions turn out right; one-third are minimally effective; and one-third are outright failures.

In no other area of management would we put up with such miserable performance. Indeed, we need not and should not. Managers making people decisions will never be perfect, of course. But they should come pretty close to batting 1.000, especially because in no other area of management do we know so much.

Some executives' people decisions have, however, approached perfection. At the time of Pearl Harbor, every single general officer in the U.S. Army was overage. Although none of the younger men had been tested in combat or in a significant troop command, the United States came out of World War II with the largest corps of competent general officers any army has ever had. George C. Marshall, the army's chief of staff, had personally chosen each man. Not all were great successes, but practically none was an outright failure.

In the forty or so years during which he ran General Motors, Alfred P. Sloan, Jr., picked every GM executive— down to the manufacturing managers, controllers, engineering managers, and master mechanics at even the smallest accessory division. By today's standards, Sloan's vision and values may seem narrow. They were. He was concerned only with performance in and for GM. Nonetheless, his long-term performance in placing people in the right jobs was flawless.

➤ *The Basic Principles*

There is no such thing as an infallible judge of people, at least not on this side of the Pearly Gates. There are, however, a few executives who take their people decisions seriously and work at them.

Marshall and Sloan were about as different as two human beings can be, but they followed, and quite consciously, much the same principles in making people decisions:

1. If I put a person into a job and he or she does not perform, I have made a mistake. I have no business blaming that person, no business invoking the "Peter Principle," no business complaining. I have made a mistake.

2. "The soldier has a right to competent command" was already an old maxim at the time of Julius Caesar. It is the duty of managers to make sure that the responsible people in their organizations perform.

3. Of all the decisions an executive makes, none is as important as the decisions about people because they determine the performance capacity of the organization. Therefore, I'd better make these decisions well.

4. The one "don't": Don't give new people new major assignments, for doing so only compounds the risks. Give this

sort of assignment to someone whose behavior and habits you know and who has earned trust and credibility within your organization. Put a high-level newcomer first into an established position where the expectations are known and help is available.

Some of the worst staffing failures I have seen involved brilliant Europeans hired by U.S. companies—one based in Pittsburgh, the other in Chicago—to head up new European ventures. Dr. Hans Schmidt and Mr. Jean Perrin (only the names are fictitious) were hailed as geniuses when they came in. A year later they were both out, totally defeated.

No one in Pittsburgh had understood that Schmidt's training and temperament would make him sit on a new assignment for the first six or nine months, thinking, studying, planning, getting ready for decisive action. Schmidt, in turn, had never even imagined that Pittsburgh expected instant action and immediate results. No one in Chicago had known that Perrin, a solid and doggedly purposeful man, was excitable and mercurial, flailing his arms, making speeches about trivia, and sending up one trial balloon after another. Although both men subsequently became highly successful CEOs of major European corporations, both executives were failures in companies that did not know and understand them.

Two other U.S. companies successfully established businesses for the first time in Europe during the same period (the late 1960s and early 1970s). To initiate their projects, each sent to Europe a U.S. executive who had never before worked or lived there but whom people in the head offices knew thoroughly and understood well. In turn the two managers were thoroughly familiar with their companies. At the same time, each organization hired half a dozen young Europeans and placed them in upper-middle executive jobs in the United States. Within a few years, each company had a solid European business and a trained, seasoned, and trusted corps of executives to run it.

As Winston Churchill's ancestor, the great Duke of Marlborough, observed some three centuries ago, "The basic trouble in coalition warfare is that one has to entrust victory, if not one's life, to a fellow commander whom one knows by reputation rather than by performance."

In the corporation as in the military, without personal knowledge built up over a period of time there can be neither trust nor effective communication.

≫ *The Decision Steps*

Just as there are only a few basic principles, there are only a few important steps to follow in making effective promotion and staffing decisions:

1. *Think through the assignment.* Job descriptions may last a long time. In one large manufacturing company, for example, the job description for the position of division general manager has hardly changed since the company began to decentralize thirty years ago. Indeed, the job description for bishops in the Roman Catholic Church has not changed at all since canon law was first codified in the thirteenth century. But assignments change all the time, and unpredictably.

Once in the early 1940s, I mentioned to Alfred Sloan that he seemed to me to spend an inordinate amount of time pondering the assignment of a fairly low-level job—general sales manager of a small accessory division—before choosing among three equally qualified candidates. "Look at the assignment the last few times we had to fill the same job," Sloan answered. To my surprise, I found that the terms of the assignment were quite different on each occasion.

When putting a man in as division commander during World War II, George Marshall always looked first at the nature of the assignment for the next eighteen months or two years. To raise a division and train it is one assignment. To lead it in combat is quite another. To take command of a division that has been badly mauled and restore its morale and fighting strength is another still.

When the task is to select a new regional sales manager,

the responsible executive must first know what the heart of the assignment is: to recruit and train new salespeople because, say, the present sales force is nearing retirement age? Or is it to open up new markets because the company's products, though doing well with old-line industries in the region, have not been able to penetrate new and growing markets? Or, because the bulk of sales still comes from products that are twenty-five years old, is it to establish a market presence for the company's new products? Each of these is a different assignment and requires a different kind of person.

2. *Look at a number of potentially qualified people.* The controlling word here is *number*. Formal qualifications are a minimum for consideration; their absence disqualifies the candidate automatically. Equally important, the person and the assignment need to fit each other. To make an effective decision, an executive should look at three to five qualified candidates.

3. *Think hard about how to look at these candidates.* If an executive has studied the assignment, he or she understands what a new person would need to do with high priority and concentrated effort. The central question is not "What can this or that candidate do or not do?" It is, rather, "What are the strengths each possesses and are these the right strengths for the assignment?" Weaknesses are limitations, which may, of course, rule a candidate out. For instance, a person may be excellently qualified for the technical aspects of a job, but if the assignment requires above all the ability to build a team and this ability is lacking, then the fit is not right.

But effective executives do not start out by looking at weaknesses. You cannot build performance on weaknesses. You can build only on strengths. Both Marshall and Sloan were highly demanding men, but both knew that what matters is the ability to do the assignment. If that exists, the company can always supply the rest. If it does not exist, the rest is useless.

If, for instance, a division needed an officer for a training assignment, Marshall looked for people who could turn recruits into soldiers. Usually every man who was good at this task had serious weaknesses in other areas. One was not particularly effective as a tactical commander and was positively hopeless when it came to strategy. Another had foot-in-mouth disease and got into trouble with the press. A third was vain, arrogant, egotistical and fought constantly with his commanding officer. Never mind, could he train recruits? If the answer was yes—and especially if the answer was "he's the best"—he got the job.

In picking members of their cabinets, Franklin Roosevelt and Harry Truman said, in effect: "Never mind personal weaknesses. Tell me first what each of them can do." It may not be coincidence that these two presidents had the strongest cabinets in twentieth-century U.S. history.

4. *Discuss each of the candidates with several people who have worked with them.* One executive's judgment alone is worthless. Because all of us have first impressions, prejudices, likes, and dislikes, we need to listen to what other people think. When the military picks general officers or the Catholic Church picks bishops, this kind of extensive discussion is a formal step in their selection process. Competent executives do it informally. Hermann Abs, the former head of Deutsche Bank, picked more successful chief executives in recent times than anyone else. He personally chose most of the top-level managers who pulled off the postwar German "economic miracle," and he checked out each of them first with three or four of their former bosses or colleagues.

5. *Make sure the appointee understands the job.* After the appointee has been in a new job for three or four months, he or she should be focusing on the demands of that job rather than on the requirements of preceding assignments. It is the executive's responsibility to call that person in and say, "You have now been regional sales manager—or whatever—for three months. What do you have to do to be a success in your new job? Think it through and come back in a week or ten days and show me in writing. But I can tell you one thing right away:

the things you did to get the promotion are almost certainly the wrong things to do now."

If you do not follow this step, don't blame the candidate for poor performance. Blame yourself. You have failed in your duty as a manager.

The largest single source of failed promotions—and I know of no greater waste in U.S. management—is the failure to think through, and help others think through, what a new job requires. All too typical is the brilliant former student of mine who telephoned a few months ago, almost in tears. "I got my first big chance a year ago," he said. "My company made me engineering manager. Now they tell me that I'm through. And yet I've done a better job than ever before. I have actually designed three successful new products for which we'll get patents."

It is only human to say to ourselves, "I must have done something right or I would not have gotten the big new job. Therefore, I had better do more of what I did to get the promotion now that I have it." It is not intuitively obvious to most people that a new and different job requires new and different behavior. Almost fifty years ago, a boss of mine challenged me four months after he had advanced me to a far more responsible position. Until he called me in, I had continued to do what I had done before. To his credit, he understood that it was his responsibility to make me see that a new job means different behavior, a different focus, and different relationships.

≫ *The High-Risk Decisions*

Even if executives follow all these steps, some of their people decisions will still fail. These are, for the most part, the high-risk decisions that nevertheless have to be taken.

There is, for example, high risk in picking managers in professional organizations—in a research lab, say, or an engineering or corporate legal department. Professionals do not readily accept as their boss someone whose credentials in the field they do not respect. In choosing a manager of engineering, the choices are therefore limited to the top-flight engineers in the department. Yet there is no correlation (unless it be a negative one) between performance as a bench engineer and performance as a manager. Much the same is true when a high-performing operating manager gets a promotion to a staff job in headquarters or a staff expert moves into a line position. Temperamentally, operating people are frequently unsuited to the tensions, frustrations, and relationships of staff work, and vice versa. The first-rate regional sales manager may well become totally ineffective if promoted into market research, sales forecasting, or pricing.

We do not know how to test or predict whether a person's temperament will suit a new environment. We can find this out only by experience. If a move from one kind of work to another does not pan out, the executive who made the decision has to remove the misfit, and fast. But that executive also has to say, "I made a mistake, and it is my job to correct it." To keep misfits in a job they cannot do is not being kind; it is being cruel. But there is also no reason to let the person go. A company can always use a good bench engineer, a good analyst, a good sales manager. The proper course of action—and it works most times—is to offer the misfit a return to the old job or an equivalent.

People decisions may also fail because a job has become what New England ship captains 150 years ago called a *widow-maker*. When a clipper ship, no matter how well designed and constructed, began to have fatal "accidents," the owners did not redesign or rebuild the ship. They broke it up as fast as possible.

Widow-makers—that is, jobs that regularly defeat even good people—appear most often when a company grows or changes fast. For instance, in the 1960s and early 1970s, the job of "international vice-president" in U.S. banks became a widow-maker. It had always been an easy job to fill. In fact, it had long been considered a job in which banks could safely put also-rans and could expect them to perform well. Then, suddenly, the job began to defeat one new appointee after another. What had happened, as hindsight now tells us, is that international activity quickly and without warning became an integral part of the daily business of major banks and their corporate customers. What had been until then an easy job became, literally, a "nonjob" that nobody could do.

Whenever a job defeats two people in a row, who in their earlier assignments had performed well, a company has a widow-maker on its hands. When this happens, a responsible executive should not ask the headhunter for a universal genius. Instead abolish the job. Any job that ordinarily competent people cannot perform is a job that cannot be staffed. Unless changed, it will predictably defeat the third appointee the way it defeated the first two.

Making the right people decisions is the ultimate means of controlling an organization well. Such decisions reveal how competent management is, what its values are, and whether it takes its job seriously. No matter how hard managers try to keep their decisions a secret—and some still try hard—people decisions cannot be hidden. They are eminently visible.

Executives often cannot judge whether a strategic move is a wise one. Nor are they necessarily interested. "I don't know why we are buying this business in Australia, but it won't interfere with what we are doing here in Fort Worth" is a common reaction. But when the same executives read that "Joe Smith has been made controller in the XYZ division," they usually know Joe much better than top management does. These executives should be able to say, "Joe deserves the promotion; he is an excellent choice, just the person that division needs to get the controls appropriate for its rapid growth."

If, however, Joe got promoted because he is a politician, everybody will know it. They will all say to themselves, "Okay, that is the way to get ahead in this company." They will despise their management for forcing them to become politicians but will either quit or become politicians themselves in the end. As we have known for a long time, people in organizations tend to behave as they see others being rewarded. And when the

rewards go to nonperformance, to flattery, or to mere cleverness, the organization will soon decline into nonperformance,
flattery, or cleverness.

Executives who do not make the effort to get their people
decisions right do more than risk poor performance. They risk
their organization's respect.

[1985]

14

Measuring White-Collar Productivity

In the United States, white-collar workers now substantially outnumber blue-collar workers, and they absorb an even larger share of the total wage bill. They account, for instance, for almost two-thirds of total hospital costs. Even in traditional blue-collar industries, automobiles, for instance, the total wage bill for white-collar workers is by now almost equal to that of the blue-collar force. Yet few managements seem much concerned with white-collar productivity. Their excuse: "No one knows how to measure it."

But this is simply not true. The yardsticks we have may be crude, but they are perfectly adequate.

The most useful one is the ratio between the number of units of output, that is, automobiles made or patient-bed-days delivered in the hospital, and the number of white-collar people on the payroll (or white-collar hours worked and paid for). This measures a company's or an industry's competitive standing. Surely a company, whatever the quality of its products or its reputation in the marketplace, is at a serious competitive disadvantage if its white-collar productivity is substantially below that of its competition, whether domestic or foreign.

This ratio further enables us to identify the location of any shortage in white-collar productivity and its causes. For in addition to the ratio between output and total white-collar employment we can usually also measure the ratio between total output and groups in the white-collar force. And the yardstick indicates how much improvement can be aimed for with a fair chance of success. It does not yield some absolute, ideal figure but compares one organization with another competing one. And surely what one company has done another one can always strive for and hope to attain, if not to better.

Finally, this measurement tells us whether a company or an industry is improving white-collar productivity or losing ground and with it competitive position.

Most, if not all, of the $1,500 difference in labor costs between a small car made in the United States and one made in Japan is accounted for by wages, benefits, and union work rules, rather than by any difference in productivity. But Japan produces quite a few more cars per hundred white-collar employees than Detroit does. And it isn't difficult to find out where Detroit lags. U.S. carmakers do not employ substantially more engineers per car made and sold than the Japanese do. They employ fewer—probably too few—white-collar people to serve dealers and customers. But Detroit does employ many more clerks, clerical supervisors, and clerical managers in recordkeeping, reporting, and controlling. It substitutes paper for information. This is a tenacious disease, but curable.

Measuring white-collar productivity has been the real "secret" of the successful profit-making hospital chain. "When we hear of a hospital that is for sale, we carefully look at its population base, its medical staff, and its equipment," one chain's chief executive officer explains. "When we find any of them substandard we don't touch the place. But seven out of every ten hospitals are in trouble because of substandard white-collar productivity. And once identified it isn't too hard to cure this. We expect a hospital, once we have bought it, to reach the white-collar productivity of the average hospital in our chain in twelve to eighteen months. That's still quite low compared with our best-managed hospitals. But it's usually enough to turn loss into a profit."

The ratio between output and white-collar employment also enables us to compare the past with the present and to set goals for the future.

To know whether white-collar productivity goes up or down is especially important as a company (or industry) grows. In a rapidly growing business, the number of blue-collar workers usually rises in direct proportion to output, other things such as technology and capital equipment remaining equal. But white-collar employment should go up far more slowly than output and sales in the growing business, perhaps only half as fast. If it rises as fast as output or sales, let alone if it rises faster, the business is in danger of becoming noncompetitive, and soon. A loss in white-collar productivity is usually the first warning of the "growth crisis" ahead, and a highly reliable one. Even though the company gains market position, it loses competitive strength. And no one is more vulnerable to competitive attack than the company that combines market leadership with noncompetitive white-collar productivity. It invites attack but lacks the means to defend itself.

Actually, white-collar productivity, like all productivity, should go up steadily. If it doesn't, it will soon go down. White-collar productivity therefore requires an improvement goal and the means to monitor progress toward it. This, too, the ratio between output and white-collar employment supplies, crudely but adequately.

There are three further highly useful measurements of white-collar productivity. They might be compared with the measurements of blood pressure and of weight in the aging human body: they give early warning of the most common and most dangerous degenerative tendencies.

The first of these is the length of time it takes to bring a new product or service successfully out of development and into the market. This may be the largest single factor determining success in a competitive market and is one in which the performance of U.S. business (especially of U.S. manufacturers) has significantly deteriorated in the past ten or fifteen years. This measurement is also the most easily available criterion of the effectiveness with which our most expensive resource, the knowledge worker, actually works.

Second, and closely related, there are the number of successful new products and services that have been introduced in a given period, especially as compared with domestic and international competition. This, too, is a measurement of the productivity of white-collar workers, and especially of knowledge workers. Again, U.S. manufacturers have deteriorated in this area during the past ten or fifteen years, both as measured against their earlier performance and as measured against foreign competition, for example, Japanese or German carmakers or Sony. By contrast, this is probably the area where America's most successfully competing industry, financial services, has improved greatly, both against its own historical record and against foreign competition.

And third, there are the number of supporting-staff people and, especially, of levels of management needed for a given output. Ideally both, and especially the levels of management, should not go up with volume at all. Perhaps in modern organizations both should actually go down, for there is something like an "information economy of scale" just as there are manufacturing "economies of scale." But surely if staff services and management levels go up as fast as output, let alone faster, the business does not manage its white-collar productivity and will soon lose competitive strength.

None of these things is particularly new or particularly sophisticated. Large American retailers have known the number of customers served by salespeople and the number of sales made since Sears, Roebuck introduced these productivity measurements around 1930. This explains why the large American retailer is still more productive than retailers elsewhere, excepting only the British chain of Marks & Spencer. And no one at Bell Laboratories can remember a time when the productivity of scientists and engineers was not evaluated and appraised on a regular basis.

Yet most of American management, and practically all of our public discussion, pays no attention to white-collar productivity. It focuses on blue-collar workers. Improving blue-collar productivity is, of course, highly important, and way overdue. But it is rearguard action. We cannot hope to compete against the vast supply of young, low-wage blue-collar workers in the developing countries through blue-collar productivity, no matter how much we improve it. The only competitive advantage the United States—and every other developed country—can have lies in making productive its one abundant resource: people with long years of schooling who are available only for white-collar work. For the rest of this century, and far into the next one, the competitive battle will be won or lost by white-collar productivity.

[1985]

15

Twilight of the First-Line Supervisor?

No job is going to change more in the next decade than that of the first-line supervisor in both factory and office. And few people in the work force are less prepared for the changes and less likely to welcome them.

Automation is one of the forces drastically altering the supervisor's role. In an automated process, workers cannot be "supervised"; each worker has to be pretty much in control of the process, has to understand it, know how to program the machines he is responsible for and reset them. In an automated process, the worker switches from being an operator to being a programmer. Instead of a supervisor he needs an assistant. He needs information and continuous training. He needs someone to make sure that parts and supplies arrive on time and in proper sequence. He needs coordination with other parts of the process.

Most rank-and-file workers have little difficulty adapting to automation. But their supervisors do. When Nissan robotized its big automobile assembly plant outside Yokohama, training rank-and-file workers for the new jobs presented few problems. But practically all the supervisors had to be moved to traditional plants. Office supervisors may face even greater and more difficult changes.

Equally traumatic will be changes in industrial relations— especially in blue-collar work. They threaten the supervisor's authority and his self-image. Companies that introduced quality circles expected resistance from the blue-collar workers; there has been practically none. But supervisors resisted strongly. The whole idea of the quality circle is that the machine operator knows more about the job than anyone else. And what then is left of the supervisor's authority?

Worse still, in quality circles and all similar programs the rank-and-file employee gets to work directly with the staff— with quality control and industrial engineering and production scheduling and maintenance. But to the traditional supervisor in American industry, control of access to staff people is central to his authority and stature. All the other changes in industrial relations on the production floor now being tried out equally diminish the authority and reduce the control of the supervisor and transfer power to the worker: flexible benefits, employee share-ownership, productivity bonuses, profit-sharing, and so on. All are based on the proposition that the worker takes responsibility, has control, tells rather than being told.

In the office there is an additional problem: a growing generation gap. Office supervisors tend to be the oldest group in the labor force. And the group largely consists of people who have missed out on promotions and who have been left behind in the rapid expansion of the last fifteen to twenty years. The people they supervise increasingly are much younger and better schooled. In a recent survey of abnormally high clerical turnover in a nationwide insurance company, the most common reasons for quitting given by former employees were "My supervisor was just plain uneducated" and "My supervisor wanted us to use quill pens when I have been trained to use word processors and computers."

It can be argued that the traditional supervisor is an anachronism and an impediment to productivity.

It's not a new argument. IBM, hardly a permissive company, accepted it twenty-five years ago when it abolished the traditional supervisor in its factories and replaced him (or her) with a manager who does not supervise at all. The IBM manager is a teacher, an expediter, and an assistant. He or she has a minimum of disciplinary power and a maximum of responsibility for making the work group take responsibility for its tasks, for the design of its jobs, for standards of production, and for teamwork. The supervisory job at IBM is largely discharged by blue-collar workers themselves, men or women whom the work group itself designates as its team leaders and to whom the manager is a resource and an assistant. But in most of American business, the supervisor is very much what he or she was many years ago, a boss, though little is left of the authority and responsibility the boss had fifty years ago, before unions and powerful staff and personnel functions came in.

In the last few years the emphasis in many companies has switched back to training the first-line supervisor—and none too soon. For we have learned that training in new production processes and new industrial relations has to start with the first-line supervisor. Only when supervisors have been trained thoroughly can we successfully train workers. For instance, wherever quality circles have been successful, they first have been test-run with the first-line supervisors, before bringing in the rank and file. The quality circle thus became the supervisor's own program and the supervisor's own tool (as it is in Japan). By the time rank-and-file employees were brought in, the supervisors had also accepted the quality circle as a way of getting recognition and status.

Similarly, in a recent major switch to flexible benefits in a large mass-production plant, the key to eventual success was the first-line supervisors and their active involvement. Before the company committed itself to the new approach it had a team of experienced first-line supervisors work out the specifics. The group worked for several months with the consulting actuaries, developed with them alternatives and options, tested various programs, and got to know thoroughly what each involved, what each meant in terms of additional benefits and/or "give-ups" for each group of employees, and what new responsibilities each of the proposed programs would impose on first-line supervisors. Only then did management sit down with the union to hammer out a major change in labor-relations philosophy and in the contract.

The training needed is for a different role rather than reaffirmation of the traditional supervisor's function. To benefit from the changes—in technology, in industrial relations, in demographics—we need a stronger, more confident, more responsible first-line supervisor. We need to do what IBM did twenty-five years ago when it determined that the job of its "managers" was to bring out and put to work the strengths of the work force: competence and knowledge and capacity to take responsibility. This is not being permissive; on the contrary, it is being demanding. But it is demanding very different things from what American business by and large (aided and abetted by traditional union contracts and union relations) has been demanding of the first line.

During and right after World War II, the first-line supervisor was the center of industrial-relations concerns. For a few short years it then seemed that first-line supervisors would unionize to defend themselves against both higher management on the one hand and the unions of the rank-and-file workers on the other. For this brief period management paid attention to the supervisor—to his training, his status, and his compensation. For the last forty years, however, American business, with some exceptions, has taken the first-line supervisor for granted. But in the next decade the supervisor will again become central to industrial relations. Indeed the status, authority, and responsibility of the supervisor—as well as his compensation and promotional opportunities—may become our most pressing and difficult problem in the management of people at work.

[1983]

16

Overpaid Executives: The Greed Effect

Egalitarianism has never had great appeal in this country except to a handful of intellectuals. Now, however, a few high incomes of a very few top corporate executives are becoming a national issue.

Executive compensation played Banquo's ghost in the 1984 labor negotiations. It is not, of course, a "bargainable issue"; had it been brought up by the union, management would surely have declared it to be irrelevant and impermissible. Yet executive compensation was clearly the biggest obstacle to management's attempts to limit wage and salary increases for the rank and file and thereby to prevent renewed inflation and improve their competitive position. There is too much resentment in union ranks over the fact that in many large companies—especially in smokestack industries—wage concessions and give-ups by unions during 1982 and 1983 were followed by substantial increases in the "total compensation package" of top executives. And wherever a top management during those years actually took compensation cuts, it has long since restored them, and usually with compound interest. If union leaders will not make that point, their members will.

Resentment over top-management compensation is by no means confined to unions and rank-and-file employees. It extends up into the ranks of professionals and managers. A large defense contractor, for instance, lost some twenty senior engineers and engineering managers in 1983—some of them men with twenty-five years of service in the company. Each quit for the same reason. Said one: "While our salary increases last year were held to 3 percent with the argument that any more would be inflationary, the nine people in the top management group voted themselves bonuses and additional stock options amounting to a 25-percent to 30-percent increase in their compensation—and that's simply dishonest." Needless to say, none of these men is antibusiness or even mildly liberal.

Resentment against this perceived greed and abuse of power in high places will likely be expressed in future tax bills: by raising the maximum tax rate on high incomes, for instance; by boosting capital-gains taxes, or by penalizing stock options given to executives. Indeed an old proposal—forgotten these past thirty or forty years—is being dusted off: to set a ceiling on the amount paid an executive in total compensation (salary, bonus, pension provision, health insurance, stock options, and so on) that is tax-deductible for the employing company.

Everyone knows, of course, that such measures will not produce one penny of added revenue; on the contrary, they will reduce it. Almost all proponents of these measures would also agree that they are likely to harm the economy. But they would argue that not to limit or to penalize excessive executive compensation would do even more harm, by provoking inflationary wage demands and by creating divisive class conflict. And this attitude is not confined to so-called enemies of business. The most ardent proponent of a ceiling on the tax deductibility of executive compensation at a recent management seminar was the conservative tax counsel of one of the nation's largest businesses.

Top managers, and especially those in big companies, will argue that attacks on executive compensation as "excessive" are totally groundless. Executive compensation, they will note, has been declining in the United States in the past thirty years, both if adjusted for inflation and if compared with the total compensation package of the rank and file, where wages and especially benefits have been going up twice as fast as inflation. Indeed, up to fairly high levels in the big companies—just below division general manager, as a rule—managerial compensation is way down by any historical yardstick. Middle-management people such as engineering supervisors or plant superintendents used to make after taxes about three times what rank-and-file blue-collar employees got. With the total compensation package for blue-collar workers in the unionized mass-production industries such as steel or automobiles running close to $50,000 a year these days—or about $43,000 a year after taxes, because more than half the blue-collar employee's compensation package is either tax-free or tax-deferred, such as payments into the pension fund—many middle managers today receive barely more than blue-collar workers. Up to fairly high management levels, the income distribution in business has become extremely egalitarian, perhaps too much so.

But the real issue is not aggregate "executive compensation." It is the compensation of a tiny group—no more than one thousand people—at the very top of a very small number of giant companies. Statistically this group is totally insignificant, to be sure. But its members are highly visible. And they offend the sense of justice of many, indeed of the majority of management people themselves. And they are seen as the embodiment of the ethics and values of American business and management.

Few people—and probably no one outside the executive suite—sees much reason for these very large executive compensations. There is little correlation between them and company performance. Our toughest competitors, the Japanese, pay their top executives far less than we pay ours: about a quarter of our top-management salaries and rarely more than eight times what they pay blue-collar workers. Yet their companies aren't doing too badly. Even in the United States, one finds glaring incongruities within the same industry: companies that pay much more than $1 million to their top man and yet do quite poorly, side by side with companies that pay barely half that and yet do much better.

Indeed, the only correlation we have goes the other way: J. P. Morgan's finding of eighty years ago that the only thing the businesses that were clients of J. P. Morgan & Co. and did poorly had in common was that each company's top executive was paid more than 130 percent of the compensation of the people in the next echelon and these, in turn, more than 130 percent of the compensation of the people in the echelon just below them, and so on down the line. Very high salaries at the top, concluded Morgan—who was hardly contemptuous of big money or an "anticapitalist"—disrupt the team. They make even high-ranking people in the company see their own top management as adversaries rather than as colleagues—such as the defense contractor mentioned previously. And that quenches any willingness to say "we" and to exert oneself except in one's own immediate self-interest.

One solution might be to establish a visible link between executive compensation and employee welfare. In the smoke-stack industries especially, managements are now trying to establish such a link between employee welfare and company performance through employee stock ownership or profit participation. One complement to this might be to link executive bonuses at the top and employment security. This has obvious drawbacks, of course. It rewards top management for keeping employment—and with it costs—high. But at least it would prevent what employees resent the most: top people getting big increases in the very year in which a company slashes blue-collar and clerical payrolls.

A simpler way would be a voluntary limitation on the total after-tax compensation package paid any employee—including the chief executive officer—to a preset multiple of the after-tax total compensation package of the rank and file. The actual effect of such a measure would be minimal; in most companies it would be nil. But the psychological impact would be considerable. If the multiple were, for example, set at 20, resulting in a maximum of $850,000 or so for top people, it would affect only some 500 executives in all of American business. If the multiple were set at 15—with a resulting maximum after-tax take of about $650,000 today—about 1,000 people would be affected. Such multiples would be eminently acceptable and would be much lower than what, according to a good many surveys, wage earners think top executives make—"50 times what I get" is the most common guess.

"But in the biggest companies," top-management people will say, "the very large executive compensation is needed because in our culture rank has to be expressed through income. Every level of management has to make more than the level just below it—and if you are General Motors or Exxon or U.S. Steel, you have twenty levels of management so that the top man ends up at $1 million-plus if the blue-collar worker is to get $50,000 a year. Anyhow, these high incomes are largely symbolic: Uncle Sam takes a very hefty slice out of them." Hierarchy is indeed the one logical explanation of top-management incomes other than plain greed. But if it is true that these large compensation packages for top people in the very big companies are badges of rank rather than "real money" (something no rank-and-file employee will ever agree with), then why not treat them as symbols? To the extent, for instance, to which the chairman and chief executive of Universal International must get more than a certain multiple of rank-and-file compensation, why not have the company give the excess in the form of a charitable contribution in his name to a beneficiary of his choosing?

There are undoubtedly other—and perhaps better—ways to balance the need for top-management compensation that is high enough to provide incentives and reward performance with the need for an equitable relationship between top-management compensation and the pay of the company's other employees. And some answers will be worked out within the next few years—unions and politicians will see to it.

[1983]

1986 Note: By 1985 excessive executive compensation did then actually become an issue in wage negotiation. That the chairman of the Chrysler Corporation, Mr. Lee Iacocca, had paid himself a multimillion-dollar bonus in the same year in which he cut blue-collar wages by 30 percent was the union's main reason for refusing to make any concessions on wages, benefits, and working conditions and for its imposing a contract on Chrysler with labor costs so high that they are likely to destroy the company should the American automobile market turn down for a few years.

17

Overage Executives: Keeping Firms Young

Most companies, especially large ones, still assume that age sixty-five is the normal retirement age for managers and executives. But more and more of them, especially in middle-management ranks and in highly specialized work, take early retirement, some as early as age fifty-two. An even larger and faster-growing group is beginning to exercise the legal right (of all but a small group of executives in "decision-making positions" with very large retirement pensions) to delay retirement until age seventy. And the compulsory retirement of federal employees and of employees in California who aren't decision-making executives with very large pensions isn't permitted anymore at any age. Therefore, unless the employer plans for the retirement of aging executives, he is likely to find that the people he would most like to keep are the ones taking early retirement while the ones he would most like to get rid of are staying on the payroll until age seventy and beyond.

So far employers, as a rule, are handling these problems on a case-by-case basis. They still think they have freedom to decide whether they want executives to stay or to leave when they are in their fifties or to ease them out when they reach sixty-five. But that practically guarantees being accused of age discrimination.

"We haven't been sued yet for age discrimination by any of our managers or professionals," the personnel vice-president of a big insurance company told me recently. "But only because we backtrack immediately when anyone as much as hints at challenging us—we must have caved in at least thirty times in the last few years."

Indeed, planning for the retirement of executives should begin when they are still in early middle age. For the law now defines the onset of *aging*—at least for purposes of nondiscrimination—as age forty-two. After that, any decision affecting an individual—a new assignment or the lack thereof, a raise or a promotion or their denial, even a lateral transfer—can, and will, be challenged as age discrimination unless the employer has a clear, well-documented policy to ensure equal treatment of all employees based on performance and its appraisal.

A lot of early retirements these past few years were involuntary and the result of employment cutbacks. But a much larger number were voluntary—and the number is rising. A sizable proportion are people who do indeed retire, or at least plan to do so, especially those with health problems. But many more only "retire" to do something else, for example, to start their own small business. *Modern Maturity,* the publication of the American Association of Retired Persons—the third-largest magazine in the country—is full of stories of successful second careers and successful business start-ups by people who are officially "retired" and "on pension." A good many of these nonretiring retirees have only waited to quit their jobs until the kids were grown up and their pensions vested. But many more —some personnel people believe it to be a substantial majority —would have liked to have stayed on but felt that their talents weren't being fully utilized or felt that they had advanced as far as they would go. Many of them are right, and they should have been encouraged to leave much earlier. But many people who take early retirement because they feel unneeded and unwanted are plain wrong, only no one tells them.

What is needed is systematic analysis of a company's executives and managers in their early or mid-forties. Which ones does the company really want to keep until they reach retirement age, that is, for an additional twenty or twenty-five years? Which ones have already peaked or are about to reach the point beyond which they are unlikely to advance and are unlikely to make any further contribution? And which ones—the most critical category—are productive, valuable people, but only within a fairly narrow, specialized range?

We know what to do about the people who have already peaked in their early forties. They should be helped to find a job elsewhere, and at an age at which they still can be placed easily, that is, before they reach their late forties. If they stay an additional ten years, they only block the advancement of younger people. The other group, the people who should be encouraged to stay rather than to seek early retirement, are the challenge. They are likely to leave unless something is done to hold them. Yet they are precisely the people who find it easiest and most tempting to take early retirement, only to move to smaller companies, to start their own businesses, or to join consulting practices. These are typically the people who want to continue what they are doing and want to continue where they are—but feel that the company no longer appreciates them, or needs them, or respects them. They are the people who need career planning the most, and *before* they have begun to feel rejected and superfluous: that is, before they reach their late forties.

The time to start is now. By 1990 the first group of the baby-boom children will be past forty, and the young executives of today will become middle-aged. Then employers, especially large employers, will suddenly find themselves with a "bulging midriff" on their executive bodies. They will suddenly have large numbers of still-young people who have had years of rapid promotions and who suddenly find themselves stuck in a terminal job. By then, a policy of identifying the ones who should stay and the ones who should leave should be in place and working.

By then also, any employer should have in place a policy for the over-sixties in managerial and professional ranks. Before the end of the 1980s, the people who began their executive and professional careers in the first big hiring wave after 1929, that in the early 1950s, will reach and pass age sixty. Unlike their predecessors, however, they won't disappear automatically five years later. The person who has switched to a "second career" at age forty-five or even fifty knows how to find and develop a third one, twenty years later. But to go out and start anew at age sixty-three or sixty-five if one has never done this earlier is difficult and discouraging.

The basic rule, and one that should be clearly established and firmly enforced, is that people beyond their early sixties should ease out of major managerial responsibilities. It is a sensible rule for anyone, and not only for the executive, to stay out of decisions if one won't be around to help bail out the company when the decisions cause trouble a few years down the road—as most of them do. The older executive should move into work one performs on one's own rather than be the "boss," work where he or she specializes and concentrates on one major contribution, advises, teaches, sets standards, resolves conflicts, rather than work as a "manager." The Japanese have "counselors," and they work very effectively, sometimes well into their eighties.

One good American example is an old executive in one of our major banks. Until age sixty-three, he was head of the bank's Asia-Pacific division and built it into a major moneymaker. Then, ten years ago, he moved out of operations and became the policymaker, strategist, and adviser on the bank's problem loans to the Third World. Now his associates have persuaded him to stay on for a few more years—but he no longer travels and no longer negotiates. The secret, as this example shows, is to identify the specific strengths of a person and to put them to work.

Isn't all this a great deal of work? Yes, but there is really no alternative. Employers in treating the aging executive will find themselves increasingly caught between the proverbial rock and the hard place. The *rock* is the law under which the employer has to prove that a personnel decision—any personnel decision—affecting an employee over forty-two does not discriminate against age.

But also, until well into the next century—until 2015 or so when the firstborn of the baby boom will themselves reach their mid-sixties—employers will be under heavy pressure from their younger people.

The baby boom did not end until the 1961 "baby bust." The baby boom's last cohorts are therefore only now coming out of the graduate and professional schools. For an additional ten years, until the babies born in 1960 reach their thirty-fifth year, we shall have very large numbers of young people in the managerial and professional ranks. And for another ten years thereafter, we will have very large groups in "the best years," the years between thirty-five and forty-five. These younger people will be highly schooled and ambitious and will expect the rapid promotions of their immediate predecessors. The company that cannot or will not satisfy this *hard place,* the expectations of the younger people, risks losing its most valuable human resource; the ambitious ones will quit and the ones who stay behind will retire on the job.

What is therefore needed are policies that satisfy both the legal imperative of keeping the aging executive on the job and the demographic imperative of creating promotional opportunities for the younger people. And, to keep the enterprise healthy, both the aging and the young have to be focused on performance, challenged, and productive.

[1984]

18

Paying the
Professional Schools

The best investment around, by far, is professional school. Whether it is engineering school or medical school, law school or library school, business school or architecture school, graduation from one of them increases a person's lifetime earning power by a substantial multiple of the *investment,* that is, of the cost of his or her education.

Not all professional schools produce the same economic returns, of course. But even the ones with the lowest "yield" (probably schools of education, social work, and library science) endow their graduates with the potential of earning well above the median American income. Yet financing professional education will become increasingly difficult, whether the school is tax-supported or private.

Costs have been rising much faster at professional schools than at undergraduate liberal-arts colleges. Yet major increases in costs are still ahead for a good many professional schools. It is in those schools, after all—and by no means only in engineering or graduate business schools—that faculty salaries are becoming so uncompetitive that there is already a serious brain drain. And with money for higher education becoming increasingly scarce, the suppliers, whether legislatures or private donors, are bound to cut back on supporting those institutions—the schools for the "elite" and the "affluent"—rather than on supporting education for the "masses" at undergraduate liberal-arts colleges.

President John R. Silber of Boston University long ago proposed to bridge the gap between the riches that universities generate for their graduates and their own penury with a loan program under which the graduates would repay their schools the full cost of their tuition over five or ten years.

The problem with that proposal is that it might deter a substantial number of the ablest applicants; going into debt for a sizable amount at the very beginning of one's career is frightening, especially to young people from low-income backgrounds.

A loan program of that kind would also grossly discriminate against a graduate who chose to dedicate his or her life to public service rather than go where the money is—the physician, for instance, who goes into research or becomes a medical missionary in Africa rather than a plastic surgeon on Park Avenue, or the lawyer who becomes a public defender rather than a corporate-takeover specialist.

If professional education is treated as an investment, however, the problem is quite simple. Investments are paid for out of the additional value they create. All that is needed to finance professional education—indeed, to put it on Easy Street—is to return to it a fraction of the valued added by it, that is, of the increase in the graduate's lifetime earning power.

This would not burden the person who chooses to become a medical missionary; his liability would be zero. And it would also not burden the colleague who rakes in the money as a successful plastic surgeon; she can afford it. A fairly small proportion of the value added through professional education —at most 5 percent of the graduate's earnings above the median income—should be adequate to support the professional school and give it financial independence. It would even be possible to support graduate schools of arts and sciences—the schools in most of our universities that are in the worst financial shape—in this way. Graduate schools of arts and sciences are, so to speak, the source of "R & D" for the professional schools, and it is shortsighted management to cut back research and development to what it can earn by "selling" its by-products.

Yet this is exactly what many of our universities are doing when they cut the budget of the graduate school of arts and sciences to what it can support by training Ph.D.s for largely nonexistent teaching jobs at colleges. The main "product" of that graduate school is knowledge and vision—and that needs to be supported adequately whether there are a great many doctoral students or only a few.

If we finance the professional schools through assessing the value added to the lifetime earning power of their graduates, and then put, say, one-tenth of the professional schools' income into the graduate schools of arts and sciences, we would, I am convinced, have a solid financial base for research and scholarship in all but the most expensive areas. We would attain a degree of financial independence that would ensure that research grants, whether from government or industry, would again become the icing on the cake rather than the cake itself.

But how would we organize this? One way—the easy but dangerous way—would be to collect through the tax system.

Let us assume that the graduates of professional schools get a distinct Social Security number. All that would then be needed would be a few lines on the annual tax return where the taxpayers would deduct an amount equal to the median family income from their taxable income, figure out 5 percent of the difference, and add the result to the tax they remit. This would be no more difficult than the calculation for the Social Security tax on the self-employed, which is already part of Form 1040.

No change in the tax law would be necessary to make the 5-percent charge tax deductible as a charitable contribution—legally it is a payment on a charitable pledge.

I would much prefer, however, a separate and nongovernment mechanism; let's call it the Academic Credit Corporation. It would be a cooperative to which universities would turn over their claims, which the cooperative would collect for all of them.

One major advantage of this is, of course, that claims would soon—perhaps within five and certainly within ten years —become bankable instruments that could be sold in the financial market or borrowed against, thus generating an early cash flow back to the professional schools, based on actuarial expectations and experience in collecting against pledges. Even more important and desirable, such a cooperative would keep the schools and their money apart from the government.

I can think of no greater contribution that our major foundations could make today than to emulate what the Carnegie Foundation did sixty years ago when it underwrote the Teachers Insurance and Annuity Association (thereby, in my opinion, ensuring the survival of private higher education in America) and underwrite the Academic Credit Corporation.

What about the possibility that requiring a pledge to repay 5 percent of value added, especially if it were irrevocable and firmly collectible, would deter applicants?

To be sure, if a weak professional school pioneered the idea, it might lose applicants, but a strong one—the medical school at Harvard University, for instance, or the Wharton School at the University of Pennsylvania—could only gain. For there are strong indications that a good many able applicants are already deterred by the high and rising cost of professional school. If they could defer payment until they were able to pay —that is, until they had the income that a professional education makes possible—they could and would enter.

Unless the professional schools find a way to get paid when their graduates are able to pay out of the value added by the professional degree, they may soon find that they have priced themselves beyond the reach of all but the children of the rich, while still not taking in enough to maintain faculties, libraries, laboratories, and research.

[1982]

19

Jobs and People: The Growing Mismatch

It is becoming fashionable to rename the personnel department "the department of human resources." But few employers, indeed, few human-resources managers themselves, yet realize that more is needed than a better personnel department. We face a growing mismatch between jobs and available labor supply.

Both are changing, but in different, often opposite, directions. As a result, the job openings increasingly do not fit the available people. In turn, qualifications, expectations, and values of people available for employment are changing to the point where they no longer fit the jobs offered.

This applies to the job most people still think of when they speak of "labor," the blue-collar job in manufacturing. Even outside the "rust bowl," blue-collar unemployment is still high enough to hold wages down. Yet some of the most desirable and best-paid blue-collar jobs are increasingly hard to fill. What formerly called for "skilled labor" now increasingly demands a *technologist,* that is, someone who has a modicum of theoretical knowledge, in, for example, installing information systems or in programming robots and automated materials-moving equipment. It is in such work that manufacturing offers the fastest-growing job opportunities. But we do not even know as yet whether old-line blue-collar workers can be retrained in large numbers for such jobs. In the hospital, the one major employment area with a need to fill such jobs in the past, upgrading traditional blue-collar labor has not worked. The "paramedics" represent a group with different backgrounds, training, expectations, and qualifications. And the technologist in the factory actually needs greater ability to acquire additional knowledge—and thus a firmer theoretical base—than did the paramedics with their narrow specializations.

Changes in jobs and their content are also creating mismatches in management. Technology is one factor. We know how to train people to do technology such as engineering or chemistry. But we do not know how to endow managers with *technological literacy,* that is, with an understanding of technology and its dynamics, the opportunities it offers, and its impact on product and process, markets, organization structures, and people. Yet technological literacy is increasingly a major requirement for managers, especially on the lower and middle levels.

But not only individual jobs are being changed; organization structures are changed as much. Technology is again a factor. As more information becomes available, fewer levels of management but more specialists of all kinds are needed. Changes in the economic and social environment are pushing businesses in the same direction. Twenty years ago, high-level specialists were, on the whole, confined to research and to data processing. Today, even a medium-size company may well have an environmental specialist, one assistant treasurer who does nothing but manage cash and liquidity and tries to protect the company against foreign-exchange losses, and another one who watches over costly benefits programs.

Our management trainees, however, are unprepared for

careers as specialists. Their aspirations and expectations point them toward managerial jobs. And in business, the values, career opportunities, and rewards still assume an organization structure in which a managerial rather than a professional appointment constitutes recognition, advancement, and reward. To be sure, thirty years ago, a few companies, notably GE, pioneered "parallel ladders" of recognition and promotion for managers and individual professional contributors. But save in strictly scientific work, this has not really worked so far.

The assistant treasurers who handle the company's foreign-exchange exposure or its benefit plans see their advancement in being promoted out of the specialist's job and into "general management," yet there are fewer and fewer promotional opportunities in general management.

In the clerical ranks similar forces have the same effects. "Electronic mail," for instance, makes most of the traditional secretary's skills obsolete. Instead, she is likely to find herself expected to define the one part of her boss's work that henceforth will be her own direct responsibility. And even the secretary who sees in this a promotion is unlikely to be prepared for the change.

Shifts in population structure and age structure may have an even greater impact on the mismatch between jobs and labor supply, at least a more visible one. The labor-force participation of married women under age fifty is now just as high as that of men. It is therefore unlikely to rise any further. But a very large number of women in the labor force—the bulk of those who entered since 1970 when the inrush of women began —are now reaching their mid-thirties. They are approaching the age at which they must decide whether to have a second child. And most, save only the minuscule proportion in executive ranks, want both a career and a family.

Most of the married women stay in the labor force after their first child. Few, it seems, drop out entirely even after the second one. But a large proportion switch to part-time work at least until the second child enters third grade. Some employers have organized for this and have created permanent part-time jobs staffed by women employees. The great majority have not. And even those who offer part-time job opportunities have, as a rule, not thought through what these permanent part-time employees require by way of benefits, opportunities, pensions, and so on. Where rights for women were the great "cause" of the late 1970s, rights for part-time workers who are women may become the cause of the late 1980s and early 1990s.

Another major factor is the moving of the baby-boom babies into middle age. Many companies are speeding up the early retirement of the over-fifties to make room for large masses of baby-boomers—the oldest of whom are now almost forty—who demand promotions into key jobs. But the oldest of the "baby-bust" babies are now themselves twenty-five years old, and entering their first managerial jobs. And they expect the same opportunities and rapid advancement their only slightly older predecessors have had. Yet these expectations are unrealistic.

When the baby-boomers entered the work force there was a vacuum in management positions. But the newcomers now will find that the pipelines are full. Most of the baby-boomers have gone as far as they will go in management and will stay in their present jobs another thirty years or so. There is thus a total mismatch between reality and the perfectly normal expectations of the young people now entering the work force. To bridge it we will not only have to change expectations; we will have to redesign managerial and professional jobs so that even able people will still be challenged by the job after five or more years in it. Increasingly, in other words, we will have to heap responsibility on people in junior positions. And, above all, we will have to find rewards and recognition other than promotion—more money, bonuses, extra vacations, perhaps a "presidential citation," and so on. In the meantime, however, an entire generation has grown up for whom promotion is the only "real" satisfaction, and failure to get one every year or two is equivalent to being a "loser."

And there is the emergence of entrepreneurship, especially in existing businesses. Existing businesses increasingly will have to learn to be innovative and to create entrepreneurship within the going concern. We know how to do this; there are any number of examples around. And people on all levels within the company and outside of it are ready to become innovators and entrepreneurs. Yet, with the exception of a fairly small number of entrepreneurial companies—Johnson & Johnson, Procter & Gamble, 3M in this country, Marks & Spencer in Britain, and so on—existing businesses, small ones even more so than large ones, know only managerial jobs, pay only for managerial performance, have only a managerial structure and managerial tools and measurements.

To attract and hold entrepreneurial people and to promote innovation and entrepreneurship, companies will have to create new structures with new relationships and new policies and supplement managerial compensation, benefits, and rewards with those appropriate to the very different realities of entrepreneurship.

To overcome the growing mismatch between jobs and labor supply, employers—especially large ones—will first have to think through and project their job needs a few years out. So far, planning mostly means anticipating the markets for products and services a few years out, analyzing technology, and projecting both on money needs. Increasingly, planning will have to project people needs as well and will, in turn, project jobs and demographic trends on products and services, technology, and money requirements. Increasingly planning will have to ask: Do these goals of ours take advantage of trends in labor supply and in the expectations, aspirations, qualifications, and values of people? Or do they run counter to them? The most successful planning in the future may well start out with trends and developments in the supply of people rather than with financial goals or market projections.

Also, companies will have to both step up and considerably change their training. American business is already the country's largest educator. But most companies have "training programs" rather than a "training policy." Few focus their training on the company's needs five years out or on their employees' aspirations. Fewer still have any idea what they are getting for all the money and effort they spend on training, let alone what they should be getting. Yet training may already cost as much as health care for employees—perhaps more.

Finally, employers increasingly will have to change what they mean by "labor market." Increasingly it will be the job seeker who is the "customer," with job opportunities and job characteristics having to satisfy the job seeker. Traditionally employers have seen the labor market as homogeneous, divided only by very broad lines: age and sex, for example, or manual workers, clerical workers, and managerial and professional workers. But increasingly the available work force is segmenting into a fairly large number of different markets, with considerable freedom for the individual to switch from one to another. Increasingly, therefore, employers will have to learn that jobs are products that have to be designed for specific buyers and both marketed and sold to them.

[1985]

20

Quality Education: The New Growth Area

That America's schools will improve—radically and quite soon —is certain.

How fast they will improve we don't yet know, though it may be faster than anyone expects. Nor is it at all clear how the changes will come about. But the economic rewards for knowledge and skill, after a half century of steady decline, are going up sharply—and so are the penalties for their absence.

It is generally believed that in this century jobs have become more demanding. But this holds true only for a minority of jobs, and, in general, only for jobs that have always had high knowledge requirements, such as physician or engineer. For a good many others, educational credentials have often risen without any real change in knowledge or skill requirements; where applicants once needed a high school diploma, for instance, they now usually need four years of college, although there isn't any discernible change in the job itself. But for the largest single group and the one that has fared by far the best in this century—low-skilled manual workers in manufacturing

—neither knowledge nor credential requirements have become any stiffer. And whereas in this group the economic rewards for acquiring knowledge or skills were extremely high a half century ago, they have gone down so sharply as to have all but disappeared.

Seventy-five years ago it took an industrial worker three full years of steady work to earn the $750 that was the original price of that low-cost miracle, the Ford Model T. And the $250 a year in cash was all such a worker earned then—and only in the most unlikely event of being fully employed ten hours a day, six days a week, and fifty weeks a year. There were no "fringes"—no Social Security, no pension, no group life insurance, no health insurance, no sickness pay, no unemployment compensation, no workmen's compensation, and, of course, no extra pay for working overtime or on Sundays.

The direct descendant of this manual laborer of yesterday, the unionized blue-collar worker in the mass-production industries—steel, automotive, electrical machinery, rubber, chemicals—costs a minimum of $50,000 a year (about one-half "fringes"), or nine times the price of a low-priced new car today. And this understates the real income gain; for today's blue-collar worker with his eight-hour day and five-day week works one-third fewer hours in a year than his predecessor did seventy-five years ago. His hourly income, as measured by automobile prices, has thus increased forty- to fiftyfold. And although the average labor cost for semiskilled work in manufacturing is well below the cost in the big, fully unionized, mass-production industries—$15 an hour as against $25 at U.S. Steel—even that represents an annual real income of $30,000, or five new cars, or a twentyfold increase in hourly income in seventy-five years.

This fundamental change in the economic position of the low-skilled worker in the developed countries is the central social event of this century. There has never been anything even remotely similar in social history. To a very large extent it reflects, of course, the rocketlike rise in productivity in the last one hundred years. But although usually called "a rise in labor productivity," it was accomplished in its entirety through higher capital investment, better machines and tools, and, above all, better management. Contrary to all Marx considered "scientific" and absolutely certain, labor, and especially the least-skilled and least-knowledgeable labor (Marx's "proletariat"), received all the fruits of increased productivity, and perhaps a little more.

This is surely one of mankind's more creditable feats. For the worker of today does not work longer and harder than the worker of 1907; he works fewer hours and, thank God, with a fraction of the backbreaking bodily toil and the accidents of yesterday. Above all, his work requires no more knowledge or skill. In fact, it is a pure euphemism to call it "semiskilled"—nothing that can be learned in three weeks, as is true of most production-line work, can be considered to need any skill. It took a good deal longer to become proficient at digging a ditch with pick and shovel.

But in most other occupations in our economy real incomes have gone up far less quickly. Indeed, the more skill or knowledge a job requires, the less its real income has risen. Salespeople in retail stores had about the same income as blue-collar workers in the early years of the century—perhaps a little more. Today they average between one-third and one-half. Doctors and lawyers had a real income at least five times that of blue-collar workers. Their total "compensation package" today is on average less than twice that of the highly unionized blue-collar workers in the steel or auto plant. The real income of teachers in the best-paying big-city systems was then about three times that of a blue-collar worker. Even adjusting for the teachers' fewer working days, longer vacation, and liberal pension plans, teachers now make a good deal less than unionized blue-collar workers.

The compression of income differentials has been greatest in manufacturing. The differential between skilled people (machinists and electricians, for instance) and semiskilled is down to 25 percent; seventy-five years ago the skilled workers earned three times as much, with a famous early Ford car ad boasting that "the Model T costs no more that a good craftsman can earn in a year." College graduates around 1910 started at around $20 a week, or three times a laborer's wages. Now their starting salaries are lower than those of laborers. Even industry's pampered darlings, the MBAs of the prestigious business schools, often work for five years before their total compensation package exceeds that of the unskilled blue-collar worker who survives the thirty-day probationary period.

One need not be a confirmed egalitarian to consider most of these developments beneficial and, indeed, elementary justice. But the by-product, neither intended nor foreseen, has been a steady devaluation of knowledge and skill, and with it a steady whittling away of the incentives for maintaining the performance capacity of the schools.

Seventy-five years ago the school was, by and large, the *only* way out of grueling poverty and total insecurity, and the only access to modest affluence, self-respect, and the respect of one's community. Knowledge and skills were, of course, no guarantee of success. But without them failure was practically certain. Hence there was enormous community pressure on the school to maintain standards and to demand performance. The demands that the destitute Jewish immigrants made on New York City's schools in the first quarter of this century have been described often. What is rarely realized is that these demands transformed what, before 1890 or 1900, had been a lackluster or even inferior school system into the educational pressure cooker described so vividly in the memoirs of the New York Jewish writers.

The Iowa farm community or the Swedish settlers in Minnesota put the same pressure on their schools, and for the same reason. "Just tell us if you have any trouble-maker or any boy who doesn't want to learn and we'll take care of him," the eighteen-year-old "schoolmarm" from New England was told by the community elders when she arrived to take on the one-room schoolhouse in the prairie town, and the elders meant it.

Jobs requiring knowledge and skill—or at least their credentials—still carry far more social prestige, of course. And many other forces act on schools besides economics. Still, since World War II, knowledge and skill have ceased to be the only economic escape hatch. The college professor still thinks it's disgraceful if his son "drops out" and goes to work on an assembly line. But the son lives just as well as his father. And what the blue-collar worker sees is that his older son, who works as a machine operator in the glass plant, earns just as much as the younger son who graduated from the state university, and earns it a good deal sooner. No wonder this worker is then willing to settle for a school that's "caring" rather than "demanding."

But this state of things is over now. It would be over even if recovery were to restore every blue-collar job, with full wages and benefits. The switch to knowledge work as the economy's growth area and the large-scale movement to new technologies mean above all that productivity will increasingly be determined by the knowledge and skill that workers put into their task. And productivity, in the end, always determines the ability to pay and the level of real incomes.

This is the reason we can say with confidence that the American school will improve—fast.

[1983]

Part III

MANAGEMENT

21

Management:
The Problems of Success

The best-kept secret in management is that the first systematic applications of management theory and management principles did not take place in business enterprise. They occurred in the public sector. The first systematic and deliberate application of management principles in the United States—undertaken with full consciousness of its being an application of management—was the reorganization of the U.S. Army by Elihu Root, Teddy Roosevelt's secretary of war. Only a few years later, in 1908, came the first "city manager" (in Staunton, Virginia), the result of a conscious application of such then-brand-new management principles as the separation of "policy" (lodged in an elected and politically accountable city council) from "management" (lodged in a nonpolitical professional, accountable managerially). The city manager, by the way, was the first senior executive anyplace called a *manager*; in business, this title was still quite unknown. Frederick W. Taylor, for instance, in his famous 1911 testimony before the U.S. Congress never used the term but spoke of "the owners and their helpers." And when Taylor was asked to name an organization that truly practiced "Scientific Management," he did not name a business but the Mayo Clinic.

Thirty years after, the city manager Luther Gulick applied management and management principles to the organization of a federal government that had grown out of control in the New Deal years. It was not until 1950 and 1951, that is, more than ten years later, that similar management concepts and principles were systematically applied in a business enterprise to a similar task: the reorganization of the General Electric Company after it had outgrown its earlier, purely functional organization structure.

Today, surely, there is as much management outside of business as there is in business—maybe more. The most management-conscious of our present institutions are probably the military, followed closely by hospitals. Forty years ago the then-new management consultants considered only business enterprises as potential clients. Today half of the clients of a typical management consulting firm are nonbusiness: government agencies, the military, schools and universities, hospitals, museums, professional associations, and community agencies like the Boy Scouts and the Red Cross.

And increasingly, holders of the advanced degree in Business Administration, the MBA, are the preferred recruits for careers in city management, in art museums, and in the federal government's Office of Management and Budget.

Yet most people still hear the words *business management* when they hear or read *management.* Management books often outsell all other nonfiction books on the bestseller lists; yet they are normally reviewed on the business page. One "graduate business school" after another renames itself "School of Management." But the degree it awards has remained the *MBA,* the Master of *Business* Administration. Management books, whether textbooks for use in college classes or books for the general reader, deal mainly with business and use business examples or business cases.

That we hear and read *business management* when the

word *management* is spoken or printed has a simple explanation. The business enterprise was not the first of the managed institutions. The modern university and the modern army each antedate the modern business enterprise by a half century. They emerged during and shortly after the Napoleonic Wars. Indeed, the first "CEO" of a modern institution was the chief of staff of the post-Napoleonic Prussian army, an office developed between 1820 and 1840. In spirit as well as in structure, both the new university and the new army represented a sharp break with their predecessors. But both concealed this—deliberately—by using the old titles, many of the old rites and ceremonies and, especially, by maintaining the social position of the institution and of its leaders.

No one could, however, have mistaken the new business enterprise, as it arose in the third quarter of the nineteenth century, for a direct continuation of the old and traditional "business firm"—the "counting house" consisting of two elderly brothers and one clerk that figures so prominently in Charles Dickens's popular books published in the 1850s and 1860s, and in so many other nineteenth-century novels, down to Thomas Mann's *Buddenbrooks* published in 1906.

For one, the new business enterprise—the *long-distance railroad* as it developed in the United States after the Civil War, the *Universal Bank* as it developed on the European Continent, or the *trusts* such as United States Steel, which J. P. Morgan forged in the United States at the turn of the twentieth century—were not run by the "owners." Indeed, they had no owners, they had "shareholders." Legally, the new university or the new army was the same institution it had been since time immemorial, however much its character and function had changed. But to accommodate the new business enterprise, a new and different legal *persona* had to be invented, the "corporation." A much more accurate term is the French *Société Anonyme,* the anonymous collective owned by no one and open to investment by everyone. In the corporation, shares become a claim to profits rather than to property. Share ownership is, of necessity, separate from control and management, and easily divorced from both. And in the new corporation capital is provided by large, often by very large, numbers of outsiders, with each of them holding only a minute fraction and with none of them necessarily having an interest in, or—a total novelty—any liability for, the conduct of the business.

This new "corporation," this new *"Société Anonyme,"* this new *"Aktiengesellschaft,"* could not be explained away as a *reform,* which is how the new army, the new university, and the new hospital presented themselves. It clearly was a genuine innovation. And this innovation soon came to provide the new jobs—at first, for the rapidly growing urban proletariat, but increasingly also for educated people. It soon came to dominate the economy. What in the older institutions could be explained as different procedures, different rules, or different regulations became in the new institution very soon a new function, management, and a new kind of work. And this then invited study; it invited attention and controversy.

But even more extraordinary and unprecedented was the position of this newcomer in society. It was the first new autonomous institution in hundreds of years, the first to create a power center that was within society yet independent of the central government of the national state. This was an offense, a violation of everything the nineteenth century (and the twentieth-century political scientists still) considered "law of history," and frankly a scandal.

Around 1860 one of the leading social scientists of the time, the Englishman Sir Henry Maine, coined the phrase in his book *Ancient Law* that the progress of history is "from status to contract." Few phrases ever have become as popular and as widely accepted as this one.

And yet, at the very time at which Maine proclaimed that the law of history demands the elimination of all autonomous power centers within society, the business enterprise arose. And from the beginning it was clearly a power center within society and clearly autonomous.

To many contemporaries it was, and understandably so, a totally unnatural development and one that bespoke a mon-

strous conspiracy. The first great social historian America produced, Henry Adams, clearly saw it this way. His important
novel, *Democracy,* which he wrote during the Grant administration, portrays the new economic power as itself corrupt and,
in turn, as corrupting the political process, government, and
society. Henry's brother, Brooks Adams, a few decades later,
further elaborated on this theme in one of the most popular
political books ever published in the United States, *The Degen-
eration of the Democratic Dogma.*

Similarly, the Wisconsin economist, John R. Commons—
the brain behind the *progressive movement* in Wisconsin, the
father of most of the "reforms" that later became the social and
political innovations of the New Deal, and, last but not least,
commonly considered the father of America's "business unionism"—took very much the same tack. He blamed business
enterprise on a lawyers' conspiracy leading to a misinterpreta-
tion of the Fourteenth Amendment to the Constitution by
which the corporation was endowed with the same "legal personality" as the individual.

Across the Atlantic in Germany, Walter Rathenau—himself the successful chief executive of one of the very large new
"corporations" (and later on to become one of the earliest
victims of Nazi terror when he was assassinated in 1922 while
serving as foreign minister of the new Weimar Republic)—
similarly felt that the business enterprise was something radically new, something quite incompatible with prevailing political and social theories, and indeed a severe social problem.

In Japan, Shibusawa Eiichi, who had left a promising
government career in the 1870s to construct a modern Japan
through building businesses, also saw in the business enterprise
something quite new and distinctly challenging. He tried to
tame it by infusing it with the Confucian ethic; and Japanese
big business as it developed after World War II is very largely
made in Shibusawa's image.

Everyplace else, the new business enterprise was equally
seen as a radical and dangerous innovation. In Austria, for
instance, Karl Lueger, the founding father of the "Christian"

parties that still dominate politics in Continental Europe, was elected lord mayor of Vienna in 1897 on a platform that defended the honest and honorable small businessman—the shopkeeper and the craftsman—against the evil and illegitimate corporation. A few years later, an obscure Italian journalist, Benito Mussolini, rose to national prominence by denouncing "the soulless corporation."

And thus quite naturally, perhaps even inevitably, concern with management, whether hostile to it or friendly, concentrated on the business enterprise. No matter how much management was being applied to other institutions, it was the business enterprise that was visible, prominent, controversial, and above all, new, and therefore significant.

By now, however, almost a hundred years after management arose in the early large business enterprises of the 1870s, it is clear that management pertains to every single social institution. In the last hundred years every major social function has become lodged in a large and managed organization. The hospital of 1870 was still the place where the poor went to die. By 1950 the hospital had become one of the most complex organizations, requiring management of extraordinary competence. The labor union in developed countries is run today by a paid managerial staff, rather than by the politicians who are nominally at the head. Even the very large university of 1900 (and the largest then had only five thousand students) was still simple, with a faculty of, at most, a few hundred, each professor teaching his own specialty. It has by now become increasingly complex—including undergraduate, graduate, and postgraduate students—with research institutes and research grants from government and industry and, increasingly, with a large administrative superstructure. And in the modern military, the basic question is the extent to which management is needed and the extent to which it interferes with leadership— with management apparently winning out.

The identification of management with business can thus no longer be maintained. Even though our textbooks and our studies still focus heavily on what goes on in a business—and typically, magazines having the word *management* in their title (for example, Britain's *Management Today* or Germany's *Management Magazin*) concern themselves primarily if not exclusively with what goes on in business enterprises—management has become the pervasive, the universal organ of a modern society.

For modern society has become a "society of organizations." The individual who conforms to what political and social theorists still consider the norm has become a small minority: the individual who stands in society directly and on his own, with no intermediary institution of which he is a member and an employee between himself and the sovereign government. The overwhelming majority of all people in developed societies are employees of an organization; they derive their livelihood from the collective income of an organization, see their opportunity for career and success primarily as opportunity within an organization; and define their social status largely through their position within the ranks of an organization. Increasingly, especially in the United States, the only way in which the individual can amass a little property is through the pension fund, that is, through membership in an organization.

And each of these organizations, in turn, depends for its functioning on management. Management makes an organization out of what otherwise would be a mob. It is the effective, integrating, life-giving organ.

In a society of organizations, managing becomes a key social function and management the constitutive, the determining, the differential organ of society.

≫ *The New Pluralism*

The dogma of the "liberal state" is still taught in our university departments of government and in our law schools. According to it, all organized power is vested in one central government. But the society of organizations is a *pluralist* society. In open defiance of the prevailing dogma, it contains a diversity of organizations and power centers. And each has to have a management and has to be managed. The business enterprise is only one; there are the labor unions and the farm organizations, the health-care institutions and the schools and universities, not to mention the media. Indeed, even government is increasingly becoming a pluralist congeries of near-autonomous power centers, very different indeed from the branches of government of the American Constitution. There is the civil service, for instance. The last president of the United States who had effective control of the civil service was Franklin D. Roosevelt fifty years ago; in England it was Winston Churchill; in Russia, Stalin. Since their time the civil service in all major countries has become an establishment in its own right. And so, increasingly, has the military.

In the nineteenth century the "liberal state" had to admit the parties, though it did so grudgingly and with dire misgivings. But the purpose of the parties was the conquest of government. They were, so to speak, gears in the governmental machine and had neither existence nor justification outside of it.

No such purpose animates the institutions of the new pluralism.

The institutions of the old pluralism, that is, of medieval Europe or of medieval Japan (the princes and the feudal barons, the free cities, the artisans, the bishoprics and abbeys) were themselves governments. Each indeed tried to annex as much of the plenitude of governmental power as it could get away with. Each levied taxes and collected customs duties. Each strove to be granted the right to make laws, and to establish and run its own law courts. Each tried to confer knighthoods, patents of nobility, or titles of citizenship. And each tried to obtain the most coveted right of them all, the right to mint its own coins.

But the purpose of today's pluralist institution is nongovernmental: to make and to sell goods and services, to protect jobs and wages, to heal the sick, to teach the young, and so on. Each only exists to do something that is different from what government does or, indeed, to do something so that government need not do it.

The institutions of the old pluralism also saw themselves as total communities. Even the craft guild, the powerful woolen weavers of Florence, for instance, organized itself primarily to control its members. Of course, weavers got paid for selling woolen goods to other people. But their guild tried as hard as possible to insulate the members against economic impacts from the outside by severely restricting what could be made, how much of it, and how and at what price it could be sold, and by whom. Every guild gathered its members into its own quarter in the city, over which it exerted governmental control. Every one immediately built its own church with its own patron saint. Every one immediately built its own school; there is still "Merchant Taylor's" in London. Every one controlled access to membership in the guild. If the institutions of the old pluralism had to deal with the outside at all, they did so as "foreign relations" through formal pacts, alliances, feuds, and, often enough, open war. The outsider was a foreigner.

The institutions of the new pluralism have no purpose except outside of themselves. They exist in contemplation of a "customer" or a "market." Achievement in the hospital is not a satisfied nurse, but a cured *former* patient. Achievement in business is not a happy work force, however desirable it may be; it is a satisfied customer who reorders the product.

All institutions of the new pluralism, unlike those of the old, are single-purpose institutions. They are tools of society to supply one specific social need, whether making or selling cars, giving telephone service, curing the sick, teaching children to read, or providing benefit checks to unemployed workers. To make this single, specific contribution, they themselves need a considerable measure of autonomy, however. They need to be organized in perpetuity, or at least for long periods of time. They need to dispose of a considerable amount of society's resources, of land, raw materials, and money, but above all of people, and especially of the scarcest resource of them all, highly trained and highly educated people. And they need a considerable amount of power over people, and coercive power at that. It is only too easy to forget that in the not-so-distant past, only slaves, servants, and convicts had to be at the job at a time set for them by someone else.

This institution has—and has to have—power to bestow or to withhold social recognition and economic rewards. Whichever method we use to select people for assignments and promotions—appointment from above, selection by one's peers, even rotation among jobs—it is always a power decision made for the individual rather than by him, and on the basis of impersonal criteria that are related to the organization's purpose rather than to the individual's purpose. The individual is thus, of necessity, subjected to a power grounded in the value system of whatever specific social purpose the institution has been created to satisfy.

And the organ through which this power is exercised in the institution is the organ we call *management*.

This is new and quite unprecedented. We have neither political nor social theory for it as yet.

This new pluralism immediately raises the question, Who takes care of the commonweal when society is organized in individual power centers, each concerned with a specific goal rather than with the common good?

Each institution in a pluralist society sees its own purpose as the central and the most important one. Indeed, it cannot do otherwise. The school, for instance, or the university could not function unless they saw teaching and research as what makes a good society and what makes a good citizen. Surely nobody chooses to go into hospital administration or into nursing unless he or she believes in health as an absolute value. And as countless failed mergers and acquisitions attest, no management will do a good job running a company unless it believes in the product or service the company supplies, and unless it respects the company's customers and their values.

Charles E. Wilson, GM's chairman (later President Eisenhower's secretary of defense), never said, "What is good for General Motors is good for the country." What he actually said is "What is good for the country is good for General Motors, and vice versa." But that Wilson was misquoted is quite irrelevant. What matters is that everybody believed that he not only said what he was misquoted to have said, but that he actually believed it. And indeed no one could run General Motors—or Harvard University, or Misericordia Hospital, or the Bricklayers Union, or the Marine Corps—unless he believed that what is good for GM, or Harvard, or Misericordia, or the Bricklayers, or the Marines is indeed good for the country and is indeed a "mission," that if not divinely ordained, is still essential to society.

Yet each of these missions is one and only one dimension of the common good—important yes, indispensable perhaps, and yet a relative rather than an absolute good. As such, it must be limited, weighed in the balance with, and often subordinated to, other considerations. Somehow the common good must be made to emerge out of the clash and clamor of special interests.

The old pluralism never solved this problem. This explains why suppressing it became the "progressive cause" and the one with which the moral philosophers of the modern age (that is, of the sixteenth through the nineteenth centuries) aligned themselves.

Can the new pluralism do any better? One solution is, of course, to suppress the pluralist institutions. This is the answer given by totalitarianism and is indeed its true essence. The totalitarian state, whether it calls itself Fascist, Nazi, Stalinist, or Maoist, makes all institutions subservient to and extensions of the state (or of the omnipotent party). This saves the "state" of modern political theory, but at the sacrifice of individual freedom, of free thought and free expression, and of any limitation on power altogether. The state (or the party) is then indeed the *only* power center, as traditional theory preaches. But it can maintain its monopoly on power only by being based on naked terror, as Lenin was the first to realize. And even at that horrible price, it does not really work. As we now know—and the experience of all totalitarian regimes is exactly the same, whether they call themselves Right or Left—the pluralist institutions persist behind the monolithic facade. They can be deprived of their autonomy only if they and society altogether are rendered unable to perform, for instance, through Stalin's purges or Mao's Cultural Revolution. What the totalitarian regimes have proved is that modern society *has* to be a "society of organizations," and that means a pluralist society. The only choice is whether individual freedom is being maintained or is being suppressed and destroyed, albeit to no purpose other than naked power.

The opposite approach to that of the totalitarian is the American one. The United States, alone among modern nations, never fully accepted the dogma of the liberal state. It opposed to it, quite early in its history, a pluralist political theory, that of John C. Calhoun's "concurrent majority." In the way in which Calhoun presented his theory in the 1830s and 1840s, that is, as a pluralism exercised through the individual states and intended to prevent the breakup of the Union over slavery, the "concurrent majority" did not survive the Civil War. But thirty years later, Mark Hanna, the founder of the modern Republican party and of modern American politics altogether, reformulated Calhoun's pluralism as a concurrent majority of the major "interests": farmers, workers, business. Each of these three "estates of the realm" can effectively veto the majority. It must not impose its will on the others. But it must be able to prevent the others from imposing their will on it. Another thirty years later, Franklin D. Roosevelt made this the basic political creed of the New Deal. In Roosevelt's system government became the arbiter whose job it is to make sure that no one interest gets too powerful. When Roosevelt came in, "capital"—*business* as a term came later, and *management* later still—appeared to be far too powerful. Farmers and workers were thus organized to offset the business power. And then, not so many years later, when the labor power seemed to become too great, farmers and business were organized to offset and balance labor power, and so on.

Each of the "interests" is free to pursue its own goals regardless of the common good; it is indeed expected to do so.

In the darkest days of World War II, in 1943 when American troops still lacked arms and ammunition, John L. Lewis, the founder of the Congress of Industrial Organizations (that is, of modern American unionism) and the powerful head of the coal miners' union, called a coal strike to get higher wages for his men, defying national wage controls. President Roosevelt attacked him publicly for endangering the nation's survival. Lewis retorted: "The President of the United States is paid to look after the nation's survival. I am paid to look after the interests of the coal miners." And while the newspapers attacked Lewis harshly, public opinion apparently felt that Lewis had only said out aloud what the Roosevelt administration had practiced all along. It gave Lewis enough support to win the strike.

This example, however, shows that the American pluralist doctrine is hardly adequate. Indeed, just as the old pluralism did, it has given birth to so many vested interests and pressure groups that it is almost impossible to conduct the business of government, let alone to conduct it for the common good.

In 1984–85 practically everyone in the United States agreed that the country needed a drastic tax reform to replace an increasingly complicated and irrational tax code, with a few tax rates and with exemptions eliminated. But no such code could be enacted. Every single exemption became the sacred cause of a vested interest. And even though some of them represented only a few hundred or a few thousand voters, each of them could and did block tax reform.

Is there a way out? The Japanese seem to be the only ones so far able to reconcile a society of organizations with the pursuit of the common good. It is expected of the major Japanese interests that they take their cue from "what is good for the country": Then they are expected to fit what is good for themselves into the framework of a public policy designed to serve the national interest.

It is doubtful, however, whether even Japan can long maintain this approach. It reflects a past in which Japan saw herself as isolated in a hostile and alien world—so that all of

Japan, regardless of immediate interests, had to hang together lest it hang separately. Will this attitude survive Japan's success? And could such an approach have a chance in the West, where interests are expected to behave as interests?

Is this a problem of management, it will be asked? Is it not a problem of politics, of government, or political philosophy? But if management does not tackle it, then almost inevitably there will be imposed political solutions. When, for instance, the health-care institutions in America, the hospitals and the medical profession, did not take responsibility for spiraling health-care costs, government imposed restrictions on them, for example, the Medicare restrictions on the care of the aged in hospitals. These rules clearly are not concerned with health care at all and may even be detrimental to it. They are designed to serve short-run fiscal concerns of government and employers, that is, designed to substitute a different but equally one-sided approach for the one-sided, self-centered approach of the health-care "interests."

This must be the outcome unless the managements of the institutions of the new pluralism see it as their job to reconcile concern for the common good with the pursuit of the special mission for the sake of which their institution exists.

≫ The Legitimacy of Management

Power has to be legitimate. Otherwise it has only force and no authority, is only might and never right. To be legitimate, power has to be grounded outside of it in something transcending it that is accepted as a genuine value, if not as a true absolute by those subject to the power—whether descent from the gods or apostolic succession; divine institution or its modern, totalitarian counterpart the scientific laws of history; the consent of the governed, popular election or, as in so much of modern society, the magic of the advanced degree. If power is an end in itself, it becomes despotism and both illegitimate and tyrannical.

Management has to have power to do its job, whatever the

organization. In that respect there is little difference between the Catholic diocese, the university, the hospital, the labor union, and the business enterprise. And because the governing organ of each of these institutions has to have power, it has to have legitimacy.

And here we encounter a puzzle. The management of the key institutions of our society of organizations is by and large accepted as legitimate. The single exception is the management of the business enterprise. Business enterprise is seen as necessary and accepted as such. Indeed, society is often more concerned with the survival of a large business or an industry than it is with that of any other single institution. If a major business is in trouble, there is a crisis and desperate attempts to salvage the company. But at the same time, business management is suspect. And any exercise of management power is denounced as usurpation, with cries from all sides for legislation or for judicial action to curb if not to suppress managerial power altogether.

One common explanation is that the large business enterprise wields more power than any other institution. But this simply does not hold water. Not only is business enterprise hemmed in in its power on all sides—by government and government regulations, by labor unions, and so on. The power of even the largest and wealthiest business enterprise is insignificant next to that of the university now that a college degree has become a prerequisite for access to any but the most menial jobs. The university and its management are often criticized, but their legitimacy is rarely questioned.

The large labor union in Western Europe and in American mass-production industries surely has more power than any single business enterprise in its country or industry. Indeed in Western Europe, both in Britain and on the Continent, the large labor union became society's most powerful institution in the period after World War II, more powerful sometimes than the nation's government. The unions' exercise of their power during this period was only too often self-serving, if not irresponsible. But even their bitterest critics in Western Europe and in the United States rarely questioned the unions' legitimacy.

Another explanation—the prevalent one these days—is that the managements of all other institutions are altruistic, whereas business is profit-seeking and therefore out for itself and materialistic. But even if it is accepted that for many people nonprofit is virtuous, and profit dubious, if not outright sinful, the explanation that profit undermines the legitimacy of business management is hardly adequate. In all Western countries the legitimacy of owners, that is, of real capitalists, and their profits is generally accepted without much question. That of a professional management is not, yet professional management obtains profits for other people rather than for itself—and its main beneficiaries today are the pension funds of employees.

And then there is the situation in Japan. In no other country, not even in France or in Sweden, was the intellectual climate of the postwar period as hostile to "profit" as in Japan, at least until 1975 or so. The left-wing intelligentsia of Japan in the universities or the newspapers might have wanted to nationalize Japan's big businesses. But it never occurred even to the purest Marxist among them to question the necessity of management or its legitimacy.

The explanation clearly lies in the image which Japanese management has of itself and which it presents to its society. In Japanese law, as in American and European law, management is the servant of the stockholders. But this the Japanese treat as pure fiction. The reality which is seen as guiding the behavior of Japanese big-business management (even in companies that are family-owned and family-managed like Toyota) is management as an organ of the business itself. Management is the servant of the going concern, which brings together in a common interest a number of constituencies: employees first, then customers, then creditors, and finally suppliers. Stockholders are only a special group of creditors, rather than "the owners" for whose sake the enterprise exists. As their performance shows, Japanese businesses are not run as philanthropies and know how to obtain economic results. In fact, the

Japanese banks, which are the real powers in the Japanese economy, watch economic performance closely and move in on a poorly performing or lackluster top management much faster than do the boards of Western publicly held companies. But the Japanese have institutionalized the going concern and its values through lifetime employment, under which the employees' claim to job and income comes first—unless the survival of the enterprise itself is endangered.

The Japanese formulation presents very real problems, especially at a time of rapid structural change in technology and economy when labor mobility is badly needed. Still, the Japanese example indicates why management legitimacy is a problem in the West. Business management in the West (and in particular business management in the United States) has not yet faced up to the fact that our society has become a society of organizations of which management is the critical organ.

Thirty years ago or so, when the serious study of management began, Ralph Cordiner, then CEO of the General Electric Company, tried to reformulate the responsibility of corporate top management. He spoke of its being the "trustee for the balanced best interest of stockholders, employees, customers, suppliers and plant communities"—the groups which would now be called *stakeholders* or *constituencies*. As a slogan this caught on fast. Countless other American companies wrote it into their Corporate Philosophy statement. But neither Mr. Cordiner nor any of the other chairmen and presidents who embraced his rhetoric did what the Japanese have done: institutionalize their professions. They did not think through what the best-balanced interest of these different stakeholders would mean, how to judge performance against such an objective, and how to create accountability for it. The statement remained good intentions. And good intentions are not enough to make power legitimate. In fact, good intentions as the grounds for power characterize the "enlightened despot." And enlightened despotism never works.

The term *enlightened despot* was coined in the eighteenth

century—with Voltaire probably its greatest and most enthusiastic exponent—when the divine right of princes was no longer generally accepted as a ground of legitimate power. The prince with the best intentions among eighteenth-century enlightened despots and the very model of the progressive, the enlightened liberal, was the Austrian emperor Joseph II (reigned 1765–90). Every one of the reforms that he pioneered was a step in the right direction—the abolition of torture; religious toleration for Protestants, Jews, and even atheists; universal free education and public hospitals in every county; abolition of serfdom; codification of the laws; and so on. Yet his subjects, and especially his subjects in the most advanced parts of his empire, the Austrian Netherlands, rose against him in revolt. And when, a few years later, the French Revolution broke out, the enlightened despots of Europe toppled like ninepins. They had no constituency to support them.

Because Ralph Cordiner and his contemporaries never even tried to ground management power in institutional arrangements, their assertion very rapidly became enlightened despotism. In the 1950s and 1960s it became *corporate capitalism,* in which an enlightened "professional" management has absolute power within its corporation, controlled only by itself and irremovable except in the event of catastrophe. "Stock ownership," it was argued, had come to be so widely dispersed that shareholders no longer could interfere, let alone exercise control.

But this is *hubris*: arrogance and sinful pride, which always rides before a fall. Within ten years after it had announced the independence of management in the large, publicly owned corporation, "corporate capitalism" began to collapse. For one, stock ownership came to be concentrated again, in the hands of the pension funds.

And then inflation distorted values, as it always does, so that stock prices, which are based on earnings expectations, came to appear far lower than book values and liquidation values. The result was the wave of hostile takeovers that has been inundating the American economy these last years and is spilling over into Europe now. Underlying it is the assertion that the business enterprise exists, and solely, for the sake of stockholder profits, and short-run, immediate profits at that.

By now it has become accepted widely—except on Wall Street and among Wall Street lawyers—that the hostile takeover is deleterious and in fact one of the major causes of the loss of America's competitive position in the world economy. One way or another, the hostile takeover will be stopped (on this see also Chapter 28 of this volume). It may be through a "crash"; speculative booms always collapse in the end. It may be through such changes as switching to different classes of common stock, with the shares owned by the outside public having a fraction of the voting power of the insiders' shares, or by giving up voting rights for publicly held common shares altogether. (I owe this suggestion to Mr. Walter Wriston, the chairman emeritus of New York's Citibank.)

No matter how the hostile takeover boom is finally stopped, it will have made certain that the problem of management legitimacy has to be tackled. We know some of the specifications for the solution. There have to be proper safeguards of the economic performance of a business: its market standing, the quality of its products or services, and its performance as an innovator. There has to be emphasis on, and control of, financial performance. If the takeover boom has taught us one thing, it is that management must not be allowed substandard financial performance.

But somehow the various "stakeholders" also have to be brought into the management process (for example, through the company's pension plan as a representative of the company's employees for whom the pension plan is the trustee). And somehow the maintenance of the wealth-producing and the job-producing capacity of the enterprise, that is, the maintenance of the going concern, needs to be built into our legal and institutional arrangements. It should not be too difficult. After all, we built the preservation of the going concern into our bankruptcy laws all of ninety years ago when we gave it priority over all other claims, including the claims of the creditors. But whatever the specifics, business management has to attain legitimacy; its power has to be grounded in a justification outside and beyond it and has to be given the "constitutional" sanction it still largely lacks.

Closely connected to the problem of the legitimacy of management is management's compensation.

Management, to be legitimate, must be accepted as "professional." Professionals have always been paid well and deserve to be paid well. But it has always been considered unprofessional to put money ahead of professional responsibility and professional standards. This means that there have to be limitations on managerial incomes. It is surely not professional for a chief executive officer to give himself a bonus of several millions at the very time at which the pay of the company's other employees is cut by 30 percent, as the chief executive officer of Chrysler did a few years ago. It is surely not professional altogether for people who are employees and not "owners" to pay themselves salaries and bonuses greatly in excess of what their own colleagues, that is, other members of management, receive. And it is not professional to pay oneself salaries and bonuses that are so far above the norm as to create social tension, envy, and resentment. Indeed there is no economic justification for very large executive incomes. German and Japanese top managers surely do as good a job as American top managers—perhaps, judging by results, an even better one. Yet their incomes are, at the most, half of what American chief executives of companies in similar industries and of similar size are sometimes being paid.

But there is also work to be done on the preparation, testing, and selection of, and on the succession to, the top-management jobs in the large business enterprises; on the structure of top management; and on performance standards for top management and the institutional arrangements for monitoring and enforcing them.

Business management is not yet fully accepted as legitimate in the West because it has not yet realized the full implications of its success. Individual executives, even those of the biggest company, are largely anonymous. They only make asses of themselves if they try to behave as if they were aristocrats. They are hired hands like the rest of us. On the day on which they retire and move out of the executive suite they become "nonpersons" even in their old company. But while in office they represent; individually almost faceless, collectively they constitute a governing group. As such their behavior is seen as representative. What is private peccadillo for ordinary mortals becomes reprehensible misconduct and indeed betrayal if done by a leader. For not only is the leader visible; it is his duty to set an example.

But then there is also the big question of what is now being called the "social responsibility" of management. It is not, despite all rhetoric to the contrary, a social responsibility of business but of all institutions—otherwise we would hardly have all the malpractice suits against American hospitals or all the suits alleging discrimination against American colleges and universities. But business is surely one of the key institutions of a society of organizations and as such needs to determine what its social responsibilities are—and what they are not.

Surely business, like anyone else, is responsible for its impacts: responsibility for one's impacts is, after all, one of the oldest tenets of the law. And surely, business, like anyone else, is in violation of its responsibilities if it allows itself impacts beyond those necessary to, and implicit in, its social purpose, for example, producing goods and services. To overstep these limits constitutes a *tort,* that is, a violation.

But what about problems that do not result from an impact or any other activity of business and yet constitute grave social ills? Clearly it is not a responsibility of business, or of any organization, to act where it lacks competence; to do so is not responsibility but irresponsibility. Thus when a former mayor of New York City in the 1960s called for "General Electric and the other big corporations of New York City to help solve the problem of the Black Ghetto by making sure that there is a man and father in the home of every Black Welfare Mother," he was not only ridiculous. He demanded irresponsibility.

But also management must not accept "responsibility" if by doing so it harms and impedes what is its first duty: the economic performance of the enterprise. This is equally irresponsible.

But beyond these caveats there is a no-man's-land where we do not even fully understand what the right questions are. The problems of New York, for instance, are in no way caused by business. They were largely caused by public policies business had warned against and fought against: primarily by rent control, which, as it always does, destroys the very housing the poor need, that is, decent, well-maintained older housing; by demagogic welfare policies; and by equally demagogic labor-relations policies. And yet when New York City was on the verge of self-destruction, in the late 1960s and early 1970s, a small group of senior executives of major New York business enterprises mobilized the business community to reverse the downward slide and to renew New York City—people like Austin Tobin of the Port of New York Authority; David Rockefeller of the Chase Manhattan Bank; Walter Wriston and William Spencer of Citibank; Felix Rohatyn of Lazard Frères, the private bankers; the top management of Pfizer, a pharmaceutical company; and several others. They did this not by "taking responsibility" for things they lacked competence in, for example, the problems of the black ghetto. They did it by doing what they were highly competent to do: they started and led the most dramatic architectural development of any major city since Napoleon III had created a new Paris and Francis Joseph a new Vienna a hundred years earlier. The black ghetto is still there, and so are all the ills associated with it, for example, crime on the streets. But the city has been revitalized.

And this did not happen because these businesses and their managements needed the city; excepting only the Port of New York Authority, they could all have moved out, as a good many of their colleagues—IBM, for instance, or General Electric, or Union Carbide—were doing. These businesses and their top managements acted because the city needed them, though, of course, they benefited in the end if only because a business

—and any other institution—does better in a healthy rather than a diseased social environment.

Is there a lesson in this? There surely is a challenge.

Altogether, for management of the big business to attain full legitimacy, it will have to accept that to remain "private" it has to accept that it discharges a social, and that means a "public," function.

≫ *The Job as Property Right*

When, in 1985, a fair-size Japanese company found itself suddenly threatened by a hostile takeover bid made by a group of American and British "raiders"—the first such bid in recent Japanese history—the company's management asserted that the real owners of the business, and the only ones who could possibly sell it, were not the stockholders, but the employees. This was considerable exaggeration, to be sure. The real owners of a major Japanese company are the banks, as has already been said. But it is true that the rights of the employees to their jobs are the first and overriding claim in a large Japanese company, except when the business faces a crisis so severe that its very survival is at stake.

To Western ears the Japanese company statement sounded very strange. But actually the United States—and the West in general—may be as far along in making the employees the dominant interest in business enterprise, and not only in the large one as in Japan. All along, of course, the employees' share of the revenues of a business, almost regardless of size, exceeds what the "owners" can possibly hope to get: ranging from being four times as large (that is, 7 percent for after-tax profits, as against 25 percent for wages and salaries) to being twelve times as large (that is, 5 percent for profits versus 60 percent of revenues for wages and salaries). The pension fund not only greatly increased the share of the revenues that go into the "wage fund," to the point that in poor years the pension fund may claim the entire profit and more. American law now also gives the pension fund priority over the stockholders and their property rights in a company's liquidation, way beyond anything Japanese law and Japanese custom give to the Japanese worker.

Above all, the West, with the United States in the lead, is rapidly converting the individual employee's job into a new property right and, paradoxically, at the very time at which the absolute primacy of stockholder short-term rights is being asserted in and by the hostile takeover.

The vehicle for this transformation in the United States is not the union contract or laws mandating severance pay as in many European countries. The vehicle is the lawsuit. First came the suit alleging discrimination, whether in hiring an employee, in firing, in promotion, in pay, or in job assignment —discrimination on grounds of race or sex or age or handicap. But increasingly these suits do not even allege discrimination, but violation of "due process." They claim that the employer has to treat the employee's job, including the employee's expectations for pay and promotion, as something the enjoyment of which and of its fruits can be diminished or taken away only on the basis of preset and objective standards and through an established process which includes an impartial review and the right to appeal. But these are the features that characterize "property" in the history of the law. In fact, they are the *only* features a right must possess to be called property in the Western legal tradition.

And as few managements yet seem to realize, in practically every such suit the plaintiff wins and the employer loses.

This development was predictable. Indeed, it was inevitable. And it is irreversible. It is also not "novel" or "radical." What gives access to a society's productive resources—gives access thereby to a livelihood and to social function and status and constitutes a major, if not the major, avenue to economic independence however modest—has always become a "property right" in Western society. And this is what the job has become, and especially the knowledge worker's job as a manager or a professional.

We still call land "real" property. For until quite recently

it was land alone that gave to the great majority of mankind
—95 percent or more—what "property" gives: access to, and
control over, society's productive resources; access to a livelihood and to social status and function; and finally a chance at
an *estate* (the term itself meant, at first, a landholding) and
with it economic independence.

In today's developed societies, however, the overwhelming majority—all but 5 or 10 percent of the population—find
access to and control over productive resources and access to
a livelihood and to social status and function through being
employees of organizations, that is, through their jobs. For
highly educated people the job is practically the only access
route. Ninety-five percent, or more, of all people with college
degrees will spend their entire working lives as employees of an
organization. Modern organization is the first, and so far the
only, place where we can put large numbers of highly educated
people to productive work and pay them for applying knowledge.

For the great majority of Americans, moreover, the pension fund at their place of employment is their only access to
an "estate," that is to a little economic independence. By the
time the main breadwinner in the American family, white collar or blue collar, is forty-five years old, the claim to the pension
fund is likely to be the family's largest asset, far exceeding in
value the equity in the home or the family's personal belong-
ings, for example, their automobiles.

Thus the job had to become a property right—the only
question is in what form and how fast.

Working things like this out through lawsuits may be "as
American as apple pie," but is hardly as wholesome. There is
still a chance for management to take the initiative in this
development and to shape the new property rights in the job
so that they equally serve the employee, the company, and the
economy. We need to maintain flexibility of employment. We
need to make it possible for a company to hire new people and
to increase its employment. And this means that we must avoid
the noose the Europeans have put around their neck: the sever-

ance pay which the law of so many Continental countries mandates makes it so expensive to lay off anybody that companies simply do not hire people. That Belgium and Holland have such extraordinarily high unemployment is almost entirely the result of these countries' severance pay laws. But whichever way we structure the new property rights which the job embodies, there will be several requirements which every employer, that is, every organization, will have to satisfy. First, there must be objective and equal performance standards for everyone performing a given job, regardless of race, color, sex, or age. Secondly, to satisfy the requirements of due process, the appraisal against these standards of performance has to be reviewed by somebody who is truly disinterested. Finally, due process demands a right of appeal—something, which by the way, as "authoritarian" a company as IBM has had for more than half a century.

The evolution of the job into a "property right" changes the position of the individual within the organization. It will change equally, if not more, the position of the organization in society. For it will make clear what at present is still nebulous: organized and managed institutions have increasingly become the organs of opportunity, of achievement, and of fulfillment for the individual in the society of organizations.

≫ *Conclusion*

There is still important work ahead—and a great deal of it— in areas that are conventionally considered "management" in the schools of management, in management journals, and by practicing managers themselves. But the major challenges are new ones, and well beyond the *field of management* as we commonly define it. Indeed, it will be argued that the challenges I have been discussing are not management at all, but belong in political and social theory and public law.

Precisely. The success of management has not changed the *work* of management. But it has greatly changed management's *meaning*. Its success has made management the general, the pervasive function, and the distinct organ of our society of organizations. As such, management inevitably has become "affected with the public interest." To work out what this means for management theory and management practice will constitute the "management problems" of the next fifty years.

[1986]

22

Getting Control of Staff Work

Corporate *service staffs*—the people who analyze and plan, supply knowledge, design policies, and give advice—have been growing at very high speed in most American organizations. Their growth is even faster in the nonprofit sector than in business. But since the 1950s at many major manufacturing companies, staff employment has grown five to ten times as fast as the number of "operating" people in production, engineering, accounting, research, sales, and customer service. The unchecked growth and excessive power of service staffs is considered by practically all our foreign critics to be a serious weakness of U.S. industry, and a major cause of its poor performance.

Staffs weren't always so bloated in America. In the 1950s many foreign visitors, especially the Japanese, came to the United States to learn how companies ought to use their staffs. It may be useful to remind ourselves of some of the lessons which our visitors put into practice in their own countries but which many American companies apparently have forgotten.

First, staff should concentrate on tasks of major importance that will continue for many years. A task of minor importance, if it is to be done at all, should be done in operations and by operating people. A task of major importance that will not last forever—for example, the reorganization of a company's management—is better handled as a one-time assignment. Then one calls in an outside consultant or, often the better way, one forms an ad hoc task force. One can get rid of either as soon as the job is done. But a staff of internal "organization consultants" will immediately build its own empire and start looking for places to "reorganize," a quest that will inevitably do damage.

Staff work should be limited to a few tasks of high priority. This is the rule most often violated in American business, especially by large companies. One personnel department I know has twenty-eight sections, each grinding out "policies," "programs," "procedures," "manuals," and "training courses"; thirty years ago it had four sections. Another company has fourteen sections in "marketing services."

Proliferation of staff services deprives them of effectiveness. Worse, it destroys the effectiveness of the people who produce results, the operating people. Every staff service is convinced that its concern is the most important area in the business, whether it is wage and salary administration, or sales forecasting, or inventory management. Each is busy, as it should be, producing policies and procedures. And each then expects operating people, from first-line supervisor to chief executive officer, to give it adequate time and attention.

Unless the number of staff tasks is closely controlled, staff will therefore gobble up more and more of operating people's scarcest resource: time. I like to use a simple test: If staff work in its totality—from planning and cash-flow analysis to a new public relations policy—requires more than three or four days a month of the working time of operating people on any level, then, except in rare moments of crisis, the staff needs to be pruned.

This means that every time the staff takes on a new task,

it should abandon an old one. "All right, you want to go into productivity research," one says to the personnel vice-president. "Which of the things you are doing now are you going to give up?"

Effective staff work requires specific goals and objectives, clear targets and deadlines. "We expect to cut absenteeism in half within three years" or "Two years from now we expect to understand the segmentation of our markets sufficiently to reduce the number of product lines by at least one third." Objectives like these make for productive staff work. Vague goals such as "getting a handle on employee behavior" or "a study of customer motivation" do not.

Every three years or so, it is important to sit down with every staff unit and ask, "What have you contributed these last three years that makes a real difference to this company?" Staff work in a business, a hospital, or a government agency is not done to advance knowledge; its only justification is the improvement of the performance of operating people and of the entire organization.

Rules for staff people are just as important as rules for staff work. Don't ever put anyone into a staff job, for example, unless he or she has successfully held a number of operating jobs, preferably in more than one functional area. For if staff people lack operating experience, they will be arrogant about operations, which always look so simple to the "planner." And unless staff people have proved themselves in operations, they will lack credibility among operating people and will be dismissed as "theoreticians."

This is so elementary a rule that even the most extreme proponent of staff supremacy, the Prussian army of the nineteenth century, strictly observed it. An officer had first to get promoted twice in troop command—from second to first lieutenant and then to captain—before he could sit for the general staff exam.

But today, in government even more than in business, we put young people fresh out of business or law school into fairly senior staff jobs as analysts or planners or staff counsel. Their arrogance and their rejection by the operating organization practically guarantee that they will be totally unproductive. By contrast, no man in Japan, whether in business or government, gets into staff work of any kind until he has had seven—or, more usually, ten—years of successful performance in three or four operating assignments.

With rare exceptions, staff work should not be a person's "career" but only a *part* of his or her career. After five or seven years on a staff job, people ought to go back into operating work and not return to a staff assignment for five years or so. Otherwise, they will soon become behind-the-scene-wirepullers, "gray eminences," "kingmakers" like those brilliant mischief-makers, the staff officers of the Prussian army. Staff work, by definition, has great authority, the authority of knowledge. But it has no responsibility; its concern is advice, plan, forecast, rather than decision, execution, results. And it is the oldest adage of politics that authority without responsibility corrupts.

Above all, the true results of staff work are more effective, more productive operating people. Staff is support for operating people and not a substitute for them.

[1982]

23

Slimming
Management's Midriff

A widely quoted article in the *Harvard Business Review* thirty years ago asked, "Is Middle Management Obsolete?" and answered a resounding yes. But instead of disappearing or even shrinking, middle management has been exploding in the last few decades. In many companies the "middle" between the first-line supervisor and the corporate top has been growing three or four times faster than sales, even before adjustment for inflation.

The growth hasn't been confined to big business; middle management in small and medium-size companies may have grown even faster: since thirty years ago many of these companies had no "management" except the owning family. And it hasn't been confined to business; middle-management growth has been even greater in government, the military, and a host of nonprofit institutions. Thirty years ago the community hospital of 250 beds had an administrator (often an elderly physician retired from practice) and a director of nursing. Now it also has three or four associate or assistant administrators, a comptroller, and half a dozen "directors": of the medical lab, of X ray, of physical therapy, of food services, of data processing, and so on. A liberal arts college I know had, in 1950, a president, a dean, an assistant dean of students who also handled admissions, and a chief clerk who kept the books. Enrollment has doubled, from five hundred to one thousand, but administrative staff has increased sixfold, with three vice-presidents, four deans, and seventeen assistant deans and assistant vice-presidents.

Some of this growth is healthy. Thirty years ago, middle management was overworked and overaged, following twenty-five years of very low birthrates and twenty years (beginning in 1929) of low hiring and slow promotions. And of course all institutions have expanded tremendously since then, with both population and the economy growing at a fast clip. Some of this growth has been imposed from without. Of the three new vice-presidents in one community hospital, one works full time on labor relations, one on government regulations. And business has grown in complexity and new performance demands. The computer which the *Harvard Business Review* thought would make middle management obsolete has instead spawned a very large number of new middle-management jobs.

But a large part, perhaps the major part, of this growth has been inflation pure and simple. The inflation in management titles has been even more severe these last thirty years than the inflation of money. In the liberal-arts college of 1950, for instance, five secretaries did the same work now being done by seven or eight deans, assistant deans, and assistant vice-presidents—and did it very well. The head of Letters of Credit in a large commercial bank was then a "supervisor" or at most a "manager"; he is a senior vice-president now. There were many large companies with only one vice-president. And title inflation has been even worse in the military and in state and local governments.

Demographics pushed for rapid growth in middle-management jobs and titles, especially in the last ten years, when the baby-boomers entered the managerial labor force. As younger people entered in large numbers, older people in the organization had to be given promotions to make room. And as entrance salaries for the young, highly educated ones went up, the older ones had to be given corresponding raises and titles to go with them.

As a result middle managements today tend to be over-staffed to the point of obesity (and by no means only in the United States—Europe may be worse). This slows the decision process to a crawl and makes the organization increasingly incapable of adapting to change. Far too few people, even in high positions with imposing titles, are exposed to the chal-lenge of producing results. And it isn't only in the armed services that "support" has grown to the point that it overshad-ows the combat troops and employs many more people. A good many businesses large and small have become equally bureau-cratic and equally suffer from gross overweight around the midriff.

Yet by the late 1980s the supply of young people is going to drop sharply as the children of the baby bust replace the baby-boom children in professional schools. By the end of the decade the supply of young management candidates may be 30 percent below what it has been in the last several years. Not only will it become progressively easier to correct middle-man-agement bulge; it will become progressively more important. To maintain the present level of middle-management jobs, let alone continue expanding, would only lead to further bidding up management wages and further inflating management titles. Now is the time to start middle-management weight control.

One means is attrition. As a job becomes vacant through retirement, death, or resignation, don't automatically fill it. Don't "make a study" either. Leave jobs open for six or eight months and see what happens; unless there is an overwhelming clamor for filling the job then, abolish it. The few companies that have tried this report that about half the "vacancies" disappeared after six months. A large university that is using the same approach reports similar results.

Above all, use attrition to cut down on the number of managerial "levels." In the past thirty years levels have increased even faster than middle-management jobs. In the large university, which is now trying to reduce management, administration levels have been growing twice as fast as administrative staff positions (which in turn grew almost three times as fast as student enrollment). And similar or worse ratios can be found in many large businesses as well as in research labs. Every additional level, however, increases rigidity. Each slows the decision-making process. And it is a law of information theory that every *relay* (that is, "level") halves the information transmitted and doubles the noise. Levels should increase much more slowly than numbers, if at all.

The justification for this managerial growth will disappear: We will no longer have green people who must be promoted fast into positions for which they are inadequately prepared and who then don't stay long enough in the jobs to become proficient before being promoted out of them again. With the age structure of the managerial population changing rapidly—the median will be above forty in 1990; in the early 1980s it was in the very low thirties—the "ninety-day wonder" in management is about to be replaced by people with years of experience. Indeed we may well see a return to the old rule that people aren't ready for a promotion unless they already know enough about their new job to perform it without supervision after a very short time. And the "span of control" can then be substantially widened as subordinates will be expected to take responsibility for upward communications and for self-control. Then, as attrition creates a vacancy on one level, one abolishes the level.

A second way to reduce middle-management bulk is to substitute job-enlargement for promotion. In the last thirty years, and especially in the last ten or fifteen, we were almost forced to emphasize promotion. As recently as 1960 senior managers tended to be quite old in most organizations. And because of the low birthrates between 1925 and 1950 and the even lower hiring and promotion rates during most of that period, there wasn't nearly enough middle management around to replace them, let alone to provide managerial staff for rapid expansion. Hence from 1960 on young people had to be promoted as soon as they showed "promise."

But for the near term the pipelines are full. How much promotional opportunity is there, for instance, for the eager and brilliant vice-president of thirty-one at a large commercial bank when the senior VP to whom he or she reports is thirty-eight, the executive VP forty-six, and the president fifty? Or for his or her counterpart in academia, the assistant dean of twenty-nine whose dean is thirty-four, the provost forty-five, and the president forty-six? The one and only way to provide satisfaction and achievement for these young managers and executives—and for the even younger people working under them—is to make jobs bigger, more challenging, more demanding, and more autonomous, while increasingly using lateral transfers to different assignments, rather than promotions, as a reward for outstanding performance.

Twenty years ago we built into the performance review of managerial people the question, "Are they ready for promotion?" Now we need to replace the question with "Are they ready for a bigger, more demanding challenge and for the addition of new responsibilities to their existing job?"

[1983]

24

The Information-Based Organization

The "office of the future" is still largely speculation. But the organization of the future is rapidly becoming reality—a structure in which information serves as the axis and as the central structural support. A number of businesses—Citibank, for instance, in the United States; Massey-Ferguson, the Canadian multinational tractor maker; and some of the large Japanese trading companies—are busily reshaping their managerial structure around the flow of information. And wherever we have been moving into genuine automation of manufacturing production, as in the Erie, Pennsylvania, locomotive plant of General Electric, we are finding that we have to restructure management and redesign it as an information-based organization.

The organization chart of an information-based system may look perfectly conventional. Yet such an organization behaves quite differently and requires different behavior from its members.

The information-based structure is *flat,* with far fewer levels of management than conventional ones require. When a large multinational manufacturer restructured itself around information and its flow, it found that seven of its twelve levels of management could be cut out. Similarly, in automated plants, for example, the Nissan auto assembly plant outside of Yokohama, Japan, and the GE locomotive plant in Erie, most of the traditional management layers between first-line supervisor and plant manager have disappeared.

These levels, it turns out, were not levels of authority, of decision making, or even of supervision. They were relays for information, similar in function to the boosters on a telephone cable, which collect, amplify, repackage, and send on information—all tasks that an impersonal "information system" can do better. This pertains in particular to management levels that "coordinate" rather than "do"—group executives, or assistants to, or regional sales managers. But such levels of management as remain in information-based organizations find themselves with far bigger, far more demanding, and far more responsible jobs. This is true particularly in respect to the first-level supervisor in the automated plant.

The information-based structure makes irrelevant the famous principle of the *span of control,* according to which the number of subordinates who can report to one superior is strictly limited, with five or six being the upper limit. Its place is being taken by a new principle—I call it the *span of communications:* The number of people reporting to one boss is limited only by the subordinates' willingness to take responsibility for their own communications and relationships, upward, sideways, and downward. "Control," it turns out, is the ability to obtain information. And an information system provides that in depth, and with greater speed and accuracy than reporting to the boss can possibly do.

The information-based organization does not actually require advanced "information technology." All it requires is willingness to ask, Who requires what information, when and where? With nothing more high tech than the quill pen, the

British asked those questions in India two hundred years ago and came out with the world's flattest organization structure, in which four levels of management staffed by fewer than a thousand Britons—most of them youngsters barely out of their teens and "lower-middle management"—efficiently ruled a subcontinent.

But when a company builds its organization around modern information technology it *must* ask the questions. And then management positions and management layers whose main duty it has been to report rather than to do can be scrapped.

At the same time, however, the information-based structure permits, indeed it often requires, far more "soloists" with far more and different specializations in all areas, from technical and research people to service professionals taking care of special groups of customers. Citibank, for instance, recently appointed a senior vice-president in New York headquarters to take care of the bank's major Japanese customers and their financial needs anyplace in the world. This man is not the "boss" of the bank's large branches in Japan. But he is not "service" staff either. He is very definitely "line." He is a soloist and expected to function somewhat the way the pianist playing a Beethoven concerto is expected to function. And both he and the "orchestra" around him, that is, the rest of the bank, can function only because both "know the score." It is information rather than authority that enables them mutually to support each other.

Automated manufacturing plants have equally found that they need a good many quality-assurance specialists. These people, though very much seniors, hold no rank. They are not in the chain of command. Yet they take over as a kind of "pinch-hitting" superboss whenever any process within the plant runs into quality problems.

The information-based system also allows for far greater diversity. It makes it possible, for instance, to have within the same corporate structure purely *managerial units,* charged with optimizing what exists, and *entrepreneurial units,* charged with making obsolete what exists and with creating a different tomorrow.

Traditional organization basically rests on command authority. The flow is from the top down. Information-based organization rests on responsibility. The flow is circular from the bottom up and then down again. The information-based system can therefore function only if each individual and each unit accepts responsibility: for their goals and their priorities, for their relationships, and for their communications. Each has to ask, What should the company expect of me and hold me accountable for in terms of performance and contribution? Who in the organization has to know and understand what I am trying to do so that both they and I can do the work? On whom in the organization do I depend for what information, knowledge, specialized skill? And who in turn depends on me for what information, knowledge, specialized skill? Whom do I have to support and to whom, in turn, do I look for support?

The conventional organization of business was modeled after the military. The information-based system much more closely resembles the symphony orchestra. All instruments play the same score. But each plays a different part. They play together, but they rarely play in unison. There are more violins but the first violin is not the boss of the horns; indeed the first violin is not even the boss of the other violins. And the same orchestra can, within the short span of an evening, play five pieces of music, each completely different in its style, its scoring, and its solo instruments.

In the orchestra, however, the score is given to both players and conductor. In business the score is being written as it is being played. To know what the score is, everyone in the information-based organization has to manage by objectives that are agreed upon in advance and clearly understood. Management by objectives and self-control is, of necessity, the integrating principle of the information-based structure.

The information-based organization thus requires high self-discipline. This in turn makes possible fast decisions and quick response. It permits both great flexibility and considerable diversity.

These advantages will be obtained only if there are understanding, shared values and, above all, mutual respect. This probably rules out the finance-based diversification of the conglomerate. If every player has to know the score, there has to be a common language, a common core of unity. And this, experience has shown, is supplied only by a common market (for example, health-care providers or the housewife), or by a common technology. Even with a traditional command-based system, diversification that rests primarily on financial control, as it does in the typical conglomerate, has never outlasted the tenure of its founder, whether ITT's Harold Geneen or Gulf & Western's Charles Bluhdorn. But if the organization is information-based, diversification in which financial control is the only common language is bound to collapse in the confusion of the Tower of Babel.

The information-based organization is not permissive: it is disciplined. It requires strong decisive leadership; first-rate orchestra conductors are without exception unspeakably demanding perfectionists. What makes a first-rate conductor is, however, the ability to make even the most junior instrument at the last desk way back play as if the performance of the whole depended on how each one of those instruments renders its small supporting part. What the information-based organization requires, in other words, is leadership that respects performance but demands self-discipline and upward responsibility from the first-level supervisor all the way to top management.

[1985]

25

Are Labor Unions Becoming Irrelevant?

Within one short year—the year 1982—three well-known American union leaders called on me for counsel—the president of a large union of government employees, the president of a large union in a primary industry, and the head of a large district of a mass-production union. Each came with his own specific concerns. Yet each one asked—and fairly soon— whether the labor union still has a function in America or is becoming irrelevant.

Each of these men believes that to remain legitimate and to continue to be accepted as the spokesman, representative, and defender of the American working people, the labor union will have to develop positions and take actions that are incompatible with its traditions, its commitments, and its rhetoric.

"It is our proudest boast," the mass-production unionist said, "that the total wage package in our industry is some 30 percent to 40 percent higher than the average wage package in American manufacturing. But would there be record unemployment in our industry, approaching the levels of the Depression, if that 30 percent to 40 percent had been put into plant modernization instead of into wages and benefits? I know that all my colleagues in the union leadership ask themselves this question. But not one dares come out with it into the open— he wouldn't last ten minutes if he did."

Ten, even five, years ago, anyone who mentioned "capital formation" or "productivity" to a labor leader was dismissed as a "tool of the bosses." At best such matters were considered none of the union's business and "what management is being paid for." By now, few inside or outside union ranks would deny that the worker's welfare depends on capital formation and productivity, even in the very short run. The two largely determine how many jobs there can be, how secure they can be, and how well paid they can be.

To focus on capital formation and productivity, however, would be tantamount to accepting that the interests of the enterprise and the interests of its employees are identical—and this would be seen as a denial of the union's very reason for existence. So far no labor leader has even tried to build concern for capital formation and productivity, that is, for workers' jobs, into union thinking, policies, and actions.

A second challenge confronting labor leaders is that the union may no longer be able to maintain the unique position it has reached this century in all developed noncommunist countries. To use traditional terms, the union has become an *estate of the realm* with substantial immunities—from taxes, from antitrust, from damage suits, for instance—and with legal privileges that are not too dissimilar to those enjoyed in earlier times by the army in Prussia or by the church in prerevolutionary France. The union is considered legitimate as no other nongovernmental institution is. And in accepting and protecting the union's "right to strike" we have given one group in society a "right to civil disobedience."

The reason for this is the union's claim to be more than an interest group. It claims to be a cause. It wants more for its members as do all other interest groups, whether farmers, druggists, or undertakers. But the union also presents itself as the champion of all "underprivileged" or "exploited" groups in society. The true strength of the labor movement in developed countries has been moral: its claim to be the political conscience of a modern secular society.

And this claim, as most of my friends in the labor movement are beginning to see, cannot be maintained any longer. It is being destroyed by demographics. No matter how fast the economy will grow, "more" for the older people inexorably means "less" for the younger, working ones—and vice versa. One of my union friends—the president of the union of government employees—said that "the generation conflict between older and younger people rather than the conflict between management and labor will be the central social conflict of the next fifty years."

Today the support of the older nonworking population, in Social Security and pension fund contributions, takes roughly 20 to 25 cents out of every dollar available for wages and salaries to the working population. If we do nothing at all, this will go up to perhaps 33 cents within ten years—in part because older people are living much longer, in part because the low birthrates of the last twenty years limit the number of young people entering the labor force.

It is inconceivable that working people will stand still for this transfer to nonworking people. In years past, we bought their acquiescence by raising wages and salaries as fast as Social Security and pension-fund contributions, or faster. But this way is barred. With wages and salaries already taking 85 percent of GNP, all we can do is create inflation, which lowers real incomes for both the older retirees and the younger people at work. We will have to decide whether older retired people are to get "more" by taking it away from younger working ones, or whether the younger working ones will get "more" by such measures as reducing early-retirement pension payments, lowering Medicare health benefits, and delaying the age of full retirement benefits.

If the labor union ignores this dilemma—as most union

leaders understandably would like to do—the members will, of necessity, form new competing organizations that bypass the union and make it irrelevant. Retired people are already doing this. But if the union takes sides it will be fractured from within in short order. In either event it will soon cease to be the "cause," or to have a unique legitimacy.

An even more difficult problem for the union arises out of the fact that employees are fast becoming the only real capitalists and the only real owners of the "means of production." In Japan this has been accomplished through lifetime employment, which in effect means that, short of bankruptcy, large businesses are run primarily for the employees who, in traditional legal terms, are the "beneficial owners."

In the United States, where pension funds now own up to 50 percent or more of our large businesses, the employees are the real owners, and their pension funds the main source of capital for productive investment. Conversely, the stake in the retirement fund is increasingly the largest single asset of the American family, once the head of the household is forty-five years or older.

"Power follows property" is one of the oldest and most thoroughly tested laws of politics. Employees—or "trustees" supposed to act for them and accountable to them—will predictably be brought into the supervision and the management of pension funds. The only possible alternative is control of the funds by government and its appointees.

The result will be what any union fears the most and fights the hardest: an organ of the employees that expresses the identity of interest between enterprise and workers, is independent of the union and bypasses it, and, inevitably, will oppose the union as an outsider. This is, in effect, what has happened in Japan. There lifetime employment, by restricting labor mobility and thereby reducing the threat of strikes, has made the union impotent in the private sector and little more than an organ of management. The alternative is for the union to claim that it represents the employees both against management and in management—whether through "co-determination" as in

Germany; through control and management of the pension funds, which is what the unions in Sweden now demand; or through board membership as, for example, at Chrysler in the United States.

But "responsibility follows power" is also a law of politics. If it is disregarded—as it was, for instance, by the union members on the board of Volkswagen in Germany who in the late 1960s delayed the company's plan to build a plant in the United States because it would have meant "exporting German workers' jobs"—the result is serious damage. In VW's case, the company's share in the American auto market fell from 8 percent in 1969 to less than 1 percent now—seriously threatening the viability and survival of the whole enterprise and the jobs of its German employees.

But if the union representatives in management and ownership act responsibly, that is, in the interest of the enterprise, they soon will be tagged as "company stooges" and accused of having "sold out to management." This happened in the 1970s to the labor representatives on the boards of the German steel and coal companies and, a few years later, to the leaders of the United Automobile Workers in America when they accepted wage concessions to save companies in severe crisis. Indeed its Canadian members revolted and split off from the automobile workers' union.

There is a precedent in political history for the resolution of this conflict: the constitutional design that integrated the *populus,* the working people of Rome, into the power structure by enabling their representatives to veto actions by the patrician Senate. But it is not a problem that can be solved by good intentions or by rhetoric. It requires a redefinition of the role and function of the "countervailing power," the union, and its reestablishment as the embodiment of the ultimate identity of interest between employer and employee.

Management, no matter who "owns" and no matter whether the institution is a business, a government agency, or a hospital, has to have considerable power and authority—power and authority grounded in the needs of the enterprise and based on competence. And power, as the drafters of the American Constitution knew, needs to be limited by countervailing power. Modern society, a society of organizations each requiring strong management, needs an organ such as the labor union —events in Poland in the last few years have amply proved this. The alternative is an uncontrolled and uncontrollable government bureaucracy. But to become again a dynamic, effective, legitimate organ, the labor union will have to transform itself drastically. Otherwise my union friends will be proved right: The union will become irrelevant.

[1982]

26

Union Flexibility: Why It's Now a Must

Within the next two years the long-range course will be set for America's smokestack labor. Will smokestack incomes and jobs continue to shrink—and perhaps even faster in good times when industry can raise money for automation? Or can employment be stabilized and real incomes be maintained, at least for a goodly majority? The decision will be made by smokestack labor itself and by its unions.

Productivity in the American smokestack industries needs to be improved considerably. But poor productivity is not the real villain. To be sure Toyota has far fewer workers on its payroll per car than does General Motors. But then Toyota buys twice as much—or more—from outside suppliers. When the figures are adjusted for this, it turns out that the Detroit-made car still requires fewer man-hours to be produced. But each of these man-hours costs GM about 50 percent more than it costs the Japanese. Yet Toyota in Nagoya or Mercedes in Stuttgart do not employ "cheap labor"; the total annual compensation package of the Japanese or West German worker is exactly the same as that of most American industrial workers outside of the smokestack industries, whether unionized or not—around $30,000 a year (1985 dollars), or $15 an hour, counting all fringes and benefits. But an hour worked in an integrated steel mill in the United States—at U.S. Steel, Bethlehem, or Armco, for instance—or at any other of the major smokestack industries costs $25: $15 in cash wages and another $10 in fringes and benefits—total compensation of $50,000 a year for a full-time worker. And no industry can overcome such a labor-cost disadvantage in a competitive market, no matter how much it increases productivity.

At the root of this—and actually a good deal more important than dollars and cents—are the basic assumptions underlying compensation in our smokestack industries. An assumption held as an article of faith, especially by lower-ranking union leaders, business agents, and local presidents, is that "big business" has oligopolic control of the market; that is, it can always, and practically without limit, pass on higher costs in the form of higher prices. The old delusion persists that "capitalists" pay wages out of "profits"—despite the fact that wages and salaries in a developed economy account for something like 85 percent of revenues and profits for at most 5 percent or 6 percent. Most labor leaders still see the work force as homogeneous and as composed of adult males who work full time and who are the sole breadwinners in their families. Finally, there is the firm belief that the value of a "benefit" is not determined by how much it does for the beneficiary, the employee, but by how much it costs the employer; if a given benefit costs the employer more it is automatically seen as a "gain for the working man" and a "union victory." These assumptions were perhaps defensible thirty years ago when cash wages accounted for 90 percent of the compensation of the American worker and fringes were really that, no more than 6 percent or 7 percent, and when it was widely believed—by Eleanor Roosevelt, for instance—that married women would be out of the American labor force altogether by 1980. Today, however, these assumptions are inane and highly deleterious, above all, for the employee.

The first need of smokestack labor, most of the workers themselves would say, is the largest number of jobs, the slowest shrinkage rate, and the greatest employment continuity. The optimum would probably be a slowing down of the rate of job shrinkage to where, despite automation and structural changes in industry, it does not exceed the drop in the number of new entrants into the labor force who are available for traditional manual jobs in industry—a drop of around 30 percent in the next eight years as a result of the baby bust after 1960.

But this is almost certainly more than can actually be achieved. The second need of smokestack labor is thus for a cushion against the consequences of job shrinkage: that is, for provision for early retirement for older people and for retraining and placement of middle-aged ones.

Third would come the need for maximum income maintenance for smokestack workers.

And fourth, there is an urgent need to restructure benefits so that they meet the realities of today's work force. We need to make sure that the beneficiary gets the most for the available benefit money.

Different people will rank these needs differently. But there will be little disagreement with the answers themselves. They do lead, however, to radically different and highly controversial compensation policies.

First, a large part of the "wage" needs to be flexible instead of being fixed: It needs to be geared to performance, to profitability and productivity, with cash wages being larger, perhaps even much larger, in good years and lower, perhaps even much lower, in poor ones. This is perhaps the sharpest break with tradition, and one that management may resist as much as union leaders. Middle managers and supervisors, in particular, will be opposed; there is nothing they resent as much as a subordinate making more than they do. But labor has also traditionally accepted pay for productivity and profitability only as a "bonus" on top of a fixed wage and has altogether rejected the idea of cutting the fixed wage in bad times. "It is unfair to penalize workers for the lack of performance of their employers" has been a stock argument. But what is needed now—and what is now in the interest of the workers themselves—is adjustment to economic fluctuations through flexible wage costs rather than through unemployment; for adjustment through unemployment in the smokestack industries is likely not to be "cyclical" and temporary but structural and permanent. One-third of the cash wages in smokestack industries—the one-third that is in excess of the prevailing American industrial wage—might thus be considered flexible and contingent on performance (and in good years it might, then, greatly exceed one-third, of course). Wherever we have done something like this, for instance, at Lincoln Electric in Cleveland, the results have been substantially higher worker incomes over long periods of time and high employment stability.

And then, to satisfy the second need, labor incomes generated through productivity and profitability might be used to cushion job attrition, to provide early retirement pensions for older workers and retraining and placement monies for the middle-aged (younger workers under thirty are usually highly mobile and able to fend for themselves).

Benefits today are the same for everyone, old and young, men and women, married and unmarried. With a work force that has become as heterogeneous as ours, this means, however, that a substantial part of the benefit money is simply wasted: some estimates run as high as 40 cents out of every dollar. If both partners of a married couple work—and among the under-fifties this is the rule now—both today have full health insurance even though only one can collect reimbursement. The wife, even if working full time, does not commonly stay long enough in one place of employment to qualify for a pension—yet she is charged the full retirement-fund contribution, in addition to full Social Security of which, even if she outlives her husband, she'll never get one penny back. The pension fund contribution and Social Security, however, already amount to more than a fifth of her cash wage—and with Social Security contributions set to go up sharply, will soon exceed a full quarter! But there is also the unmarried man around twenty-eight who at his age does far better by putting an extra 15 percent or 20 percent of his income into a retirement account rather than getting a higher and highly taxed cash wage. Conversely the same employee, twenty years later, at forty-eight and with children of college age, might greatly benefit by trading a smaller retirement contribution against a larger cash income, and so on. With benefits uniform and totally inflexible, the union, understandably, has to push to get every benefit for everyone. Each of the gains helps only a minority of the members but penalizes all of them by creating unemployment as the industry becomes progressively less able to compete. What smokestack labor needs—and what incidentally the Japanese have had all along—is a "total compensation package." The total amount available per hour or per employee is fixed. But the individual employee can choose how much of the package should be cash income and how much benefits, and among benefits which of the available options provide the most real "benefit" to the individual according to his or her status in life and family-cycle. Whenever such flexible benefits have been introduced the result has been both a measurable increase in employee satisfaction, if not in real incomes, and a sharp cut in benefit costs, sometimes amounting to one-third or more.

Whenever I discuss these matters with union leaders, they nod and say, "You're absolutely right; that's what's needed." But then they immediately add: "But why should we stick out our necks and propose something so difficult, so novel, and so different from anything we've told our members all these years? We aren't paid to look after the interest of the companies; management is." But this is a total misreading of reality. The smokestack companies have alternatives. They can move labor-intensive work to the Third World—beginning with Mexico in our own backyard—where there is abundant low-cost manufacturing labor. They can automate—and technologically we now can easily multiply the speed of automation. But also unionization in the private sector of the American economy has now been going down steadily for thirty years and has already fallen to below the proportion of the labor force that was organized before the present mass-production unions were born in the big unionization wave of the New Deal—and there is no law of nature that demands unionization in smokestack industries. It is smokestack labor and its union leaders who have no choice. Either they take the initiative in developing new concepts and policies for wages and benefits, or they face rapid shrinkage and eventual disappearance of their jobs and with them of their unions. And isn't the labor leader, in the famous phrase of the founder of our smokestack unions, John L. Lewis, "paid to look after the interests of his members"?

[1983]

27

Management as a Liberal Art

Three foreigners—all Americans—are thought by the Japanese to be mainly responsible for the economic recovery of their country after World War II and for its emergence as a leading economic power. Edwards Deming taught the Japanese statistical quality control and introduced the "quality circle." Joseph M. Juran taught them how to organize production in the factory and how to train and manage people at work. What is now the "latest" import from Japan and the "hottest management discovery"—the "just-in-time" inventory delivery system (the Japanese word for it is *Kanban*)—was introduced to Japan by Juran, who had been instrumental in developing it for America's World War II production effort.

I am the third of these American teachers. My contribution, or so the Japanese see it, was to educate them about management and marketing. I taught them that people are a resource rather than a cost, and that people therefore have to be managed to take responsibility for their own as well as for the group's objectives and productivity. I taught them that communication has to be upward if it is to work at all. I taught them the importance of structure but also that structure has to follow strategy. I taught them that top management is a function and a responsibility rather than a rank and a privilege. And I also taught them that the purpose of a business is to create a customer, and that a business only exists in contemplation of the market.

All these things the Japanese could have learned from my books and they have, indeed, been my most avid readers—some of my management books have sold proportionately many more copies in Japan than they have in the United States. But my real impact in Japan was through the three- to four-week seminars that I ran in Japan every other year from the late 1950s to the mid-1980s for top people in government and business. My effectiveness in these seminars did not, however, rest on my knowledge of management techniques. It rested squarely on my interest in Japanese art and my acquaintance with Japanese history.

This interest of mine began as a result of a purely accidental visit to a Japanese art exhibition way back in 1934 when I was a young bank economist in London. My fascination with Japanese art, which resulted from this visit, led me to ask, What in their history, society, and culture explains the ability of the Japanese to have anticipated, sometimes centuries earlier, the most recent trends in Western modern art, beginning with impressionism and progressing through expressionism and cubism to abstract art?

Thus I found myself soon face-to-face with a mystery, a still largely unexplained mystery: How did the Japanese, alone of all non-Western people, manage to build a modern nation and a modern economy on technology and institutions imported from the West, and yet, at the same time, maintain their basic national identity and integrity? At first glance, nothing that the Japanese did in the late nineteenth century appeared different from what anybody else did at the time. The new kingdoms in the Balkans such as Bulgaria, the South American republics, or Persia similarly imported a broad range of Western institutions—a parliament and a navy modeled after the British, an army modeled after Prussia, a constitutional monarchy and government ministries modeled after Germany, universal education (again on the German model), universities modeled after America, banking modeled after France and Germany, and legal codes copied from the Germans, Swiss, and French. Yet only in Japan did these foreign imports "take." Morcover, they flourished as effective modern institutions and, at the same time, served to maintain a Japan as distinct, as clearly identified, and as cohesive as it had been when it was totally isolated from intercourse with the foreign world.

I have always been attracted to the unexpected success; in my experience, it holds the key to understanding. It occurred to me that there had been no more unexpected or more unique success than that of the Japanese after the Meiji Restoration of 1867. But I soon realized that this had not been the first such Japanese achievement. The Japanese had had a very similar success twelve hundred years earlier when they adopted the institutions and the religions of what was then the world's most advanced civilization, the China of the T'ang Dynasty, and used them to create a totally different and uniquely Japanese government, society, culture, religious life, and art. And they repeated this success on a lesser scale several times during their subsequent history. The more I explored the issue, the more mystified I became. What did, however, become increasingly clear was that the Japanese achievement rested on a unique ability to use imported tools, whether social institutions or material techniques, to embody Japanese values and to achieve Japanese objectives.

And so, when I first found myself working with senior executives in Japanese government and business, it came naturally to me to lead off with the question "How can *your* values, *your* traditions, *your* culture and its beliefs be used to perform the objective, impersonal tasks of a modern economy and to harness modern technology for social and economic performance?" In my earlier books, I had pointed out that although unemployment insurance in the West, originally a British invention, protected the worker's income, it did not satisfy the worker's need for psychological and social security. This, I had argued, required *employment* security as well. I had argued further that the need for security required gearing wage and employment policies to the family life cycle and its needs. Finally, however, I had pointed out that flexibility in labor costs was equally essential.

Thus, because I knew a little Japanese history, I was able to help the Japanese leaders who participated in my seminars to work out the combination of high employment security, high labor-force flexibility, and a wage structure in tune with the family cycle and its needs—the combination that has since become known in the West as *lifetime employment* and which, for thirty years, has given Japan, in all its earlier history until World War II a country of violent class wars and bloody worker revolts, unprecedented industrial cooperation and harmony. Similarly, the one reason that the "marketing concept" I presented in my seminars has "taken" in Japan—whereas in the United States, the country of its birth, it is still being preached rather than practiced—is surely that marketing as a technique could be embedded in the deeply rooted Confucian ethics of mutual relationships. A sale to a customer thus creates a "relationship," and with it a permanent commitment.

These days I am always being asked to explain the success of the Japanese, especially as compared with the apparent malperformance of American business in recent years. One reason for the difference is *not,* as is widely believed, that the Japanese are not profit conscious or that Japanese businesses operate at a lower profit margin. This is pure myth. In fact, when measured against the cost of capital—the only valid measurement for the adequacy of a company's profit—large Japanese companies have, as a rule, earned more in the last ten or fifteen years than comparable American companies. And that is the main reason the Japanese have had the funds to invest in global distribution of their products. Also, in sharp contrast to governmental behavior in the West, Japan's government, especially the powerful Ministry of International Trade and Industry (MITI), is constantly pushing for higher industrial profits to ensure an adequate supply of funds for investment in the future—in jobs, in research, in new products, and in market development.

One of the principal reasons for the success of Japanese business is that Japanese managers do not start out with a *desired* profit, that is, with a *financial* objective in mind. Rather, they start out with *business* objectives and especially with *market* objectives. They begin by asking "How much market standing do we need to have leadership?" "What new products do we need for this?" "How much do we need to spend to train and develop people, to build distribution, to provide the required service?" Only then do they ask "And how much profit is necessary to accomplish these business objectives?" Then the resulting profit *requirement* is usually a good deal higher than the profit *goal* of the Westerner.

Second, Japanese businesses—perhaps as a long-term result of my management seminars twenty and thirty years ago—have come to accept what they originally thought was very strange doctrine. They have come to accept my position that the end of business is not "to make money." Making money is a necessity of survival. It is also a result of performance and a measurement thereof. But in itself it is not performance. As I mentioned earlier, the purpose of a business is to create a customer and to satisfy a customer. That is performance and that is what a business is being paid for. The job and function of management as the leader, decision maker, and value setter of the organization, and, indeed, the purpose and rationale of an organization altogether, is to make human beings productive so that the skills, expectations, and beliefs of the individual lead to achievement in joint performance.

These were the things which, almost thirty years ago, Ed Deming, Joe Juran, and I tried to teach the Japanese. Even then, every American management text preached them. The Japanese, however, have been practicing them ever since.

I have never slighted techniques in my teaching, writing, and consulting. Techniques are tools; without tools, there is no "practice," only preaching. In fact, I have designed, or at least formulated, a good many of today's management tools, such as management by objectives, decentralization as a principle of organizational structure, and the whole concept of "business strategy," including the classification of products and markets.

My seminars in Japan also dealt heavily with tools and techniques. In the summer of 1985, during my most recent trip to Japan, one of the surviving members of the early seminars reminded me that the first week of the very first seminar I ran opened with a question by a Japanese participant, "What are the most useful techniques of analysis we can learn from the West?" We then spent several days of intensive work on break-even analysis and cash-flow analysis: two techniques that had been developed in the West in the years immediately before and after World War II, and that were still unknown in Japan.

Similarly, I have always emphasized in my writing, in my teaching, and in my consulting the importance of financial measurements and financial results. Indeed, most businesses do not earn enough. What they consider profits are, in effect, true costs. One of my central theses for almost forty years has been that one cannot even speak of a profit unless one has earned the true cost of capital. And, in most cases, the cost of capital is far higher than what businesses, especially American businesses, tend to consider as "record profits." I have also always maintained—often to the scandal of liberal readers—that the *first* social responsibility of a business is to produce an adequate surplus. Without a surplus, it steals from the commonwealth and deprives society and the economy of the capital needed to provide jobs for tomorrow.

Further, for more years than I care to remember, I have maintained that there is no virtue in being nonprofit and that, indeed, any activity that could produce a profit and does not do so is antisocial. Professional schools are my favorite example. There was a time when such activities were so marginal that their being subsidized by society could be justified. Today, they constitute such a large sector that they have to contribute to the capital formation of an economy in which capital to finance tomorrow's jobs may well be the central economic requirement, and even a survival need.

But central to my writing, my teaching, and my consulting has been the thesis that the modern business enterprise is a human and a social organization. Management as a discipline and as a practice deals with human and social values. To be sure, the organization exists for an end beyond itself. In the case of the business enterprise, the end is *economic* (whatever this term might mean); in the case of the hospital, it is the care of the patient and his or her recovery; in the case of the university, it is teaching, learning, and research. To achieve these ends, the peculiar modern invention we call management organizes human beings for joint performance and creates a social organization. But only when management succeeds in making the human resources of the organization productive is it able to attain the desired outside objectives and results.

I came to this thesis naturally, for my interest in management did not start with business. In fact, it started when I decided to become a writer and teacher rather than continue a promising career as an investment banker. My interest in modern organization, in business and management, began with an analysis of modern society and with my conclusion, reached around the time World War II began, that the modern organization and especially the large business corporation was fast becoming the new vehicle of social integration. It was the new community, the new order of a society in which the traditional vehicles of integration—whether small town, craft guild, or church—had disintegrated. So I began to study management with an awareness of economic results, to be sure, but also searching for principles of structure and organization, for constitutional principles, and for values, commitments, and beliefs.

There is a good deal of talk these days of the "culture" of a company. But my book, *The Practice of Management,* published more than thirty years ago, ends with a chapter on the "spirit" of an organization, which says everything to be found in such current best-sellers as *In Search of Excellence*. From the beginning I wrote, taught, and advised that management has to be both outside-focused on its mission and on the results of the organization, and inside-focused on the structure, values, and relationships that enable the individual to achieve.

For this reason, I have held from the beginning that management has to be a discipline, an organized body of knowledge that can be learned and, perhaps, even taught. All of my major books, beginning with *Concept of the Corporation* (1946) and *Practice of Management* (1954) and progressing through my most recent one, *Innovation and Entrepreneurship* (1985), have tried to establish such a discipline. Management is not, and never will be, a *science* as that word is understood in the United States today. Management is no more a science than is medicine: both are practices. A practice feeds from a large body of true sciences. Just as medicine feeds off biology, chemistry, physics, and a host of other natural sciences, so management feeds off economics, psychology, mathematics, political theory, history, and philosophy. But, like medicine, management is also a discipline in its own right, with its own assumptions, its own aims, its own tools, and its own performance goals and measurements. And as a separate discipline in its own right management is what the Germans used to call a *Geisteswissenschaft*—though "moral science" is probably a better translation of that elusive term than the modern "social science." Indeed, the old-fashioned term *liberal art* may be the best term of all.

[1985]

Part IV

THE
ORGANIZATION

28

The Hostile Takeover and Its Discontents

Almost every week these last few years there has been a report of another "hostile takeover bid," another stock-market maneuver to take over, merge, or split up an existing publicly held company against determined opposition by the company's board of directors and management. No such wave of stock-market speculation has hit the United States since the "bears" and the "bulls" of the 1870s, when the Goulds and the Drews and the Vanderbilts battled each other for control of American railroads. The new wave of hostile takeovers has already profoundly altered the contours and landmarks of the American economy. It has become a dominant force—many would say *the* dominant force—in the behavior and actions of American management, and, almost certainly, a major factor in the erosion of American competitive and technological leadership. Yet the papers usually report it only on the financial page. And very few people, outside of business, really quite know what goes on or, indeed, what a hostile takeover really is.

The hostile takeover usually begins with a *raider*—a company or an individual who is legally incorporated and works through a corporation—buying a small percentage of the target company's share capital on the open market, usually with money borrowed expressly for this purpose. When, and as the raider expects, the target's board of directors and its management spurn his takeover bid, the raider borrows more money —sometimes several billion dollars—buys more of the target's shares on the market, and goes directly to the target's stockholders, offering them substantially more than the current share price on the stock exchange. If enough of the target's shareholders accept to give the raider complete control, he then typically unloads the debt he has incurred in the takeover onto the company he has acquired. In a hostile takeover the victim thus ends up paying for his own execution.

The raider not only now controls a big company: he has made a tidy profit on the shares he bought at the lower market price. Even if the takeover attempt fails, the raider usually wins big. The target may only be able to escape the raider by finding a *white knight,* that is, someone who is less odious to the management of the target company and willing to pay even more for its shares, including those held by the raider. Alternatively, the target company pays ransom to the raider—which goes by the Robin Hood–like name of *greenmail*—and buys out the shares the raider acquired at a fancy price, way beyond anything its earnings and prospects could justify.

Hostile takeovers were virtually unknown before 1980. Harold Geneen, who built ITT into the world's largest and most diversified conglomerate in the 1960s and 1970s, made literally hundreds of acquisitions—perhaps as many as a thousand. But he never made an offer to a company unless its management had first invited him to do so. Indeed, in a good many of Geneen's acquisitions the original initiative came from the company to be acquired; it offered itself for sale. In those days it would have been impossible to finance hostile takeovers: no bank would have lent money for such a purpose. But since 1980 they have become increasingly easy to finance.

At first, hostile takeovers were launched by large companies intent on rapid growth or rapid diversification. This phase reached a climax in 1982 with a months-long battle of three giants: Bendix (defense and automotive), Martin-Marietta (defense, aerospace, and cement), and Allied (chemicals). Bendix began the fight with a hostile takeover bid for Martin-Marietta, which promptly counterattacked with a hostile takeover bid for Bendix. When these two, like two scorpions in a bottle, had finished each other off, Allied joined the fray, paid ransom to an exhausted Martin-Marietta, took over Bendix, and in the process ousted the Bendix management that had started the battle.

Since then, raiders increasingly are individual stock-market operators whose business is the hostile takeover. Some, like Carl Icahn, range over the lot, attacking all kinds of business. T. Boone Pickens, originally a small, independent oil producer, specializes in large petroleum companies—his targets have included such major companies as Gulf Oil, Phillips Petroleum, and Union Oil. Ted Turner of Atlanta specializes in the media and was embroiled in a hostile takeover bid for the smallest of the three television networks, CBS. But there are dozens of smaller raiders abroad, many of them looking for fast-growing medium-size companies, especially companies in such currently "sexy" fields as electronics, computers, or biotechnology. Others primarily raid financial institutions. Practically all of them do so on money borrowed at high interest rates.

≫ Why the Raider Succeeds

How many hostile takeover bids there have been, no one quite knows. Conservative estimates run to four hundred or five hundred, with at least one-half ending in the disappearance of the target company either because the raider succeeds or because the target finds a white knight. Such a massive phenomenon—whether considered destructive or constructive—surely bespeaks fundamental changes in the underlying economic structure and the environment of American business and the American economy. Yet to my knowledge there has so far been practically no discussion of what might explain the takeover phenomenon, of its meaning, and of the policy questions it raises.

What, for instance, explains the *vulnerability* of companies, among them a good many big, strong, well-established ones? Few of the raiders have much financial strength of their own. Most have little managerial or business achievement behind them. In the 1960s and early 1970s, the managements of big, publicly owned companies were widely believed to be impregnable; nothing short of the company's bankruptcy could threaten, let alone dislodge, them. It was then considered almost a "self-evident truth" in highly popular books (those of John Kenneth Galbraith, for instance) that we had moved into "corporate capitalism" as a new and distinct "stage," one in which professional managers perpetuated themselves and ran the country's big business autonomously, ruling without much interference from any of their supposed "constituencies." But in the last few years, any number of companies, and particularly large companies doing well by any yardstick, have been swallowed up by hitherto unknown and obscure newcomers despite the most vigorous defense by their management.

These raiders often have no capital of their own, but have to borrow every penny they need to buy a small percentage of the company's stock and then to make their takeover bid. By now, to bar a hostile takeover bid even giants like General Motors are forced into expensive and complicated subterfuges such as splitting their shares into a number of different issues, each with different voting rights. What has happened to corporate capitalism and to the absolute control by professional autonomous management, seemingly so firmly established only a little while ago?

Fundamentally, there are three explanations for this extreme vulnerability of established companies to the hostile takeover.

One explanation is inflation.

Then there are structural changes within the economy

that make a good many of yesterday's most successful companies no longer appropriate to today's economic realities.

Finally, *corporate capitalism*—that is, the establishment of a management accountable only to itself—has made managements and companies exceedingly vulnerable. They have no constituencies to come to their succor when attacked.

Inflation distorts: It distorts values. It distorts relationships. It creates glaring discrepancies between economic assumptions and economic realities. The fifteen years of inflation in America which began during Lyndon Johnson's presidency and continued into the early 1980s were no exception. And the most predictable, indeed the most typical, distortion of inflation is between the value of assets and their earning power. *In any inflation the cost of capital goods tends to rise much faster than the price of the goods they produce. It thus becomes economical to buy already existing capital assets rather than to invest in new facilities and new machines.* So any company that is rich in fixed assets is worth more when dismembered—that is, when its capital assets are being sold as pieces of real estate, as factories, as machinery and equipment—than it is worth on a realistic price/earnings ratio based on the value of its output. This is one of the distortions that the raiders exploit.

The stock market values companies on the basis of their earnings. It values them, in other words, as "going concerns." It does not value them on their liquidation value. As a result, a company heavy with fixed assets—and especially a company that also has a lot of cash with which the raider, after the takeover, can repay himself (and make a sizable profit to boot) —becomes a most inviting target. This situation accounts for one-quarter, perhaps even one-third, of all the successful hostile takeovers.

Equally important are the tremendous structural changes in the American and world economies in the last fifteen years. They have made inappropriate a good many of the traditional forms of economic integration. The best example is probably the large, integrated petroleum company. One need not sympathize with Mr. T. Boone Pickens, the raider who successfully forced one of the country's largest and proudest petroleum companies, Gulf Oil, into a shotgun marriage with a white knight and almost succeeded in taking over two other old and well-established petroleum companies, Union Oil and Phillips. But Pickens has a point. He has forced the petroleum companies at which he leveled his guns to do something sensible: that is, to split the company into two parts, one making and selling petroleum products, one keeping reserves of crude oil in the ground.

Large integrated petroleum companies have performed poorly since 1980 or 1981. Their earnings basically reflect a crude oil price of around $12 or $15 a barrel, which is what the market price would have been all along had there been no OPEC cartel. But all of them have tried desperately, since the OPEC oil shock of 1973, to build up underground crude oil reserves for the future. And these reserves were priced in the market, and especially by people looking for a long-term tax shelter, on the expectation of a petroleum price many times the present price, twenty or thirty years hence. In fact, to justify what the market was paying for crude and crude oil reserves in the ground, one would have to assume a petroleum price of around $100 a barrel by the year 2015 or so; otherwise, on a discounted cash-flow basis, the present valuation of these proven underground reserves could not possibly be justified.

Whether the expectation of high petroleum prices twenty or thirty years hence is rational is not the point. (Every historical experience would indicate that the only rational expectation is for the petroleum prices thirty years hence to be lower than they are today—but this is another issue.) The fact is that it makes little sense today to be an "integrated" petroleum company. The interests of the people who want the earnings of the present petroleum company, and the interests of the people who look for a long-term tax shelter (and who, in other words, do not care much about present earnings), are not compatible. Therefore Pickens's proposal, that the integrated petroleum company split itself into two pieces, made sense.

A similar situation exists in the steel industry, and in fact in a good many of the traditional large-scale, integrated, capital-intensive materials producers. Every one of these situations invites a raider.

But perhaps the biggest single reason companies are vulnerable to the raider is "corporate capitalism" itself: that is, autonomous management, accountable to no one, controlled by no one, and without constituents. It has made management arrogant. And far from making management powerful, corporate capitalism has actually made it impotent. Management has become isolated and has lost its support base, in its own board of directors, among its own stockholders, and among its own employees.

Wherever a management threatened by a raider has been able to organize a "constituency," it has beaten off the hostile takeover. One example is Phillips Petroleum in Bartlesville, Oklahoma, which mobilized the employees and the community; this was enough to defeat Pickens. But where managements have given in to the temptation to become omnipotent they have in effect rendered themselves impotent. When they are then attacked, they have nobody to support them if someone offers a few dollars above the current market price to the company shareholders.

≫ *Where the Cash Comes From*

The vulnerability of the victims does not, by itself, explain how the raiders finance their takeover. To mount a hostile takeover bid for a large company takes a very large war chest. One and a half billion dollars is just about the minimum needed to attack a big company. In some recent cases the amount went up to $4 billion. It has to be in cash, as a rule. To be sure, if the takeover bid succeeds, the target company then pays. But the money has to be available from the beginning—that is, when it is by no means sure that the takeover bid will succeed. If the takeover bid is launched by an individual, as more and more of them have been in recent years, there usually is no security whatever for the cash that the raider has to borrow.

The raider himself usually has negligible assets, certainly compared to the sums needed. Even if the takeover bid is being launched by another large company, the amount needed to finance it is usually way beyond anything the company could normally raise as additional debt. *Yet the only "security" for the loan that a raider has to obtain is the promise of repayment if the raid is successful.* This is hardly what was once normally considered a "bankable" loan, yet the raiders have had no difficulty obtaining these loans. Indeed, when the financing of hostile takeover bids switched (mostly for regulatory reasons) from being done by means of bank loans to being done by means of bonds, the market promptly named the bonds *junk bonds,* and with good reason. Nevertheless, there is no difficulty in getting such bonds underwritten and issued, with commercial banks being avid buyers.

Bank loans—or junk bonds—to finance hostile takeovers are available for the same reason that enabled countries like Brazil, Zaire, or Argentina, in the early 1980s, to obtain loans from Western banks in amounts that were clearly beyond their capacity to pay interest on (let alone to repay the loan itself), and for the same reason that large money-center banks, such as Continental Illinois in Chicago, were willing, indeed eager, to snap up highly speculative and sometimes fraudulent loans often to nonexistent oil and gas speculators. *The American commercial bank is pinched by the shrinkage of its traditional sources of income and almost desperate to find new ones, and especially to find borrowers willing to pay very high interest rates.* And the raider who makes a hostile takeover bid is, of course, perfectly willing to promise very high interest rates; after all, he will not pay them—the company he is aiming to take over will, after it has succumbed.

Commercial banks, as every textbook states, make their living as *liquidity arbitrageurs*: They obtain their money from "demand deposits" which have perfect liquidity—that is, the right to withdraw the money at any time. The bank then lends out that money for longer periods of time (from ninety days to three years is the ordinary time span of a commercial loan); so the amounts owed to the bank have far less liquidity than the amounts it owes. This, then, justifies the bank's charging a substantially higher interest rate, with the difference between the interest rate on what the bank lends out and the interest rate on what the bank borrows being the bank's income.

Increasingly, this does not work anymore, for the bank either is not able to be the liquidity arbitrageur or does not get paid for it. One reason is, of course, that zero-interest demand deposits, once prescribed by the regulatory authorities, have all but disappeared. Historically, businesses have provided the bulk of the demand deposits. But few businesses these days keep large cash supplies, and the typical checking account of individuals now pays 5.5 percent interest. Adding to this the costs of administration, acquisition, and so on, the bank probably ends up paying 8 or 9 percent for the money on deposit in customers' checking accounts—which means that even demand deposits no longer provide a substantial "interest spread." And most American consumers today keep in their checking account only a minimum balance. The rest is in accounts that pay much higher interest, such as money-market accounts, which still allow high liquidity.

On the demand side, too, the liquidity arbitrage has become far less profitable. Increasingly, American businesses do not finance themselves through commercial loans, but through *commercial paper*—the business version of an installment loan. This, however, bypasses the banking system. The company with a temporary cash surplus directly buys commercial paper issued by another company with a temporary cash need. But the "spread" on commercial paper between what the borrower pays and what the lender gets is much lower than that between the traditional noninterest on demand deposits and the bank's lending rate on commercial loans. That spread may be 1.5 percent as against 4 or 5 percent previously.

By now, most U.S. banks, especially the larger ones, know that they cannot hope to continue to build their business on the "spread" of interest rates between what they pay for their money and what they charge for it. They will have to shift their income base to fees and commissions. But even those few banks which accepted this ten years ago and which since then have been working hard on shifting their source of income from being paid for money to being paid for information and service —Citibank in New York was probably the first, and is by far the leader—still have a very long way to go. And in the meantime the banks are hurting for sources of income. Hence the pressure on them to look for borrowers willing to pay higher interest—or at least to promise they will—whether they be Oklahoma wildcatters, military governments engulfed by inflation in their own country (such as Brazil and Argentina), or takeover raiders.

≫ The Lure of Easy Money

That the raiders can obtain money they need still does not explain why the shareholders team up with the raider to take over, merge, or liquidate the company they own.

They do not do so, it is abundantly clear, because they believe the takeover will be advantageous to the company. On the contrary, the shareholders clearly know that the takeover bid is usually a disaster for the company. Increasingly, they sell their shares to the raider only if they get cash, that is, if they get out of the company and have nothing to do with it anymore. Or, if they take securities in exchange, they immediately sell them. And yet, again and again, the shareholders, in their great majority, either accept the bid of the raider or turn it down only if a white knight offers more than the raider does. But then they also immediately sell whatever the white knight has given them in exchange against their holdings in the company that has disappeared.

The shareholders who control our large, publicly held companies simply have no choice but to accept the raider's offer. They are forced, perhaps even legally forced, to accept the raider's bid if it is higher than the currently quoted price for the stock. This is essentially a result of the shift of share ownership from individuals to institutions who are "trustees," and especially to pension funds. Pension funds (increasingly also mutual funds) are the legal "owners" of the publicly owned companies of America, with their holdings amounting to about 50 percent of the common shares. The percentage is even higher for large companies because the institutional holders concentrate on them. The people who manage these large and growing aggregations of capital, especially the pension fund managers, are trustees rather than owners. They are trustees both for the management of the companies which owe the pensions to their employees and for the ultimate beneficiaries, the employees and future pensioners. As trustees they have, however, little choice about whether they want to sell their shares if someone bids substantially above what the same shares fetch at the market price. They have to accept. If they were to say no, they would lay themselves open to an enormous and uninsurable liability. The trustees could be sued by both the management of the company and the ultimate beneficiaries, the employees, were those shares, six months later, quoted below the price the raider had offered. Trustees do not have the right to superimpose *their* judgment on what a "prudent man" would do. And a prudent man surely will take the bird in the hand, especially if there is no reason to believe that there is a bird in the bush.

Pension fund managers are also under tremendous pressure to show better-than-average returns—and yet are unable to do so as a rule. The pension funds of most American businesses are *defined-benefit* plans: The company promises to pay the employee upon retirement a fixed proportion of the employee's salary, usually 60 percent or so of the last five years' earnings. What the employee is to receive is fixed, or rather will be fixed by the time the employee reaches retirement. What the company contributes, however, is flexible. The contribution payable by the company goes down if the pension fund increases in value—if, for instance, it shows a high return or profit from its investments. If the pension fund does not show earnings, or shows earnings lower than anticipated, the company's contribution goes up.

This is in sharp contrast to plans based on a *defined contribution,* under which what the company pays in each year is fixed, with the employee upon retirement receiving either a fixed stipend or a variable one which depends upon what the earnings of the pension fund have been.

In the defined-benefit plan, therefore, management constantly pushes the pension fund manager to show profits, especially from investments, so that the company's contribution can be minimized. But this is a total delusion. It is in fact an impossibility. The pension funds by now *are* the American stock market. And if one is the market, one cannot possibly beat it. The performance record of the pension funds bears this out. It has been abysmal, almost without exception. In fact, the desire to "beat the market" is in itself the reason that most pension funds have performed substantially worse than the market. As a result, the pension funds waste their substance by supporting a huge stock market that only fritters away in commissions the money that should go to the future beneficiaries. In the long and checkered history of investment and finance, there is probably no more uniformly dismal record than that of American pension fund management in the last twenty years.

And yet company managements still believe that their fund can "beat the odds"—the way each slot machine player in Las Vegas believes that he can beat them. And the pension fund manager who does not operate short term, and who refuses to speculate, to trade, and to show "results" over the next three months, is likely to lose the account quickly. There is probably no more competitive industry around. This makes irresistible an offer by the raider to pay $55 for a share that is quoted at $40 on the market.

Pension fund managers know that the raider's bid is deleterious to the company whose stock they own. But they cannot consider the welfare and interests of their "property." They are not owners. They are of necessity speculators, even though they are legally vested with the owner's power. And so they behave as speculators. They have to accept the raider's bid unless a white knight makes a better offer.

» *The Dangers of Defensiveness*

The wave of hostile takeovers is a result of profound structural changes in the American economy. But it is in itself a serious disorder. There is a great deal of discussion about whether hostile takeovers are good or bad for the shareholders. There can be absolutely no doubt, however, that they are exceedingly bad for the economy. They force management into operating short term. More and more of our businesses, large, medium-size, and small, are not being run for business results but for protection against the hostile takeover. This means that more and more of our businesses are forced to concentrate on results in the next three months. They are being run so as to encourage the institutional investors, on which all publicly traded companies today depend for their supply of capital, to hold onto the company shares rather than to toss them overboard the moment the first hostile takeover bid appears.

But worse still, companies are being forced to do stupid things to prevent themselves from being raided. It is, for instance, becoming dangerous for any company to be liquid. Liquidity can only attract the raider who can expect to repay himself, and the debt he incurs in bidding for the company, out of the company's own cash. And thus companies who find themselves in a liquid position, no matter how much cash they may need only a few months further on, hasten to squander the cash—for instance, in buying up something that is totally alien to their own business and has only one advantage: it absorbs a lot of money. Even worse, companies increasingly cut back on expenses for the future, such as research and development. One of the most ominous developments for the future of America is the speed with which the Japanese are taking over the markets of the rapidly industrializing countries: Brazil, for instance, or India. They do so because they can invest in the distribution system in these countries in anticipation of the future market. American company managements are perfectly aware of this. But when asked why they do not do likewise, they tend to say, "We cannot afford to set aside this money and invest it in tomorrow. We need it to make a good showing in next month's or next quarter's profits."

The fear of the raider is undoubtedly the largest single cause for the increasing tendency of American companies to manage for the short term and let the future go hang. The fear of the raider demoralizes and paralyzes. The impact on the morale of management people and of professional people in the company can hardly be overestimated. And worse still, after the successful takeover, the morale in a company is destroyed, often forever. The people who can leave, do. The others do their minimum. "What's the point in my trying to do a good job if the rug will be pulled out from under me tomorrow?" is a frequent comment. Add to this that the raiders, in order to reimburse themselves, usually start out by selling off the company's most promising businesses. Hence the impact of a takeover on morale is total catastrophe.

Altogether, the record is poor for all companies that have been merged, especially into a conglomerate or into a business with which they had little in common: for example, the typical financial conglomerate. Only three out of every ten such acquiring companies do as well two years later as they did before the merger. But the record of companies that have been acquired in a hostile takeover is uniformly dismal.

Clearly the hostile takeover cannot be justified as leading to a more efficient allocation of resources. Most of them have no aim except to enrich the raider. To achieve this end, he offers the stockholders more money for their shares than they would get on the market, which is to say, he bribes them. And to be able to pay the bribe he loads a heavy debt on the company that is being taken over, which by itself severely impairs the company's potential for economic performance. The fact that, almost without exception, the result of the hostile takeover is also a demoralization and severe impairment of the human organization disproves the argument that the hostile takeover results in a more efficient allocation of resources. Actually, all it proves is that "resources" in the modern business enterprise are not primarily bricks and mortar—or even oil in the ground. They are the human organization.

There are indeed cases where a human organization becomes more productive by being dissociated from its former enterprise, by being set up separately—in fact, a good many of today's large organizations, and especially the conglomerates, would greatly increase their productivity by being split into smaller units, or by establishing parts as separate businesses. But this is not what the hostile takeover accomplishes. On the contrary, the most valuable parts of the acquired business are invariably put on the block after a hostile takeover so as to raise money to pay off some of the debt. And this impairs both their productivity and that of the remaining assets.

There are serious questions about resource allocation in the American economy. But the hostile takeover is clearly not the right tool to bring about a more efficient allocation. It does severe damage to the true productive resource, the human organization, its spirit, its dedication, its morale, its confidence in its management, and its identification with the enterprise that employs its people.

Even if hostile takeovers are "good for the shareholders" —and they are "good" only for the very shortest time—they are surely not good for the economy. They are indeed so bad that we will be forced to put an end to them, one way or another.

One way to do so might be to emulate the British and create a "takeover panel" with the power to stop takeover bids considered to be contrary to the best long-term interest of the enterprise and the economy. Whether such a panel could be set up in this country—or whether it would just become another troublesome government agency—is very debatable. The way the British are doing it would immediately run afoul of our antitrust laws.

It is therefore more probable that we will put an end to the hostile takeover—or at least put serious obstacles in its path—by abandoning the concept of "one share, one vote" and go to shares that, although participating equally in profits (and in the proceeds of a liquidation), have unequal voting power, at least as long as the company shows adequate financial results. General Motors has already gone this way, and quite a few smaller firms are following. This would not be a radical departure. The British, for many years, had the *private limited company,* in which management held the voting power as long as it showed specified results. Similarly, the Germans, for well over a hundred years, have had the *Kommanditgesellschaft auf Aktien,* in which management holds the majority of the voting power even though it has a very small minority of the share ownership—again, as long as there is adequate performance and results. In other words, a shift to a system in which different classes of shares have differential voting power—with Class A shares, for instance, having one hundred times the votes of Class B shares—would only need a few fairly simple safeguards to be functional: One, vesting the Class A shares, with their superior voting power, in a truly independent and strong board of directors rather than in management, a board on which independent outside directors have a clear majority (which is what the Germans require, by the way). Second, making the extra voting strength of the Class A shares conditional on the company's showing specified results and adequate performance. Thus a two-class system of shares would control the hostile takeover and yet give protection against managerial malperformance and even against managerial mediocrity.

But perhaps the takeover wave will come to an end with a whimper rather than a bang by losing its financial underpinnings. It would not take much to bring this about. One default on one big loan to finance a hostile takeover, one "billion-dollar-scandal" similar to the Penn Square collapse in Oklahoma that brought down Chicago's mighty Continental Illinois Bank—and there would be no more money available to finance hostile takeovers. And in the long history of finance, every single scheme that lured lenders into advancing money for economically nonproductive purposes by promising them returns substantially above the going market rate has come to a bad end sooner or later—and usually sooner.

Even if we control the hostile takeover, however, there will remain the underlying structural problems of which the hostile takeover is only a symptom. It clearly raises basic questions about the following: the role, functions, and governance of pension funds; the legitimacy of management; and finally, the purpose of business enterprise, especially large enterprise. Are the stockholders the *only* constituents to whom all other interests, including that of the enterprise itself as a going concern, must be totally subordinated?

≫ *Where Wall Street Meets Las Vegas*

Abatement of the boom in hostile takeovers can, paradoxically, only aggravate the pension fund problem. It would eliminate the windfall profits pension funds now reap by accepting the inflated prices the raider offers. These windfall profits are, by and large, the only way for pension fund managers to obtain the quick stock-market gains that their bosses, the company's managers, expect and demand of them. If they are eliminated, company managers will predictably put even greater pressure for quick results on the people who manage their company's pension fund; and those in turn will put even greater pressure for short-term results on the companies in the shares of which the fund invests—thus pushing businesses even further toward managing for the short term, which, as by now everybody agrees, is a significant factor in the steady erosion of America's competitive position in the world economy. As long as American pension funds are based on "defined benefits," no relief is in sight.

It might have made sense for the labor unions to push for defined benefits when pension funds first became widespread some thirty years ago. For under that system, the employer shoulders all future risks. Actually, in the negotiation of the contract that set the pattern for today's pension fund, the General Motors contract in the spring of 1950, the United

Automobile Workers strongly opposed defined benefits and wanted "defined contributions" instead.* It was the company that chose defined benefits, even though General Motors' president at the time, Charles E. Wilson, recommended a defined-contributions plan as financially much sounder. He as well as Reuther were, however, overruled by GM's finance committee, and the rest of the country's pension plans then followed GM's lead. Yet the choice of defined benefits—as we now realize, a major blunder—was based on the same delusion that makes people in Las Vegas believe that they will "make a fortune" if only they keep on feeding more quarters into the slot machine.

Under defined benefits the company commits itself to paying the future pensioner a fixed percentage of his wage or salary during his retirement years. The contribution the company makes is then dependent on the value of the fund's assets in a given year, as against the present value of the future pension obligation. The higher the fund's present value the lower the current contribution, and vice versa. And so management deluded itself into believing that an an ever-rising New York stock market is a law of nature—or at least of history—and that, therefore, under a defined-benefits plan, it would be the stock market, through its preordained continuing rise, that would eventually provide the money to discharge the pension obligation rather than the company itself. Indeed, quite a few managements then promised their boards of directors that the defined-benefits plan would in the long run become a "money spinner" for the company and would produce income well above anything it would have to put into the plan.

And then the second delusion: Practically every company adopting a defined-benefits pension plan did so with the firm belief that its own pension plan, if only administered "professionally," would "beat" *even* an ever-rising market.

*I had occasion to discuss this issue repeatedly with Walter Reuther, then head of the UAW, when the contract was under negotiation. Reuther feared, groundlessly as it turned out, that "defined benefits" would make the worker conscious of the identity of interest between himself and the employer and thus alienate him from the union.

There is, of course, no law that prescribes an ever-rising stock market. Stock markets historically have not even been particularly effective as hedges against inflation: The American market in the last twenty years, for instance, barely kept pace with it. Indeed a large pool of money which over any long period of time grows at all, let alone as fast as the economy, is the rarest of all exceptions—neither the Medici nor the Fuggers, nor the Rothschilds nor the Morgans, succeeded in this endeavor. Similarly, no large-company pension fund, to the best of my knowledge, has over the last twenty or thirty years done as well as the stock market. The only performance that counts in the pension fund is performance over the long run, because the obligations extend over twenty-five years or longer. Indeed, some of the large defined-contributions funds have produced better results for their beneficiaries, the employees and future pensioners, and at lower cost to the employers, than the great majority of the large defined-benefits plans. This is most definitely true of the largest of the defined-contributions plans, that of the employers and employees of the American nonprofit institutions, the Teachers Insurance and Annuity Association.

The misconceptions that led American management into opting for defined benefits thus practically guaranteed from the beginning that the funds would have to become "speculators" and increasingly short term in their focus.

The choice of defined benefits also explains in large part the poor *social* performance of the American pension fund. For it was conceived, as Walter Reuther quite rightly suspected, as much to be a social as to be a financial institution. It was conceived to create a visible center of common interest between employer and employee. Indeed, what General Motors had in mind was very similar to what the Japanese, acting quite independently a few years later, achieved by "lifetime employment." But unlike lifetime employment the American pension fund has not created any community of interest in the worker's mind.

The laws that govern the private pension plans in America define their managers as "trustees" for the eventual beneficiaries, the employees. In reality the managers of defined-benefits plans are of necessity appointed by and accountable only to company management. For the one at risk is the employer—and so the fund has to be run to reduce, as much as possible, the burden on the employer. As a result, the employees feel no responsibility for the fund. It is "deferred wages" rather than a "stake in the company." The employees do not feel that it makes any difference how the fund performs. And they are right: Unless the company goes bankrupt it does not make any difference to them. They also, in a defined-benefits plan, cannot in any meaningful way be brought into the decision-making process through the pension fund, the actual owners of America's productive resources.

A defined-contributions plan is no panacea, but it minimizes the problems. The right model was easily available thirty years ago—for the Teachers Insurance and Annuity Association goes back much further, to the early 1920s. The TIAA runs on "flexible contributions" rather than on defined contributions. The contribution made each year into the plan by a university, or a nonprofit organization such as the Boy Scouts, or for a minister in a Protestant denomination, is a fixed percentage of salary. It goes up as the employee advances. It thereby also—an important point—automatically adjusts the annual contribution to inflation. And yet this annual premium is known and predictable. And because of this, the TIAA can, and does indeed, invest for the long term, which in turn explains why its results have been better than those of any of the large defined-benefits plans. At the same time, the TIAA, precisely because the employer has discharged his obligation in full once he remits a fixed percentage of the employee's salary, has been able to bring the future beneficiaries, that is, today's employees, into the government of the institution. University faculty do not consider the TIAA the "employer's pension fund"; it is "our pension fund," in which they take an active interest and which to them meaningfully symbolizes the basic identity of economic interest between their employer, that is, the university, and themselves.

Pension plans are beginning to change, albeit very slowly. Many companies, especially medium-size ones, now encourage employees to make their own pension provisions, often out of company-provided funds, for example, through an Individual Retirement Account. That at least makes possible a rational (that is, a long-term) investment policy. But for the foreseeable future the bulk of our corporate pension plans will remain committed to the defined-benefits formula. The principal legal owners of our large companies, the large pension funds, will therefore continue to be forced to act as speculators rather than as investors, let alone as owners. And thus there will, for the foreseeable future, be a need to protect the economy's wealth-producing resources—that is, its businesses, and the pension funds themselves—against the pressure to manage for the immediate, the short term, the next month, the next quarter, and above all against the takeover.

≫ Demise of the Corporate Guardians

Corporate capitalism—the rule of autonomous managers as the "philosopher-kings" of the modern economy accountable at best to a professional code but not controlled by shareholders or by any other constituency—was first proclaimed more than fifty years ago by Adolph Berle and Gardner Means in their 1932 classic, *The Modern Corporation and Private Property.* "Control," Berle and Means argued, had become divorced from "property." Indeed, property was no longer ownership. It had become investment, concerned only with dividends and capital gains but not with the welfare or the governance of the property itself.

From the beginning, anyone with any knowledge of political theory or political history could have predicted that this would not work. Management, one could confidently say, would not last any longer as philosopher-king than any earlier philosopher-kings had, which was never very long. Management has power. Indeed, to do its job, it *has* to have power. But power does not last, regardless of its performance, its knowledge, and its good intentions, unless it be grounded in some sanction outside and beyond itself, some "grounds of legitimacy," whether divine institution, or election, or the consent of the governed. Otherwise, power is not legitimate. It may be well-meaning, it may perform well, it may even test out as "highly popular" in surveys and polls. Yet illegitimate power always succumbs to the first challenger. It may have no enemies, but no one believes in it, either, and no one owes it allegiance.

This should have been obvious to American management fifty years ago when Berle and Means first pointed out that there was no more real ownership in the American corporation. After all, that the philosopher-king—that is, power grounded in performance rather than in legitimacy—would not last had been known since Aristotle's dismissal of Plato's philosopher-king, all of twenty-three hundred years ago. But American management did exactly what all earlier philosopher-kings have done—for example, the "enlightened despots" of eighteenth-century Europe. It gloried in its good intentions. And American managements busily engaged in removing what they considered as the last obstacle to their enlightened rule, an independent and powerful board of directors. And then, when the investors of Berle and Means became the speculators of the pension fund, management found itself powerless against the first challenger, the raider. The hostile takeover bid is thus the final failure of corporate capitalism.

But we do need management. The business enterprise needs a government, and it needs a government that has power, has continuity, and can perform. In other words, it needs a government that has legitimacy. How can legitimacy be restored to the management of America's large, publicly owned companies?

One step, surely the first one, is to restore an independent and strong board of directors. Indeed, as has already been pointed out, where such a board exists, raiders, by and large, have been beaten off. Even shareholders whose only interest is the quick buck are likely to listen to a strong and independent board that has standing and respect in the community and is not dismissed as management's puppet. The hostile takeover may thus finally succeed in bringing about the reform and restoration of the strong, independent board of directors which a great many voices within the business community have been demanding for many years.

But such a board would not and could not be a representative of the shareholders alone. The board member who commands enough respect to be listened to is likely to be an *independent director,* that is, somebody who does not represent any constituency, including the nominal owners, but rather the integrity and the interest of the enterprise itself. The hostile takeover is thus almost certain to speed up a development that is already under way: the emergence of professionally qualified men and women who serve on a very small number of boards, maybe no more than four at a time; who have independent respect and standing in a broader community based on their achievements and known integrity; and who take seriously their responsibilities, including the responsibility to set performance goals for top management and to police them, to monitor the behavior and ethics of top management, and to remove even the proudest chief executive officer who does not live up to the standards set by the board in the interest of the enterprise.

But is this not simply replacing one set of philosopher-kings by another group of technocrats or wise men? To be sure, independent outside board members, unlike a company president, do not fight for their own jobs when they resist a takeover. But they still do not represent any identifiable constituency, neither do they have any grounds of legitimacy other than disinterested performance and knowledge. Will the large public corporation in America have to learn to mobilize new constituents, to bring in other "interests" to balance the former owners now become speculators, and to create new bonds of allegiance?

Reportedly, would-be raiders refrain from making a hostile takeover bid for a company in which employees hold a substantial portion of the shares. They know that employee-owners are not likely to accept the raider's offer. Most employees stand to lose more, of course, if their jobs are endangered than they can possibly gain by getting more for their stock. Above all employees identify with the company and are personally and emotionally attached to its remaining independent. And the most spectacular defeat of a hostile takeover bid was not achieved by a management with a strong performance record. It was the previously mentioned defeat of the bid for Phillips Petroleum in Bartlesville, Oklahoma, when the town itself rallied to the defense of its major employer.

Thirty years ago it was popular in American big business to talk of management as being the "trustee for the best-balanced interests of stockholders, employees, plant community, customers, and suppliers alike." In many cases, of course, this was pure phrase meant to clothe with respectability the managerial philosopher-king and his enlightened despotism. But even where there was more to this assertion than self-interest, nothing has been done as a rule to convert the phrase into reality. Few attempts have been made to institutionalize the relationship of these supposed "constituencies" to the enterprise and its management. Will this now have to be undertaken in earnest to safeguard both enterprise and management? And what form should such institutional relationships take?

≫ The Challenge to Free Enterprise

The question being most hotly debated currently is whether hostile takeovers are good or bad for shareholders. But what other groups may have a legitimate stake in the fight for the control and survival of the enterprise is probably more important, though less discussed. Does the modern, publicly owned, large enterprise exist *exclusively* for the sake of the shareholders? This is, of course, what orthodox "capitalism" asserts. But the term *free enterprise* was coined forty or fifty years ago to assert that the shareholder interest, although important, is only one interest and that the enterprise has functions well beyond that of producing returns for the shareholder —functions as an employer, as a citizen of the community, as a customer, and as a supplier. The British, in establishing a "take-over panel," have expressly recognized that a decision on mergers and takeovers affects the public interest. So far in the United States, this is expressed only negatively, that is, in forbidding mergers that violate antitrust laws. Will we have to bring in considerations of the impact on other groups and on the community and economy as a whole—and in which form? That is the central question. The answers this country will give to it will largely define the future shape of the American economy.

If the answer is, however, that the speculator's interest— never mind that the speculator has legal title as an owner—is the only interest to be considered, the free-enterprise system is unlikely to survive. It will rapidly lose public support. For most people, even though they do benefit—however indirectly (that is, as ultimate beneficiaries in a pension fund)—from the speculator's game, stand to lose more from the hostile takeover as employees, whether blue-collar or managers, and as citizens of a community. And more and more people are concerned with the hostile takeover as a moral issue. It deeply offends the sense of justice of a great many Americans.

Most Americans today are employees of an organization. There is a good deal of evidence that people in an organization, and especially managerial and professional people, will accept even the most painful adjustment, such as the closing of a business or the sale of parts of it, if the rationale is economic performance or the lack thereof. But this of course is not the rationale for the purchase or sale of the human organization or of its parts in the hostile takeover. There the only rationale is to enrich somebody who has nothing to do with the performance of the enterprise and who, quite admittedly, has not the slightest interest in it. And this goes against the grain of employees who feel that the hostile takeover treats them as "chattel" and not as a "resource," let alone as human beings. "Is the hostile takeover even compatible with our laws against peonage and involuntary servitude?" the middle-level executives in my advanced-management classes have been asking me of late.

Almost a hundred years ago the United States decided that the rights of the creditor are not absolute and amended its bankruptcy laws to put maintenance and restoration of the "going concern" ahead of the rights of the creditor, which till then had ruled when a business got into difficulties. This has worked remarkably well. The protection of the going concern during reorganization has indeed proved to be in the ultimate interest of the creditor, too. Will we now do the same thing with respect to the hostile takeover and give consideration to the protection of the going concern as a resource, and to the interests of employees, whether blue-collar, white-collar, or managerial; of the community; of suppliers and customers? Actually we are already moving in this direction through extending the protection of the bankruptcy laws to nonbankrupt going concerns threatened by subjection to one single interest. The Johns-Manville Corporation—a leading producer of asbestos and other building materials—successfully invoked the bankruptcy laws to preserve itself as a going concern and to protect its shareholders and its employees against a tidal wave of asbestos-damage liability suits. Continental Airlines similarly used the bankruptcy laws successfully to preserve itself against union wage claims that had become unbearable when deregulation made airfares and airline routes hotly competitive. It is by no means inconceivable that a clever lawyer will similarly construe the bankruptcy laws to preserve the going concern against the hostile takeover—and that the courts will go along as they did in the Johns-Manville and Continental Airlines cases. But one way or another—by law, by moving to multitier stock ownership, or by judicial exegesis—we surely will find a way to protect the going concern against hostile takeovers that subordinate all other interests—employees, the enterprise's long-range growth and prosperity, and the country's competitive position in an increasingly competitive world economy—to short-term speculative gain.

[1986]

29

The Five Rules of Successful Acquisitions

The merger boom of the last few years is not based on business reasons. It is financial manipulation, pure and simple. But an acquisition must make business sense, or it does not work even as a financial move. It leads to both business and financial failure.

There are five simple rules for successful acquisitions, and they have been followed by all successful acquirers since the days of J. P. Morgan a century ago.

1. An acquisition will succeed only if the acquiring company thinks through what it can contribute to the business it is buying, not what the acquired company will contribute to the acquirer, no matter how attractive the expected "synergy" may look.

What the acquiring company contributes may vary. It may be management, technology, or strength in distribution. Money alone is never enough. General Motors has done very well with the diesel-engine businesses it bought; it could and did contribute both technology and management. It got nowhere with the two businesses to which its main contribution was money: heavy earthmoving equipment and aircraft engines.

2. Successful diversification by acquisition, like all successful diversification, requires a common core of unity. The two businesses must have in common either markets or technology, though occasionally a comparable production process has also provided sufficient unity of experience and expertise, as well as a common language, to bring companies together. Without such a core of unity, diversification, especially by acquisition, never works; financial ties alone are insufficient. In social science jargon, there has to be a "common culture" or at least a "cultural affinity."

3. No acquisition works unless the people in the acquiring company respect the product, the markets, and the customers of the company they acquire. The acquisition must be a "temperamental fit."

Though many large pharmaceutical companies have acquired cosmetic firms over the last twenty to thirty years, none has made a great success of it. Pharmacologists and biochemists are "serious" people concerned with health and disease. Lipsticks and lipstick users are frivolous to them.

By the same token, few of the big television networks and other entertainment companies have made a go of the book publishers they bought. Books are not "media," and neither book buyers nor authors—a book publisher's two customers—bear any resemblance to what the Nielsen rating means by "audience." Sooner or later, usually sooner, a business requires a decision. People who do not respect or feel comfortable with the business, its products, and its users invariably make the wrong decision.

4. Within a year or so, the acquiring company must be able to provide top management for the company it acquires. It is an elementary fallacy to believe one can "buy" management. The buyer has to be prepared to lose the top incumbents in companies that are bought. Top people are used to being

bosses; they don't want to be "division managers." If they were owners or part-owners, the merger has made them so wealthy they don't have to stay if they don't enjoy it. And if they are professional managers without an ownership stake, they usually find another job easily enough. To recruit new top managers is a gamble that rarely comes off.

5. Within the first year of a merger, it is important that a large number of people in the management groups of both companies receive substantial promotions across the lines— that is, from one of the former companies to the other. The goal is to convince managers in both companies that the merger offers them personal opportunities.

This principle applies not only to executives at or near the top, but also to the younger executives and professionals, the people on whose dedication and efforts any business primarily depends. If they see themselves blocked as a result of an acquisition, they will "vote with their feet," and as a rule they can find new jobs even more easily than displaced top executives.

Most executives accept these five principles, at least since the debacle of the conglomerate merger movement in the late 1960s. But they argue that the principles don't apply to an inflationary period when acquisitions have a financial and macroeconomic rather than a business rationale.

Here the German experience during the great inflation of the early 1920s offers a convincing rebuttal. The "merger boom" of that period was as hectic as anything seen in the United States in the 1980s. And there were four great "raiders": Hugo Stinnes, Alfred Hugenberg, Friedrich Flick, and Germany's leading steel maker, the Krupp Works. Only Hugenberg and Flick succeeded. Hugenberg bought out newspapers and built the first modern newspaper chain in Germany. He survived, indeed prospered, until Hitler, whom he had helped put into power, dispossessed him. Flick bought only steel and coal companies and survived both World War II and imprisonment as a Nazi war criminal to build yet another, even bigger, business empire before he died a few years ago.

Stinnes, who as late as 1919 had been a totally unknown coal wholesaler, by 1922 dominated German industry as no single man has ever dominated the industry of a major country. But nine months after the German inflation ended, the Stinnes empire—a heterogeneous collection of steel mills, shipping lines, chemical companies, banks, and other unrelated businesses—was in bankruptcy and being dismantled.

As for Krupp, for decades before Germany's richest and politically most powerful firm, it survived, but it never recovered. It could never manage the heterogeneous businesses it had bought—shipyards, a truck manufacturer, and machine-tool companies, among others. Eventually Krupp was bled white by its acquisitions. In the early 1970s, the Krupp family was ejected from ownership and management alike, with control of the half-dead company being sold to the Shah of Iran at a fire-sale price.

The New York stock market—at least since its recovery from its infatuation with conglomerates in the 1960s—certainly senses the importance of the five acquisition rules. This explains why in so many cases the news of a massive acquisition triggers a sharp drop in the acquiring company's stock price.

Nevertheless executives, of acquirers and targets alike, still largely ignore the rules, as do the banks when they decide to finance an acquisition bid. But history amply teaches that investors and executives, in both the acquiring and acquired company, and the bankers who finance them soon come to grief if they do judge an acquisition financially instead of by business principles.

[1981]

30

The Innovative
Organization

It is widely believed that large companies cannot innovate. This is simply not true: Merck, Citibank, and 3M are but three examples of highly innovative corporate giants. But it is true that to innovate successfully, a company has to be run differently from the typical "well-managed" business, whether large or small.

The innovative company understands that innovation starts with an idea. Ideas are somewhat like babies—they are born small, immature, and shapeless. They are promise rather than fulfillment. In the innovative company executives do not say, "This is a damn-fool idea." Instead they ask, "What would be needed to make this embryonic, half-baked, foolish idea into something that makes sense, that is feasible, that is an opportunity for us?"

But an innovative company also knows that the great majority of ideas will turn out not to make sense. Innovative ideas are like frogs' eggs: of a thousand hatched, only one or two survive to maturity. Executives in innovative organizations therefore demand that people with ideas think through the *work* needed to turn an idea into a product, a process, a business, or a technology. They ask, "What work would we have to do and what would we have to find out and learn before we can commit the company to this idea of yours?"

These executives know that it is as difficult and risky to convert a small idea into successful reality as it is to make a major innovation. They do not aim at "improvements" or "modifications" in products or technology. They aim at innovating a new business. And they know that *innovation* is not a term of the scientist or technologist. It is a term of the businessman.

For innovation means the creation of new value and new satisfaction for the customer. Organizations therefore measure innovations not by their scientific or technological importance but by what they contribute to market and customer. They consider social innovation as important as technological innovation. Installment selling may have had a greater impact on economics and markets than most of the great advances in technology in this century.

Innovative companies know that the largest market for a successful new idea is usually unexpected. In developing dynamite, Alfred Nobel was trying to find a better military explosive. But dynamite is too unstable to be used in bombs and shells; instead it was used for removing rock and replaced the pick and shovel in mining, railroad building, and construction. IBM built its dominance of the large-computer market by realizing that the greatest demand for computers would come not from science and defense—the two uses for which the computer had been designed—but from such mundane applications as payroll, billing, and inventory control.

Innovative companies do not start out with a "research budget." They end with one. They start out by determining how much innovation will be needed for the business to stay even. They assume that *all* existing products, services, processes, and markets are becoming obsolete—and pretty fast at that. They try to assess the probable speed of decay of whatever exists and then determine the "gap" that innovation has to fill for the company not to go downhill. They know that their program for innovation must include promises several times the size of the innovation gap, for not more than a third of such promises, if that many, ever becomes reality. And then they know how much of an innovative effort—and how large an innovative budget—they need as the very minimum.

"But," says the chief executive of a highly successful innovative company, "then I double the size of the effort and of the budget. After all, the competition is no dumber than we are and may be luckier."

Smart companies know that money does not produce innovation; people do. They know that in innovative work, quality counts far more than quantity. They do not spend a penny unless there is a first-rate person to do the work. Successful innovations rarely require a great deal of money in the early and crucial stages. But they do require a few highly competent people, dedicated to the task, driven by it, working full time and very hard. Such companies will always back a person or a team rather than a "project" until the innovating idea has been proved out.

But these organizations also know that the majority of innovative ideas, however brilliant, never bring "results."

So they treat innovative work quite differently from the existing, ongoing business in respect to planning, budgets, expectations, and controls.

Typically innovative companies have two separate budgets: an operating budget and an innovation budget. The operating budget contains everything that is already being done. The innovation budget contains the things that are to be done differently and the different things to be worked on. The operating budget runs to hundreds of pages, even in a middle-size company. The innovation budget even in the giant business rarely runs to more than forty or fifty pages. But top management spends as much time and attention on the fifty pages of the innovation budget as on the five hundred of the operating budget—and usually more.

Top management asks different questions about each budget. On operations it asks, "What is the least effort needed to keep things from caving in?" And "What is the least effort needed to give the best ratio between effort and results? What, in other words, is the optimization point?" But for innovations, top management asks, "Is this the right opportunity?" And if the answer is yes, top management asks, "What is the *most* this opportunity can absorb by way of resources at this stage?"

Innovative companies know that returns on innovation behave radically differently from returns in the ongoing business. For long periods, years in many cases, innovations have no "returns"; they have only costs. But then returns should increase exponentially: An innovation is unsuccessful if it does not return the investment several hundredfold, for the risks are simply too great to justify a lower return.

To expect from innovative efforts the steady 10 percent rate of return and 10 percent growth rate—the yardstick of the "sound financial manager"—is foolishness. It is expecting both too much and too little. Innovative companies therefore keep such efforts out of the return-on-investment figures for ongoing businesses and do not use these figures to measure the soundness of an innovative idea and its progress, or the compensation of people working on them. The oldest rule, probably formulated by du Pont sixty years ago, is that the new will not be included in the figures for the ongoing business until its end result—the new product or service—has been on the market for two or three years and is past its infancy.

Yet, innovative companies closely control these efforts. One never hears talk of "creativity" in innovative companies— *creativity* is the buzzword of those who don't innovate. Innovative companies talk of work and self-discipline. They ask, "What is the next point at which we should review this project? What results should we expect by then? And how soon?" When an idea fails to meet the targets two or three times in a row, the innovative company does not say, "Let's redouble our efforts." It says, "Isn't it time we did something else?"

Above all the innovative company organizes itself to abandon the old, the obsolete, the no longer productive. It never says, "There will always be a market for a well-made buggy whip." It knows that whatever human beings have created becomes obsolete sooner or later—usually sooner. And it prefers to abandon its obsolete products itself rather than have them made obsolete by the competition.

Every three years or so, the innovative company therefore puts on trial for its life every product, process, technology, service, and market. It asks, "Knowing what we now know, would we now go into this product or service?" And if the answer is no, the company does not say, "Let's make another study." It says, "How do we get out?"

One way might be to stop putting additional resources in and keeping the product or service only as long as it still gives a yield—I coined the term *cash cow* for this twenty years ago. Or, the Japanese are past masters at this, one finds uses and markets where the old technology or the old product is still genuinely new and confers competitive advantage. Or one abandons. But one does not pour good money after bad. Organized abandonment of the obsolete is the one sure way for an organization to focus the vision and energies of its people on innovation.

We clearly face a period in which the demands and opportunities for innovation will be greater than at any time in living memory—as great perhaps as in the fifty years preceding World War I, during which new technical or social inventions, almost immediately spawning new industries, emerged on average every eighteen months.

Telecommunications, automation of manufacturing processes around the microprocessor, the "automated office," rapid changes in banking and finance, medicine, biogenetics, bioengineering, and biophysics—these are only a few of the areas where change and innovation are already proceeding at high speed. To compete in this environment, companies will need to muster large sums of money to boost their research budgets, even in a severe depression. But what will be required above all are the attitudes, policies, and practices of the innovative organization.

[1982]

31

The No-Growth Enterprise

Every company I know still proclaims "10 percent growth a year" as its objective. But many, in a great many industries, are quite unlikely to grow in the next few years, no matter how well the economy is doing. At the best they will grow no faster than population, that is, very slowly. This will not only hold true for businesses. It applies even more to nonbusinesses such as schools, universities, and hospitals. Yet few executives today have ever managed a no-growth organization.

The most important requirement is to maintain, and indeed to improve, the quality of the human resource, and especially the professional and managerial groups. Once a company or an industry ceases to attract and to hold competent people, dry rot has set in; and the resulting long-term decline is exceedingly difficult to reverse. Even in depression times, competent people do not stay where they have no challenge and no opportunity and do not see achievement and performance.

The no-growth company therefore has to make its jobs big and challenging, especially at the entry level. This is a 180-degree shift from what we have been doing these past thirty years. During most of this time, up into the late 1970s, expansion was fast. But good young people were still quite scarce; the baby-boom age-group joined the labor force in substantial numbers only in the mid-1970s. Hence we tended to make entry-level jobs small and easy and to build layers of management to give close supervision to inexperienced people. Above all, we tended to promote very quickly anyone who showed ability to perform. Now we will have to change these practices.

Above all, we will have to build challenge and recognition into the job again, rather than overstress promotion to the exclusion of everything else. The university and the military have been even more promotion-focused than has been business. Typically in these last decades, the young man or woman who received the promotion—the young woman who made assistant vice-president in the bank or the young man who made captain in the Air Force—immediately asked, "And what do I have to do now to get the next promotion right away?" Now we will have to structure jobs so that the young people ask, "What can I do to make the job bigger, more challenging, more achieving, more rewarding?" And we will have to learn again that recognition, both through money and through other means, has to motivate to improve performance on the job. Indeed, in the no-growth company, a vacancy is an opportunity to abolish a job or a management level rather than an opening for a promotion.

Still the no-growth organization also needs opportunities for advancement so that it can attract young people and can hold performers. Otherwise it will soon decline into organizational senility. It has to do what military services learned long ago: get rid of the middle-aged who have reached their plateau in the organization and will not be promoted further.

In the United States it is possible (as it is almost impossible anyplace else) to put a younger person over an older one. But even in the United States it is not easy and is not done very often. Unless the middle-aged who are not going to be promoted further are moved out of the management ranks, younger people will be blocked behind them and will either leave or, worse, retire on the job and turn rancid. The military retires such people. Business, or the hospital or the university, can't do this, if only because it couldn't bear the costs. No-growth companies will have to learn to place such people in a second career. Usually such people aren't "burnt out"; they are simply bored and need to be "repotted," need the challenge of a new job, of a new environment, and of new associates. But unless the no-growth company establishes clearly both that it will not keep on forever those professionals and managers who stop advancing and that it then takes responsibility for helping such people find new assignments and challenges, it will soon find itself unable to attract new young people and will age and go downhill.

And if the business does not grow bigger, it has to become better. Any organization needs challenging goals. If it is no longer realistic to say "We plan to double in size within ten years," then the goal has to be "We plan to double our productivities within ten years"—of capital, of key physical resources, and of people at work. Improving productivity is always a realistic goal and can always be done. All it normally requires is commitment all the way down from the top and conscientious, hard, unspectacular work day in and day out. And the institution that works seriously on its productivity will also soon have the means to reward its people.

There are also some "don'ts"—things not to do in the no-growth company. Don't rush into "growth industries." Mindless diversification does not work. There is no "easy business." Also, in most no-growth institutions the main earnings stream for many years ahead will have to come from the existing mundane business. And if this business is neglected in the excitement of diversification into growth business or into cash cows, everything will go down the drain—including the red-hot acquisition. The first question to ask in diversification and acquisition is always "What do we have to contribute that will make a decisive difference to the new venture or the new acquisition?" If the answer is "nothing" (or "nothing except money"), the result will predictably be catastrophe.

And then the company must avoid making "no growth" a self-fulfilling prophecy. Managing the no-growth company requires asking all the time "What are our strengths? And where are there new opportunities to apply them productively, whether because of changes in population and demographics, or in markets and distribution, or in technology?" For an organization that maintains its human-performance capacity and improves its productivities is highly likely to encounter, and fairly soon, major new growth opportunities.

Opportunities will knock on the doors of even a stagnating industry. The major American railroads in the past ten years are a good example. Twenty years ago, their resurgence would have been considered to be as unlikely as Lazarus's resurrection. Growth opportunities will even knock in a long, deep depression. There were plenty of them in the 1930s for any organization—whether business, hospital, or university—that kept on getting better. IBM, for instance, then laid the foundation for its growth from a small, marginal supplier into a world-class giant. But opportunity only knocks on the doors of those that deserve it.

[1983]

32

Why Automation Pays Off

Automation, wherever installed in a manufacturing plant, has paid for itself within three years, and often much faster. And it has given the plant the ability to compete even against low-cost foreign producers. Yet in every seminar I have been running these past few years, a plant manager gets up and says, "I can't convince my top management that automation pays." And all the other manufacturing people in the group shout, "Amen!"

The payoff from automation is indeed both fast and high. But very little, if any, of it shows up in the measurements that most U.S. manufacturing plants, especially smaller ones, use. Our conventional accounting figures measure the costs of doing. The main benefit of automation lies, however, in eliminating—or at least in minimizing—the costs of *not* doing. To convince their top managements that automation pays, manufacturing people therefore will have to develop new and more appropriate measurements of costs.

"Good quality is cheap; it is poor quality that is expensive" has been a truism in quality control for fifty years. Yet few plants know how expensive poor quality really is. The accounting system assumes that the process works the way it is designed to work: that is, that it produces the desired quality, uniformly and throughout. A good many manufacturing plants measure the *yield,* the percentage of finished products that come up to acceptable quality standards. But that is only the top of the quality iceberg. It does not show where, in the process, things went wrong. It does not show how much time and money has already been spent in earlier stages to fix problems. It does not show how many pieces have been taken off the line and scrapped as substandard without ever reaching final inspection. These costs are hidden in the conventional accounting figures, in overtime and overhead, in scrappage, in overstaffing, and so on. Even in well-managed "high-quality" plants they often run as high as a third of total manufacturing costs, sometimes higher.

Automation builds quality standards and quality control into every step of the process. Equally important, it spots and advertises a deficiency in quality the moment it occurs and at the place where it occurs. And it does so at no extra cost. Wherever we have fully automated—in Japan; in the Erie, Pennsylvania, locomotive plant of General Electric; or in the Fiat engine plant in Termoli, Italy—the quality savings greatly outweigh the savings in payroll and manpower, maybe two or three times. In fact, quality savings alone are likely to repay the costs of automation within two or three years.

The second major economic benefit of automation also lies in a cost of not doing: the cost of "downtime" when production is being changed from one model to another. During that time when tools are cleaned, molds and dies removed and new ones put in, machine speeds reset, and so on, nothing moves. And in preautomated processes, downtime often runs to hours, if not to days. Conventional cost accounting does not, however, capture downtime; it is a cost of not doing. Cost accounting assumes that the line will produce the number of pieces for which it has been designed; if it is 80 an hour, then cost accounting figures that each piece costs 1/80th the line's cost per hour. This works fine if there are very large runs of uniform products, say in the plant that produces half a million uniform radiator grilles for Chevrolets. But in the overwhelming majority of plants the runs are much shorter, models change constantly, and there is downtime and more downtime—during which people have to be paid, the plant has to be heated and lighted, and so on—all, however, without any production. In an automated process, production changes can be built into the process. As a result, downtime is cut to the bone and often eliminated. Again, the cost savings of cutting downtime usually exceed those in payroll and manpower and often pay for the entire investment in automation within a few years.

Finally, the reduction—or elimination—of downtime often gives a plant an entirely new capacity to generate revenues, in addition to cutting its costs sharply. It enables it to turn out an optimally profitable product mix and to serve more profitable markets. This can be particularly important for smaller and more specialized companies, for example, a maker of electric wiring devices or a small foundry. In the United States and Western Europe, automation is still seen as something for the "big boys." But experience in Japan, where the government provides low-interest loans for small-plant automation, would indicate that automation is, above all, the most advantageous manufacturing system for the small plant. It gives it lower costs through quality and downtime savings and also gives it higher revenues through more profitable product mixes and market mixes.

Top managements and boards are right in refusing to make the large capital investments that automation requires simply because automation is "advanced." It is not even enough to be told that American manufacturing industries (and those of any other developed country) will survive only if they automate— though it is true enough. Top managements are right in insisting on some measurement of the expected benefits, some estimate of the return on the investment in automation. But they are wrong—as are their manufacturing people who so loudly complain in management conferences and technical journals about the "conservatism" of their bosses—when they believe that these benefits are "intangible" and have to be taken on faith. The cost of poor quality and downtime to firms can actually be dug out of the available cost data fairly fast by any competent production account (and then verified by a cheap and quick sampling run).

Determining what additional revenues automation might make possible requires a little more: a conventional market study. But to estimate the benefits of automation also requires a change in the way most managements still look at the manufacturing process and its cost structure. It requires a change from a focus on the cost per piece produced to a focus on the total costs of the manufacturing process. But this, after all, is what accountants and accounting textbooks have been preaching and teaching for at least twenty-five years.

[1985]

33

IBM'S Watson: Vision for Tomorrow

Everybody knows that Thomas Watson, Sr. (1874–1956), built IBM into a big computer company and was a business leader. But "everybody" is wrong. Thomas Watson, Sr., did not build the IBM we now know; his son, Tom Watson, Jr., did this after he moved into the company's top management in 1946, only thirty-two years old (though the father stayed on until 1956 as a very active chairman). The father's IBM was never more than medium-size; as late as 1938 it had only $35 million in sales. Of course, it did not make or sell computers; its mainstays were punch-card machines and time clocks.

Instead of being a business leader, Thomas Watson, Sr., did not attain personal success and recognition until he was well past sixty. Twice in the 1930s he personally was on the verge of bankruptcy. What saved him and spurred IBM sales during the Depression were two New Deal laws: the Social Security Act in 1935 and the Wage-Hours Act of 1937–38. They mandated records of wages paid, hours worked, and overtime earned by employees, in a form in which the employer could not tamper with the records. Overnight they created markets for the tabulating machines and time clocks that Thomas Watson, Sr., had been trying for long years to sell with only moderate success.

In 1939, when I was working in New York as correspondent for a group of British papers, I wanted to write a story on Watson and IBM. I had become interested in the company because of the big pavilion it had put up at the New York World's Fair and thought a story on so small a frog behaving like a big shot might be amusing. "Forget it," my editor wrote back. "We are not interested in a story on an unsuccessful company which as far as anyone can tell is never going to amount to much." And Watson was then already sixty-five years old.

But Thomas Watson, Sr., was something far more important than a successful businessman who built a big company. He was the seer and, very largely, the maker of what we now call postindustrial society and one of the great social innovators in American history. Fifty years ago he had the vision of "data processing" and of "information." In the midst of the Depression and half broke himself, he financed the research that produced both the theoretical foundations for the computer and the first highly advanced model of it.

Fifty years ago or more he also invented and put into practice what in this country is now known, studied, and imitated as Japanese management—needless to say, he did so without the slightest knowledge of Japan and without owing anything to the then-nonexistent Japanese practices.

In fact, Watson's problem was that he was far ahead of his time, in his vision as well as in his practices.

I first met Watson in the early 1930s. He had been elected president of the American section of the International Chamber of Commerce—a job nobody else had wanted—and I, then a very young reporter, was sent to interview him. But the interview made absolutely no sense to my editor and never appeared. Of course, Watson delivered himself of the platitudes expected from the Chamber of Commerce, about free trade, about international cooperation, and about "the role of the businessman as an ambassador of peace." But then he started to talk of what clearly was his real interest—things he called *data* and *information.* But what he meant by those terms—it was not at all what anyone else at the time meant by them—he could not explain. Indeed, newspapers usually put him down as a crank.

I doubt that Watson himself *understood.* He had a vision —he *saw.* But unlike most seers, Watson *acted* on his vision.

Some kind of computer would have come without him. There were a good many people at the time working at fast calculating machines, especially under the impetus of World War II, with its need for navigational equipment for fast-moving airplanes, for firing mechanisms for long-range cannon shooting at invisible targets way beyond the horizon, for aerial bombs, and for antiaircraft guns. But without Watson it could have been a very different computer, a "calculating machine" rather than an "information processor." Without Watson and his vision the computer would have emerged as a "tool" rather than as a "technology."

Watson did not invent a single piece of hardware. He had no technical education, indeed little formal education altogether, having gone to work as a salesman of sewing machines, pianos, and organs in his native upstate New York when barely eighteen. He also had no technical talent, or much grasp of mathematics or of theory altogether. He was definitely not an inventor in the mold of Edison or his contemporary Charles Kettering. The computers that he sponsored, financed, and pushed for—one finished in 1943, another four years later, in 1947—contributed little by way of hardware and engineering solutions even to IBM's own early commercial computer in the 1950s.

But Watson saw and understood the computer fifteen years before the term was even coined. He knew right away

that it had to be radically different from a high-speed calculator. And he did not rest until his engineers had built the first
operational true "computer." Watson specified very early—in
the late 1930s at the latest—what computer people now call the
architecture of a computer: capacity to store data; a memory,
and random access to it; ability to receive instructions and to
change them, to be programmed, and to express logic in a
computer language. Watson's 1947 Selective Sequence Electronic Calculator (SSEC) was much more powerful and far
more flexible than any machine then in existence or being
planned. Its 12,500 vacuum tubes and 21,400 relays could, for
instance, solve partial differential equations. It was, above all,
the first—and for several years the only—machine to combine
electronic computation with stored programs, with its own
computer language, and with the capacity to handle its instructions as data: that is, to change, to correct, and to update them
on the basis of new information. These are, however, precisely
the features that distinguish a computer from a calculator.

When IBM embarked on designing a computer to be sold
in large quantities, it applied hardware largely developed by
others—mainly university labs at MIT, Princeton, Rochester,
and Pennsylvania. But it was all designed to Watson's original
specifications. This explains why the 650, IBM's first successful
commercial machine, immediately became the industry leader
and the industry standard when it was introduced in 1953; why
it sold eighteen hundred units during its first five years on the
market—twice as many as the best market research had predicted total computer sales worldwide to come to in the entire
twentieth century; and why it gave IBM the world leadership
in computers the company still holds.

The early *technical* history of the computer is quite
murky. And what part Watson and IBM, or anyone else,
played in it is remarkably controversial. But there is no doubt
at all that Watson played a key role in the *conceptual* history
of the computer. There are many others who were important,
if not central, in the engineering of the computer. But Watson
created the computer age.

The story begins in 1933 when IBM, on Watson's orders, designed a high-speed calculator for Columbia University's scientists and built it out of standard tabulating-machine parts. Four years later, in 1937, Howard Aiken, a Harvard mathematician, suggested that IBM try to link up several existing machines—designed originally for bookkeeping purposes—to create an even faster calculator for the time-consuming and tedious computations needed by astronomers. The work, Aiken estimated, would take a few months and would cost around $100,000. Instead, the work took six years and the cost was well over half a million dollars. For instead of the high-speed calculator Aiken had in mind, Watson went ahead and produced a computer.

First Watson specified an all-electronic machine; all earlier designs, including IBM's own machines, were electromechanical with levers and gears doing the switching. Of course, *electronic* then meant using vacuum tubes—the transistor was well into the future. And the resulting machines were therefore big and clumsy, tended to overheat, and used a great deal of electricity. Still, no one at the time even knew how to use electronic devices as switches—the key, of course, to computer technology. Even the needed theoretical work had yet to be done. For Watson and IBM to decide to desert the well-known and thoroughly familiar electromechanical technology for the totally unexplored electronics was a leap into the dark, but it was the decision that made the computer possible.

Watson's second specification was equally innovative. His project envisaged what no engineer at the time even dreamed of: a computer memory. Howard Aiken in his research proposal had been concerned with rapid calculation; he wanted a "numbers-cruncher." His idea was to build something that would be able to do very quickly what traditional adding machines and slide rules did slowly. IBM added to this the capacity to store data. And this meant that IBM's projected machine would be able to process information. It would have a data bank—a term that, of course, did not exist at the time—and would be able to refer back to it. Thus it could memorize and analyze. It could also—and this is crucial—correct and update its own instructions on the basis of new information.

And this then meant—another one of IBM's then quite visionary specifications—that IBM's machine was going to be capable of being *programmed,* that is, of being used for any information capable of being expressed in a logical notation. All the designs then being worked on were for single-purpose machines. The best known of these, called ENIAC, constructed at the University of Pennsylvania during the World War II years for Army Ordnance and completed in 1946, was, for instance, designed to do high-speed calculations for fast-firing guns. But it could do little more, as it had neither memory nor programming capacity. IBM, too, had specific applications in mind—especially calculations for astronomical tables. But, perhaps because Watson knew firsthand of the data-processing needs of a host of institutions—public libraries, the Census Bureau, banks, insurance companies, and the like—his specifications called for a machine capable of being programmed for all kinds of data. IBM's machine was a multipurpose machine from the start. This, then, also meant that when IBM finally had a computer that could be manufactured and sold—in the early 1950s—it was both willing and able to supply the users whose demand actually created the computer industry, but of whom no one had even thought in the early stages of computer design: business people who wanted computers for such mundane, unscientific purposes as payroll and inventory. Watson's insistence on memory and program thus explains in large measure why there is a computer industry.

Because of Watson's specifications of memory and program, the IBM research project of 1937 helped create computer science. The "analytical machine" that Watson tried to develop needed both computer theory and computer language—again, of course, terms that did not exist then. It needed, of course, first-class engineering, as did all the other calculating machines then designed. But it also created, or at least stimulated, the first computer scientists.

This research produced a prototype in late 1943—called

the Automatic Sequence Controlled Calculator (ASCC)—and Howard Aiken did do astronomical calculations on it, in early 1944. But it was far too advanced for the manufacturing technology of its time. In fact, only recently have the materials and the technology become available to manufacture the kind of computer for which Watson organized the research in 1937. Watson then donated the prototype, together with money to run and maintain it, to Harvard and immediately commissioned the work on the next design—the work out of which the SSEC evolved several years later. Its first public demonstration, on January 27, 1948, in New York City—at which it calculated all past, present, and future positions of the moon—ushered in the computer age. Even now, thirty-five years later, the computer that popular cartoons show, with its blinking lights and whirling wheels, is the SSEC as it was displayed at this first public demonstration. And looking at Watson's specifications in retrospect, this is precisely what must have been in his mind's eye all along.

As significant as Watson the computer seer is Watson the social innovator. He was even further ahead in his social vision than he was in his vision of data and information and had perhaps even more of an impact—and was equally (or more) misunderstood by his contemporaries.

Watson became a national figure in 1940, when *Fortune* published a violent, mudslinging attack on him. It insinuated that Watson was the American Führer and tried altogether to make him the symbol of everything repulsive in American capitalism. And it also fixed the popular perception of Thomas Watson as a reactionary and as a paternalist, a perception that still lingers on. But today it is clear that Watson's real offense was to be far ahead of his time.

Rereading the story in 1983, forty-three years later, I saw right away that what had most irked the *Fortune* writer in 1940 was Watson's ban on liquor in IBM's employee clubs and at IBM parties. He was indeed passionately opposed to alcohol— I once heard that his father or one of his uncles had been an alcoholic. But whatever Watson's reasons, it is perhaps not such a bad idea to keep work and liquor apart.

Then, of course, there was Watson's regimentation of his sales force, that is, his demand that IBM's salesmen wear dark suits and white shirts. But what Watson tried to do, as he had explained to me in my interviews with him a year before the *Fortune* story, was to instill self-respect in salesmen and respect for them among the public. When Watson began, the salesman was a "drummer," disreputable and a smelly crook, who spent his evenings in the small town's whorehouse unless he spent it debauching the farmer's innocent daughter in the hayloft. Watson, who had been a drummer himself, had deeply suffered from the contempt for his calling and was determined that his associates have self-respect and be respected. "I want my IBM salesmen," he had said in his 1939 talks with me, "to be people to whom their wives and their children can look up. I don't want their mothers to feel that they have to apologize for them or have to dissimulate when they are being asked what their son is doing" (and there was a clear implication, I thought then, that he was speaking of his own mother).

Watson's heinous crime, however, and the one the *Fortune* writer could not forgive him for, was that he believed in a worker who took responsibility for his job, was proud of it and loved it. He believed in a worker who saw his interests as identical to those of the company. He wanted, above all, a worker who used his own mind and his own experience to improve his own job, the product, the process, and the quality. Watson's crime—and it was indeed seen as a crime in the late 1930s, when a vulgar Marxism infested even fairly conservative members of the intelligentsia—was to make workers enjoy their work and thus accept the system rather than feel exploited and become revolutionary proletarians.

The way Watson did this was, first, to give his employees what we now call lifetime employment. As in Japan today, there was no contractual obligation on the part of Watson's IBM not to lay off people. But there was a moral commitment. In the first Depression years, 1931 and 1932, IBM did indeed lay off a few people, but Watson immediately stopped it. His refusal later, in the darkest Depression years of 1933 and 1934, to lay off workers could have bankrupted IBM. And employment security for workers has been IBM practice for fifty years now.

In the mid-1930s Watson abolished "foremen." They became "managers," whose job it was to assist workers, to make sure that workers had the tools and the information they needed, and to help them when they found themselves in trouble. Responsibility for the job itself was placed firmly on the work group.

The worker, Watson argued, knew far better than anyone else how to improve productivity and quality. And so around 1935 he invented what we now know as quality circles and credit to the Japanese. The industrial engineer was to be a "resource" to the work group and its "consultant," rather than the "expert" who dictated to it. Watson also laid down that the individual worker should have the biggest job possible rather than the smallest one, and as far back as 1920 he initiated what we now call job enrichment. (And after the old man's death his son, in 1958, put into effect his father's old idea and put *all* employees on a monthly salary, abolishing both the hourly wage and the distinction between blue-collar and white-collar employees.)

Finally, every employee at IBM had the right to go directly to the company's chief executive officer, that is, to Watson, to complain, to suggest improvements, and to be heard—and this is still IBM practice.

Much earlier Watson had invented what the Japanese now call continuous learning. He began in the early 1920s with his salespeople, who were called into headquarters again and again for training sessions to enable them to "do better what they are already doing well." Later Watson extended continuous learning to the blue-collar employees in the plant, and in the 1940s he hired Dwayne Orton, a college president from San Francisco, to be the company's director of education.

These practices very largely explain IBM's success. They exorcised the great bugaboo of American business, the employees' alleged resistance to change. They enabled the company in the 1950s and 1960s to grow as fast as any business had ever grown before—and perhaps faster—without much internal turbulence, without horrendous labor turnover, and without industrial strife. And because Watson's salesmen had all along been used to learning new things, middle-aged punchcard salesmen without experience in computers or in big-company management could overnight become effective executives in a big high-technology company.

But forty years ago Watson's policies and practices were very strange indeed. They either made Watson look like a crank, which is what most people believed, or they made him into the sinister force the *Fortune* writer saw. Today we realize that Watson was only forty or fifty years ahead of his time. Watson was actually one year older than Alfred Sloan. But whereas Sloan in the 1920s created modern management by building General Motors, and with it the modern "big corporation," Watson ten years later and quite independently created the "plant community" that we know to be the successor to Sloan's "big business enterprise" of the 1920s. He created in the 1930s the social organization and the work community of the postindustrial society.

The first ones to see this, by the way, were the Japanese. Again and again I have been laughed at in Japan when I talk about Japan's management embodying Japanese values. "Don't you realize," my Japanese friends ask, "that we are simply adapting what IBM has done all along?" And when I ask how come, they always say, "When we started to rebuild Japan in the 1950s, we looked around for the most successful company we could find—it's IBM, isn't it?"

Watson also anticipated the multinational. And this, too, no one in 1940 could understand.

Watson very early established foreign branches of IBM, one in France, one in Japan, and so on. IBM actually had little foreign business at the time, and Watson knew perfectly well that he could have handled whatever there was through exporting directly. But he also realized that the IBM he envisaged for the future, the IBM of what we now call data processing and information handling, would have to be a multinational company. And so he created, more than fifty years ago, the structure he knew IBM would have to have and would have to know how to manage were it ever to become the company he dreamed of. He also saw that the central problem of the multinational is to combine autonomy of the local affiliate with unity of direction and purpose of the entire company. This is in large measure the reason that Watson deliberately created what to most people seemed such extreme paternalism—today we would call it the IBM culture. Way back in 1939 he tried to explain it to me. "Foreign affiliates," he said,

> must be run by natives of their own country and not by expatriates. They must be accepted as members of their own society. And they must be able to attract the best people their own country produces. Yet they have to have the same objectives, the same values, the same vision of the world as the parent company. And this means that their management people and their professional people share a common view of the company, of the products, and of their own direction and purpose.

Most other multinationals still struggle with the problem Watson foresaw—and solved—fifty years ago.

Watson was an autocrat, of course. Visionaries usually are. Because visionaries cannot explain to the rest of us what they see, they have to depend on command.

Watson was a generous person but a demanding boss and not one bit permissive. But he demanded the right things: dedication and performance to high standards. He was irascible, vain, opinionated, a publicity hound, and an incorrigible name-dropper. And as he grew older he became increasingly addicted to being grossly flattered. But he was also intensely loyal and quite willing to admit that he had been wrong and to apologize. The people who worked for him feared him—but almost no one left.

Of course, he did not fit into the intellectual climate of the New York of the late 1930s. He was already sixty-five at that time and his roots were in the small rural towns of the 1880s, with their church socials and their service-club luncheons, with communal singing and pledges of allegiance to the flag—all the things that the "smart set" of the time had learned to sneer at as the marks of the "booboisie." And what was worse and made Watson a menace was that his employees shared Watson's values, rather than those of the intellectuals, and loved to work for him.

Watson was an extraordinarily complex man who fit into no category. He was among the first American businessmen to use modern design and modern graphics for the company logo and company stationery, products, and offices. But he did so mainly because it was the cheapest way to make his company stand out—and he had no advertising money. To get attention for IBM he used the slogan THINK, which he had invented at NCR. His salesmen used THINK notebooks by the thousands —again, it was the only advertising he could afford. And although he himself didn't have much of a sense of humor, he made up a good many of the THINK jokes and saw to it that they got wide circulation—again, to get attention for his company. Finally he hit upon the brilliant idea of building a huge pavilion at the 1939 New York World's Fair as the only way to make millions of visitors from all over the world aware of his then still small and practically unknown company and, as he told me at the time, "at the lowest cost per thousand viewers anyone ever had to pay."

Watson's popular image is that of the hidebound conservative, and he lent credence to this view by wearing the stiff Herbert Hoover collar long after it had gone out of fashion. But, almost alone among the businessmen of his time, he was an ardent New Dealer and a staunch supporter of Franklin D. Roosevelt. Indeed, FDR offered him major posts in his administration: first secretary of commerce, and then ambassador to Great Britain (when Watson said no, the job went to Joseph Kennedy instead). And at the very end of his life Watson urged

President Eisenhower to return to New Deal principles and was upset over Ike's insistence on reducing the government's role in economy and society.

Watson had a most unusual personal history, perhaps the most unusual one in the annals of American business. He started out dirt poor as a teenage drummer—not much more than a peddler. He rose to become the star salesman for the then-new National Cash Register Company of Dayton, Ohio, which was the first business-machine company in history. In about fifteen years he had become the company's sales manager. But then the company was indicted for antitrust violations, with which, we now know, Watson had little or nothing to do.

The trial was a sensation, for National Cash had been *the* growth company of the early 1900s. Watson drew a stiff fine and a one-year jail sentence. This conviction was set aside two years later, in 1915, by the Court of Appeals, and the government then dropped the case. But Watson had lost his job; both his career and his reputation were in tatters. It was an experience that marked him for life, an experience that he never forgot.

Already forty, he then had to begin all over again as general manager for a small and until then quite unsuccessful company that owned the punch-card patents. It was not until he was past sixty, in the mid-1930s, that he succeeded in establishing this company, by then renamed IBM, on a firm footing.

Watson—and this, I think, makes the man singularly interesting—was a uniquely American type and one the establishment has never understood throughout our history. He was possessed of a towering intellect but was totally nonintellectual. He belongs to the same type as Abraham Lincoln, who similarly offended the establishment of his day, the cosmopolitan, polished, learned Bostonians who considered themselves so superior to the yokel president in whose cabinet they were forced to serve. He was also similar in many ways to America's first great novelist, James Fenimore Cooper, who was also sneered at, despised, and pilloried by the intellectuals and the establishment of his time, such as the New England Transcendentalists. They could not make sense of the powerful, tragic, and prophetic vision in which Cooper foretold the end of the American Dream in such books as *The Pioneers* and *The Prairie.*

This American type is totally native and owes nothing to Europe—which is one reason that the intellectuals of his time do not know what to do with him. Typically the men of this type have a gift for words—and Watson fully shared it. But they are not men of ideas. They are men of vision. What makes them important is that, like Watson, they act on their vision.

[1983]

34

The Lessons of
the Bell Breakup

Such discussion of the Bell System breakup as there has been, and there has been remarkably little, has centered mainly on the consequences for the shareholders and on share and bond prices. Yet few governmental actions since World War II will have such profound impact on American society, on American technology, and even on national security, as the antitrust suit against AT&T and the subsequent dissolution of the Bell System. Few so immediately affect every individual in the country. The antitrust suit and its sequel raise serious and disturbing questions about those twin pillars of the American political economy: regulation of business and antitrust.

≫ Antitrust: The Cynics' View

For antitrust cynics—and among economists they outnumber the "true believers" about ten to one—it is almost axiomatic that no major antitrust suit is ever brought until the alleged monopoly is already on the skids. For it is only then that competitors appear; their complaints that the monopoly is not collapsing fast enough push the antitrust machinery into action. And thus the antitrust suit, the cynics contend, achieves the very opposite of what the antitrust champions intend. By forcing the monopolist to stop defending yesterday, it restores his leadership position and gives him a near-monopoly on tomorrow.

This surely applies to America's most celebrated antitrust suit, the one that resulted in the breakup of John D. Rockefeller's Standard Oil Trust three-quarters of a century ago. The "monopoly" that Standard Oil had was on kerosene, which had been *the* petroleum product until Henry Ford's Model T created a mass market for gasoline. In 1911, when Standard Oil was broken up, the gasoline market was still secondary but was growing fast, while kerosene was already in full decline and being replaced in all but rural areas by electric lights. And the gasoline market in the United States, and even more outside of it, was quickly taken over by aggressive newcomers such as Shell in England, Royal Dutch on the European continent, or Gulf and Texaco in the United States. Yet Rockefeller stubbornly clung to kerosene, on which indeed Standard Oil had a near-monopoly worldwide. It was only after antitrust had succeeded in breaking up the trust—in the process also dislodging the Rockefellers from active management—that the successor Standard Oil companies were free to concentrate on gasoline. Ten years later, they had 70 to 80 percent of the U.S. gasoline market and almost 50 percent of the gasoline market in the outside world.

Similarly, IBM would never have achieved worldwide leadership in the computer market had an antitrust suit not been brought against the company in the mid-1940s for monopolizing the punch card. But by 1947, punch cards were already becoming obsolete. IBM had actually done most of the work needed to give it leadership in the technology of tomorrow: the computer. But its stubborn defense of the punch card paralyzed it to the point that it actually stifled research on computers and on marketing them. The antitrust suit enabled the proponents of tomorrow in IBM management, especially the founder's son, Thomas Watson, Jr., to shift the company's efforts from defending the past to attaining leadership in the future.

The next antitrust suit against IBM, the one the government finally abandoned in 1982 as hopelessly confused, was also brought at the very moment when minicomputers and personal computers first arose to challenge IBM's domination of the domestic market, and when the Japanese first became serious competitors in mainframe computers worldwide. The suit probably pushed IBM out of being content to be number one in mainframes and into frantic efforts to do something it had earlier spurned: enter the market for small and personal computers.

There is little doubt that the antitrust suit against AT&T (the Bell System), which ended in January 1983 with the split-up of the system, was similarly brought when the company's monopoly had already been breached. It certainly forced the company to give up defending yesterday. What we do not know yet is whether it will, as the earlier suits did, enable AT&T to dominate the communications market of tomorrow: The challenge is clearly there.

≫ *A Phone in Every Room*

Some thirty years ago, AT&T made the critical decision that would eventually lead to its being broken up. The company then ran its own Advanced Management School in Asbury Park, New Jersey, to which the "comers" in upper-middle management were sent for several weeks of intensive training, usually just before being promoted into their first senior management jobs. The assignment for one of these classes during the final week at Asbury Park was to think through objectives and strategy for the Bell System, now that it had achieved its original and long-term objective of providing universal access to telephone service for everyone in the United States. (As it happened, I was the guest lecturer at Asbury Park that week and in charge of the sessions.) The assignment was to work out one recommendation for Bell System top management. But the class could not agree and ended up—to everyone's intense annoyance—with a majority and a minority report.

The majority recommended that Bell change its basic posture in the market. Whereas for more than sixty years the emphasis had been on providing everyone in the country with minimum service at lowest cost, the emphasis henceforth, the report proposed, should be on making people use their telephones as much as possible. This would mean pushing extensions in addition to the single telephone on the wall of the kitchen. It would mean selling more than one line to a customer (an extra phone for teenage children, for instance). It would also mean making the phone "interior decoration" rather than "utility" (Princess phones, for instance), or phones in colors other than black.

"All this is necessary," the minority agreed,

> but it's not nearly enough. In fact, it's only rear-guard action and good for—at most—20 years. The traditional telephone market is saturated; let's face it. The growth, and it is already fast and speeding up, is in long distance and in transmitting signals other than voice such as television programs and computer data. What is needed in addition to hard selling of traditional local service is a basic change in policy. Indeed, what is needed is a redefinition of the "system." We have always defined it as local services connected to each other by long distance lines. We now need to redefine "system" as a national and increasingly international information processor with local outlets. Specifically, this means first changing the basic pricing policy. Traditionally, we have priced so as to give the local subscriber the lowest possible cost while long distance users have paid a good deal more than the full cost of interconnection and of access to the local user. This way, long distance has been priced way above cost, and has in effect heavily subsidized local

service. This needs to be changed so that the local subscriber pays the full cost and pays for access to the network. And then we ought to shift from having telephone rates regulated by 48 states, each only concerned with getting minimum service at minimum cost for local subscribers, to national regulation; for instance by the Federal Communications Commission, with the emphasis on getting optimum national service at the lowest cost to the nation. Our traditional policies were rational when local service was our first priority and the growth sector. It is becoming deleterious to the company as well as to the nation, now that the growth opportunities have changed.

Bell System's top management took these recommendations very seriously and studied them carefully. In the end, it decided to adopt the majority report. It was, we know by hindsight, the wrong decision. But there probably was no choice. To go along with the minority would have meant forty-eight battles with forty-eight state public utility commissions. Moreover, thousands of Bell Telephone people throughout the country had been inculcated for years with the local-service creed and would have resisted any change. As it was, they strenuously resisted even the majority recommendation. "I have always been proud to provide public service and now they want me to be a huckster," one Bell System friend said when he saw the first phones in "decorator" colors. Another friend, the chief engineer for one of the operating companies, had been complaining for years that his four teenaged children monopolized the phone in his home. But when he heard that his company was going to push separate "teenager lines," he exclaimed, "This is immoral," and immediately took early retirement.

There also did not seem to be any risk in at least postponing the shift in emphasis from local service to the fast-growing, nonlocal services. Bell, after all, was regulated. Thus it was considered in those days to be immune to antitrust and to be able to exclude all would-be competitors. It was an inevitable decision, but the wrong one.

≫ *The Shortsighted Hard Sell*

The hard-sell campaign that the majority had recommended became a tremendous success. Within ten years it converted the home telephone from a utility into a convenience, if not into fashion and glamour. Few marketing campaigns in American history have been nearly so successful. Ironically, this great success in the end seriously damaged AT&T. It created a debilitating conflict between customer expectations and regulatory reality. AT&T's marketing campaign made customers avid for novelty, for rapid change, for new features. But the regulatory realities—largely a reflection of AT&T's earlier values—resisted novelty, rapid change, and new features. All forty-eight state regulatory commissions in the continental United States had long ago been taught by AT&T that their job was to ensure universal access to minimum telephone service at lowest cost. This meant, specifically, that AT&T was not permitted to write off equipment still in good physical condition, even though technically obsolescent, unfashionable, or "basic" rather than "sophisticated." AT&T's campaign created a market for rapid change in telephone equipment, whether receivers or switchboards. But AT&T kept hundreds of thousands—perhaps even millions—of obsolete models that were older but still perfectly serviceable and therefore could not be written off or junked. And so AT&T found itself caught between not satisfying the very demand it had worked hard to create and taking enormous losses on old equipment that might have endangered its financial integrity. Estimates of the writeoff run into the billions. AT&T, understandably trying to hedge, only created a market for potential competitors.

At the same time, the forecast of the minority report proved correct: Nonlocal service, long-distance telephoning, television transmission, and data transmission grew exponentially. In total numbers, calls within local areas still outnumber nonlocal calls. But both in demands on the system and in revenues, nonlocal services became, around 1970, the telephone system's center of gravity and its dominant, if not its only, growth sector. By now, Americans spend two dollars on long-distance calls for every dollar they spend on local service. For the subsidized local subscriber, this was good news. But it also meant that nonlocal rates, and especially long-distance rates, became increasingly divorced from costs, all the more so as the rapid rise in the volume of nonlocal traffic brought about a drastic reduction in its costs. AT&T did the intelligent thing: It offered large discounts to volume users. But this only increased AT&T's vulnerability, for it meant that anyone able to become a wholesaler—that is, anyone who could place enough individual long-distance calls to qualify for the wholesale discount—could underbid AT&T's rates and still make a handsome profit.

Finally, telecommunications technology exploded—largely as a result of the scientific contributions of AT&T's own Bell Labs. The transistor, switching theory, and information theory all came out of Bell Labs in the 1950s, and so did a good deal of computer logic and computer design. As a result of these breakthroughs, the telephone has virtually disappeared as unique technology. From AT&T's vantage point, the computer —for instance, in an office switchboard or in a central station —is an adjunct to the telephone; from the vantage point of an IBM, the telephone is simply a computer terminal.

No monopoly in history has ever survived even one such change, let alone several. If competition is forbidden by law, it comes in through a black market, but it comes in. Sooner or later, and usually sooner, the law is then changed one way or another. This is exactly what happened to AT&T. "Extensions" into which phones can be plugged had been quite rare; AT&T's big market push in the 1960s made them commonplace. This then created the market for competitors who, at first semilegally, offered "decorator phones," "fun phones," and other, still officially forbidden, attachments. Then competition moved in on the office switchboard. AT&T had spent millions to develop electromechanical switchboards to take the place of the old, manually operated ones. But the competition offered computerized switchboards that leapfrogged over AT&T's equipment. The technology to do so had come from AT&T. But because of its inability to write off, let alone to junk, old equipment that had become technically obsolete while remaining in perfect physical condition, AT&T had to stick with electromechanical, that is, outdated, instruments. Finally wholesalers came in—MCI, Sprint, and a host of others —who offered long-distance service to individual subscribers at 30 to 50 percent below AT&T's rates. AT&T invoked its traditional right as a regulated monopoly to keep these competitors out. But the courts, reversing a century of decisions and long-settled legal doctrine, ruled in case after case that a regulated industry is not exempt from antitrust, and that AT&T could not discriminate against competitors, ban their equipment, or penalize competitors' products in any way. In one important area, the impact on AT&T was immediate and substantial. In 1960, AT&T supplied almost all of the office switchboards used in America. Its share of the switchboard market by 1984 had fallen to less than one-third, with the bulk of new equipment being supplied by companies like ROLM that began as computer manufacturers.

The biggest loss has been in long distance. As late as 1981, AT&T's Long Lines Department still handled 90 percent of all long-distance calls in the country. By the middle of 1984, its share had dropped to 60 percent. Above all, AT&T has lost the most profitable market segments: The larger users increasingly either build their own system to link their plants and offices throughout the nation or switch to telephone discounters such as MCI and Sprint.

≫ *From "Ma Bell" to "Monster Bell"*

AT&T was thus increasingly forced on the defensive and increasingly trapped between the need to maintain high long-distance rates to subsidize local service and the need to cut long-distance rates to stanch the bleeding. Still, AT&T might have survived had it not been for inflation. The inflation of the

1970s eroded both the financial and the political base of the Bell System. And it undermined AT&T's self-confidence.

Employees within AT&T's own operations rarely know that their company has been one of the biggest nongovernmental financial institutions in the world. Not only has the company been the capital markets' heaviest borrower year in and year out, for the telephone business is highly capital-intensive; AT&T has also been the country's biggest lender. It has had to finance every single telephone subscriber for many years.

Traditionally, the subscriber did not buy the telephone connection to his home or his place of business, neither did he buy the equipment. The telephone company furnished both and was repaid out of operating revenues. And it took an average of five or six years until the subscriber's payments fully reimbursed the telephone company for the installation investment. Originally this was necessary; very few people in the telephone's early years would have been willing or able to pay the fairly large sums needed to buy the equipment. But in the years before World War I, Theodore Vail—AT&T's president from 1905 until his death in 1920 and the architect of the Bell System—turned this necessity into virtue and profit. He realized that AT&T could borrow at far lower interest rates than an individual possibly could; historically, AT&T has paid between 3 and 4 percent for its money. AT&T could thus finance the customer at a very low rate—4.5 to 5.5 percent on historical average—and yet make a handsome profit. This not only gave AT&T tremendous financial strength and security; it also enabled the company to lower rates for local service even more. Thus everybody profited.

But this very best of all possible financial worlds came to a rude end when the inflation of the 1970s pushed the interest rates AT&T had to pay to 13, 14, and 15 percent. While the interest rate to AT&T changed, the rate to the telephone subscriber remained frozen. Financing the subscriber then became a dangerous drain. *Market growth,* that is, new subscribers applying for service, became a threat, which explains why the Bell Companies have been doing worst where population has been growing fastest (as in Southern California). Despite its automation, the telephone is still quite labor-intensive. And so, as inflation pushed up wages, AT&T and its operating companies were forced to ask for higher rates. But because financing of new subscribers—and additional installations for old subscribers as well—turned a riskless profit-making venture into a big financial loss, AT&T was forced to ask for even higher rate increases well beyond the rate of inflation.

In most parts of the country and for most services, the telephone, adjusted for inflation, still costs a good deal less than it did in 1950 or perhaps even in 1960. And American telephone service is still cheaper than telephone service anywhere else, with the possible exception of Canada. But for more than 60 years, the American public had known only declining telephone rates—and local subscriber rates had been declining both the fastest and the most consistently. Now, all of a sudden, telephone rates were going up, and local service rates were going up the fastest.

There surely has been far less "public uproar" over rising telephone rates than newspaper stories and television commentators have reported. For the most part, the public contented itself with writing a few letters to the editor. But the political impact was considerable. Governors, state legislators, and public utility commissioners realized that they could get headlines and gain popularity by publicly resisting requests for higher telephone rates and denouncing the "telephone monopoly."

The psychological effect on the people at AT&T was devastating. Big companies—and big institutions generally, including universities, hospitals, and labor unions—tend to suffer from the dangerous delusion that the customer "loves" them. They are then shocked when they find out that a totally unsentimental and totally ungrateful customer only asks, "What will you do for me tomorrow?" But no institution in the United States—certainly no other business—has been so concerned with its standing in public opinion and so convinced of its being "loved" as the Bell Telephone System. This was by no means confined to top management. The lower ranks were even more deeply imbued with the Bell mystique.

And so the fairly mild protests against AT&T and its operating companies, protests which at General Motors would probably have been mistaken for expressions of endearment, came to the telephone employees as rejection by the beloved. A good many middle-management people I know in the Bell System feel as if their lives had been in vain. They had devoted their entire careers to serving the public, only to be attacked as greedy and reviled as profiteers. All along they had been confident of the public's support, and now, when for the first time they needed the public in a time of financial erosion and increasing competition, the public was turning against them.

It was just then, when all the traditional foundations of the Bell System were tottering, that the Justice Department, on November 21, 1974, brought an antitrust suit asking for the breakup of the Bell Telephone System.

≫ *Breakup . . . Without a Fight*

The AT&T suit has been documented more fully than any other antitrust suit in American history. Yet it is full of puzzles.

It is reasonably certain that the suit was brought only because of the political vacuum in the White House at the end of the Nixon presidency, which freed the antitrust lawyers in the Justice Department of political restraints. But why did the government pursue the suit? A presidential commission in the Carter administration condemned it as contrary to the national interest. Half a dozen members of the Ford, Carter, and Reagan cabinets recommended that it be dropped. And the Pentagon said publicly, on more than one occasion, that a standardized national telephone system under unified central management is absolutely essential for defense and must not be broken up. Yet neither Ford, nor Carter, nor Reagan did anything to stop the suit. Why?

The Justice Department, for its part, did little to push the suit. It waited six years, until January 1981, before bringing the suit to trial. And then it immediately adjourned the trial in the hope of a settlement offer from the company. The only rational explanation is that the higher-ups in the antitrust division were under pressure from their own "true believers" to bring the suit but expected to lose it.

AT&T's behavior was equally puzzling. AT&T has worked harder on public relations than any other large corporation in America. Yet its efforts to mobilize public opinion through the close contacts it had built up over the years with newspapers, local politicians, and academics were pathetically inadequate. Bell System's executives knew from the very beginning that much higher rates for those least able to afford them, the individual subscribers, would inevitably result from separating local from long-distance service, which was the antitrust division's first and central demand. Indeed, anyone on the outside, even if only superficially acquainted with the economics of the telephone, knew this. Yet I know of no attempt to alert customers or even the various public utility commissions. Bell System management also knew—it was again obvious—that any change would mean both substantial layoffs and sharp wage reductions for Bell System workers. Like all protected industries, the Bell System was able to pass on wage increases to its customers and thus had been forced to keep both employment and wages artificially high. Yet apparently no attempt was made to enlist the 600,000 Bell workers or their union, the Communications Workers of America, on the company's side in opposition to the antitrust suit. The union itself did not say one word about the suit that so clearly endangered it—perhaps even its very survival—even though opposition from the pro-union members of the Congress would almost certainly have put a fast stop to the suit. And Bell System management never, it seems, publicized the strong Pentagon protest. And yet, Bell System top management was emotionally committed to fighting the antitrust suit all the way without making any concessions and considered the suit to be both totally without merit and totally immoral. Indeed, judging from the plentiful published documents, top management in AT&T was preoccupied for several years with fighting the suit and had time for little else. Had Bell's top management lost its nerve? Was it so overcome by its vicissitudes, and especially by its seeming rejection by the American public, as to have become virtually paralyzed?

All of a sudden, in the closing weeks of 1981, Bell capitulated. It voluntarily offered to divest itself of the operating companies and to restrict itself to long-distance and overseas operations, to the manufacture and sale of telephone equipment, and to telecommunications research. The decision came without any warning and as a surprise to everyone in the Bell System, where it was then generally believed that the suit would surely drag on until around 1990 and would finally be fought out in the Supreme Court. Instead, Bell accepted voluntarily most of what antitrust had asked for.

The only rational explanation for the sudden about-face of the Bell System top management is that it found itself forced to redefine its own role and function. Since Theodore Vail's days in the early years of the century, AT&T has always seen itself as a "private company in the public service" rather than as a "private business." It was in this tradition that Bell System top management felt itself duty-bound to fight the government antitrust suit as likely to damage the American economy, to penalize the poor, and to endanger America's technological leadership (as we shall see, all perfectly legitimate concerns). But then, for six long years, no one in the public noticed their plight and came to their support—neither the media nor the administration nor the public utility commissions of the states, nor the labor union, nor even the Pentagon, which probably had more at stake in the antitrust suit than anybody else. And then, though one can only guess, the Bell System top-management people might have said to themselves, "If no one accepts us as defenders of the public interest, we have to do what the law tells us is our duty, that is, look after the interests of the company and its shareholders."

And so, once they had capitulated, they acted with amazing speed. Two years later, on January 1, 1984, the Bell System breakup was complete. AT&T accepted competition in long-distance service and in providing instruments and equipment to the public. In return, AT&T was relieved of all responsibility for local service and with it of the responsibility to subsidize the local subscriber. This responsibility is now being shifted to seven independent large regional companies. Neither the operating companies nor AT&T has to finance the customer's equipment any longer. They are now free to sell it. AT&T by 1987 will be free to set long-distance rates and thereby to fight back against competition that its former rate structure created and indeed subsidized. For the first time since the 1920s, when earlier antitrust fears made the Bell System sell its European manufacturing operations (after which it confined itself to North America, and since the 1950s to the continental United States), AT&T can compete worldwide. And it can engage in any business whatever, for instance, selling computers and office equipment.

But what specifically is the future for the operating companies and for AT&T? And what does the Bell breakup mean for the American telephone user and for American national security?

» Regional Difficulties

Every one of the new regional companies into which the Bell System has been split has committed itself publicly to bold entrepreneurship and aggressive marketing, for instance, to leadership in cable television. But the future of the operating companies will depend on something far more mundane: on their ability to succeed in the traditional business of offering common-carrier service for a diversity of electronic messages going from one telephone instrument to another.

The former Bell System operating companies all face several highly turbulent years fighting for the rate increases they need to survive. Rates are already going up sharply and will continue to do so. Yet the antitrust suit promised, of course, that the consumer would greatly benefit from the breakup of the Bell monopoly. But in addition to losing the subsidy from long distance, the operating companies have to pay a good deal more for the money they need now that they are no longer sheltered monopolies. And they have to raise very large sums of money for equipment and facilities.

Second, they have to complete the shift they have only begun: from owning, leasing, and installing equipment to selling it. Within ten years, the operating companies will have to transfer to the customer the burden of paying for telephone instruments, and also for the connection from the nearest telephone line to the user's building. They will not be able to finance equipment for the user, or be able to absorb the labor costs of installing and repairing equipment. Eventually this may lead to a new and profitable business—if and when interest rates come down. The Bell Companies may be able to start finance companies that will offer the consumer five- to eight-year installment finance on attractive terms. But this is well into the future. In the meantime, companies will have to persuade both the public and the public utility commissions of the forty-eight continental states (AT&T does not operate in Alaska and Hawaii) to allow them to withdraw from a service consumers and public utility commissions have been taking for granted for a century. We will thus inevitably see more attempts to guarantee low-cost telephone service for the poor, such as the recent California Universal Telephone Law. But this simply means that the subsidy to the local users that business—that is, high-volume long-distance users—formerly paid will now be provided by the taxpayer.

But perhaps even more difficult will be the labor problem. What the operating companies need is something like a one-quarter to one-third reduction in total employment and a one-quarter to one-third reduction in hourly labor rates and in the total labor cost burden. Historically, public utility commissions have automatically allowed the telephone company to pass along all employment costs and all wage increases. This is unlikely to continue, in part because rates have become highly politicized, in part however because unions—especially large, mass-production unions—have lost so much of their political power. Elected officials, such as public utility commissioners, are now clearly more afraid of taxpayers than they are of the union vote. And Bell workers, as employees of a protected industry, have achieved wage benefit levels higher than Bell's competitors pay.

There are 600,000 members of the Communications Workers of America, and any reduction of staff and pay will hit hardest at installers and repairmen, the most highly paid but also the most completely unionized of all Bell workers. Yet they know that striking is not going to help them much; telephone service is so highly automated that most subscribers would not notice even a very long strike. Labor relations, in other words, are bound to be bitter on both sides, and turbulent.

Each of these tasks is difficult and represents a complete break with Bell System tradition. Each is going to cause raucous quarrels, bitterness, and bad publicity. But each will have to be tackled.

≫ Learning to Compete

It is far more difficult to predict the future of AT&T, the former parent of the Bell System, now that it has been released from all parental responsibility—providing local service, installing and financing equipment—and from restrictions on the sale and pricing of its products, and the restriction to do business only within the continental United States. Or, rather, one has to predict "futures." For AT&T is not one, but four major businesses, each quite different though interlocked with the others.

First there is nonlocal telephone service. For some additional time, AT&T may still labor under a fairly heavy competitive penalty. The competing long-distance services have lobbied, and with considerable success, to delay for a year or two AT&T's proposal to levy "access charges" on local telephones, charges that would have curtailed the competitors' rate advantage and have enabled AT&T to cut its own long-distance rates fast and sharply. But even after the penalty is finally removed (in 1987), AT&T will face an uphill struggle to get back the long-distance users it has lost, and especially the big ones among them. Whether it can ever regain its leadership is doubtful. A good many of the best long-distance customers, the very large ones such as the big multiplant companies or the very big banks, have been pushed by AT&T's high long-distance rates into building their own private telephone systems. And so have several of the competing services. The biggest, MCI, is actually planning to build its own transatlantic circuits.

Even murkier is the future of AT&T's second unit, the huge manufacturing subsidiary, Western Electric. In number of employees (150,000), Western Electric ranks tenth among American manufacturing companies; in sales ($12 billion) it ranks twenty-second. But in profitability it ranks well below 300, with a laughable return of 2.5 percent on sales and a return of 7 percent on assets—less than one-third of such comparable engineering companies as General Electric or IBM, and a good deal less than half of the minimum return an engineering company needs to defray its cost of capital. But, of course, Western Electric never had to compete, as the Bell System bought everything it turned out. It never was run for profit, but as a supplier to the operating companies. And it never had any credit losses, or inventories to write off, or marketing expenses.

Now, almost overnight, Western Electric will have to compete for every order it gets. Under the antitrust settlement, the operating companies have to consider every supplier rather than favor one of them—and the state public utility commissions will make very sure they do. All of the world's traditional telephone equipment makers—Siemens from Germany; Ericsson from Sweden; the ITT companies from this country, Great Britain, Germany, France, and Belgium; NEC from Japan; and half a dozen others—are already in the American market hawking their wares to Ma Bell's orphans. And the mightiest and the most aggressive new competitor, IBM, is moving full speed into the telephone business. It has bought ROLM, Western Electric's most dangerous competitor in the switchboard field, and acquired a big stake in Intel, a leading manufacturer of the semiconductors that go into telephones and telephone switching gear.

On top of all this, Western Electric must break into a world market that it once dominated, but from which it retreated sixty years ago. It needs the volume. As long as Western Electric had to make everything the Bell Companies bought, and as long as the companies in turn had to buy everything Western Electric made, Western Electric had to produce an unknown but very large number of items that were neither the right products for its plants nor even remotely profitable. Obviously, it will not be able to sell these products from now on. And where, except in the export market, could it possibly get the volume to fill this capacity? The developing world is *the* market for truly advanced telecommunications equipment today, simply because developing countries (such as Singapore, Colombia, Kuwait) do not have large quantities of older equipment still functioning that would be too good to replace overnight. Thus, Western Electric has energetically moved out of the United States into a partnership with, for example, Olivetti, the large Italian office equipment and minicomputer maker. Yet the world market is already oversupplied with telephone manufacturers, and the big telephone orders—typically orders from national governments, of course—require the kind of financial encouragement that large exporters in Europe or Japan get from their governments as a matter of national policy, but that does not exist in the United States.

Western Electric has formidable assets in design, in engineering, in manufacturing—in everything, in fact, but marketing. It also has no choice but to try. But still there is no evidence that a frog can turn into a prince, and that is roughly what Western Electric is trying to do.

≫ *Does Bell Labs Have a Future?*

The third of AT&T's main units and the best known, Bell Telephone Laboratories, poses the most difficult decision. When the Bell System split itself up, top management announced that there would be no change whatever in the role and function of the system's famed Bell Labs. But this, no matter how sincerely intended, is unlikely. Indeed, Bell Labs faces the most radical change in its history and its mission.

However, the antitrust settlement is only a minor factor in this, only the trigger. Bell Labs in its traditional form had actually become increasingly untenable for a long period of time, largely as a result of its own successes and contributions. Bell Laboratories' discoveries and inventions have largely created modern "electronics"; they thereby eliminated the "telephone" as a distinct technology. To do what Bell Labs was founded to do in 1925 and did magnificently for 50 years—that is, to produce *all* the science and technology that a telephone needs—had become literally impossible. No one lab, no matter how good or how big, can possibly do this anymore. Everything in electronics, but also in solid-state or molecular physics, in metallurgy or in plastics, in crystallography or in computer sciences, and in a host of other disciplines, has a direct and immediate application to telephoning. And conversely, even the world's biggest telephone system is not large enough as an outlet for the discoveries and inventions that come out of Bell Labs. Indeed, in a wide array of areas, from the transistor to fiber optics, and from switching theory to computer logic, the Bell System has been no more adequate as a conduit for Bell Labs' scientific contributions than an eyedropper would be to channel a mountain freshet. The main users have been others —that is, nontelephone industries—with Bell Labs' getting little out of its contributions other than an occasional footnote in a scientific paper.

The antitrust suit probably delayed by a decade the tackling of this problem. But now it must be faced. Under the new arrangement Bell Laboratories' expenses can no longer be paid for by the operating companies. They can, of course, contract with Bell Labs for specific work if they so choose, but they no longer have an obligation to contribute. Considering the pressures on the operating companies to hold down costs, the forty-eight public utility commissions are certain to look with a very skeptical eye on any payment from the operating company in their state to Bell Labs. Bell Labs, in other words, suddenly may have only a fraction of its former economic base.

For several years it had been clear that Bell Labs could go in two directions. It could become a standard industrial lab of a big engineering company, comparable to the labs of GE, RCA, or du Pont. This does not necessarily condemn it to mediocrity; the GE lab can match Nobel Prize winners with any scientific institution in the world. But it is a very different role from that to which Bell Labs has been accustomed.

And then there would be a far bolder but also far riskier course: to convert Bell Labs into something totally new, a worldwide *scientific* laboratory in telecommunications and electronics, in business for itself, a lab that would aim at making a profit by taking research assignments from whoever is willing to pay for them, by developing its own patents and products to sell and to license, and so on. AT&T would still be the parent company of such a Bell Lab, but otherwise it would be just another client and would be dealt with at arm's length. Nothing like this has ever been done. And no one knows whether it could succeed. But it clearly is the alternative to Bell Labs' becoming another, though very good, industrial laboratory subordinated to a major manufacturing company.

The Bell System breakup, which deprived it of its financial base in the operating companies, surely tips the balance toward Bell Labs' becoming Western Electric's research and development department. It is hardly coincidence that one of the first organizational changes AT&T made after the breakup of the Bell System on January 1, 1984, was to put Bell Labs into the same organizational group as Western Electric and to subordinate it to the same management.

≫ *The Risk to Defense Communications*

Almost no one, so far, has publicly even mentioned AT&T's fourth major business: national defense communication. Yet it may be the most important, and the one most severely affected by the breakup of the Bell System.

Communications, everyone agrees, are the nerve system of modern defense. If communications do not function, defense collapses. Communications, everyone further agrees, are the one major area where the United States has so far enjoyed unquestionable superiority. Everyone also agrees that an enormous amount of work and effort will be needed simply to maintain our defense communications. For we now know that what we have is highly vulnerable to magnetic fields created by explosions in space. For "defense communications in the United States," read AT&T. What gave the United States its superiority in defense communications were precisely the features of the Bell System that were abandoned in the antitrust settlement: complete integration of universal access, local service with universal long-distance service; complete compatibility throughout the system under unified central control; and, finally, integration of research on all levels, from pure science to product design and operational application. It was precisely because the antitrust suit challenged these features of the Bell System that the Pentagon strongly protested against it. But in the aftermath of Vietnam, nobody listened. What will happen now that the breakup of the Bell System is an accomplished fact? How much compatibility must there be in the nation's telephone system; in telephone receivers, switchboards, and central stations; in long-distance circuits and long-distance service; in the ability to switch automatically from a damaged circuit to another route, so as to support mobilization, the organization of war production, and the transportation of defense material, let alone military command in time of war?

Under the antitrust settlement, defense communications are going to be fragmented. AT&T is bidding on the government's long-distance business, but a lot of "discounters," especially MCI, are also trying to get it. So is Bell Atlantic, the regional operating company serving Washington, D.C. There is going to be a host of suppliers offering different kinds of equipment to all government agencies, including the Defense Department. And AT&T is altogether forbidden to offer *end-to-end* services—that is, connections to local telephones—except for a few highly specialized installations at the Department of Defense and the Strategic Air Command.

But surely there is a point beyond which the fragmentation of our communication system endangers the nation. Pearl Harbor, we now know, happened in large part because a Navy telephone circuit was out of order at the critical time, while no interconnection existed to other undamaged circuits. Would we risk similar disaster if we have a number of competing long-distance systems rather than one integrated one, and if long-distance and local service are separated managerially, technically, and in their equipment?

We may thus soon be faced with the need to rethink the Bell antitrust decision as far as it affects national security. One possibility, and it is being seriously studied in the Pentagon, is for the military to build its own communications system. No one knows how much it would cost, but it would be extremely expensive; one guess is about $100 billion. It would also weaken the civilian telephone system by taking away from it its largest user and the one most willing to try out new technology and to pay for it.

But there emerged in April 1984 a totally different proposal: to repeal the antitrust settlement with respect to all governmental telecommunications and to turn all of them—local service, long distance, and equipment—back to AT&T. In fact, AT&T has already applied to the Federal Communications Commission for a waiver of the antitrust decree to allow it to submit such a bid to the government. I suspect that the Pentagon will strongly support AT&T; indeed, I suspect that the Pentagon has encouraged AT&T to make this bold move. Whether AT&T's request will be granted is, of course, quite doubtful. There is no precedent in antitrust history for anything so bold and so radical.

AT&T's request would go a long way toward nullifying the antitrust decree's central feature: the absolute separation of long distance from local service. And it would do so with respect to the country's largest single telephone user, the federal government, with a total telephone bill of nearly $2 billion. Above all, what AT&T is asking is for the government to admit, at least implicitly, that the breakup of the Bell System was a major and potentially disastrous mistake. Not only will all other providers of telephone service—former Bell operating companies, as well as all long-distance discounters and equipment manufacturers other than Western Electric—fight AT&T's request, but within the government and in the Congress there will also be enormous opposition.

Still, it might be the only solution. And if AT&T's request for a waiver is not granted, we shall sooner or later have to tackle the question of defense communications—and probably sooner. Some thoughtful people I know in the military, who are by no means alarmists, think the question might come up before the end of the next presidential term in 1988.

≫ *The Achievements—and Problems—of Regulated Monopolies*

The AT&T suit was by far the biggest antitrust action ever taken, and not only because AT&T was the country's biggest nongovernmental enterprise. It also had far more dramatic results than any previous antitrust suit ever aimed at or achieved. What, then, are its lessons for regulation and for antitrust—two pivotal American institutions—both, by the way, almost exact contemporaries of the Bell Telephone System?

The regulated monopoly was one of America's most innovative and most successful contributions to the art of government. In one simple concept it solved what had seemed an insoluble dilemma: either to leave a "natural monopoly" to free

enterprise and thereby give it a license to extort, or to nationalize it and thereby condemn it to almost certain bureaucratic
arrogance, high costs, and inefficiency. Without exception,
America's regulated monopolies have given better service and
have done better than nationalized counterparts in the rest of
the developed world. The Bell Telephone System was, of
course, the premier example, giving the country the world's
finest telephone service at rates up to 50 percent below those
of any other industrialized country. American electric utility
costs, too, are almost everywhere lower than those of electric
utilities elsewhere with comparable energy sources (for example, coal, oil, or water power).

But even a regulated monopoly can become dysfunctional.
As soon as there is any competition, as soon as there is an
alternative way of producing the same consumer satisfaction or
of filling the same consumer want, regulation becomes counterproductive. It no longer "regulates," but it still forbids and
stifles. It can no longer protect its industry and maintain its
monopoly. But it can, and will, make it difficult for its industry
to compete, to modernize itself, to meet the new threat. Yet
there is no mechanism for abolishing outmoded regulation.

What then happens is messy, capricious, expensive, and
bound to hurt a good many people, innocent bystanders included. The outcome is unpredictable and quite unlikely to be
what is most rational and most in the national interest. In some
cases we have left things to blind chance. One example is what
is now happening in financial services. It bears not the slightest
resemblance to what anyone would have foreseen or advocated
when it first became apparent twenty years ago that our financial rules, demarcation lines, and regulations would rapidly
become obsolete and meaningless. But with respect to the railroads, the outcome, equally left to chance, is quite different.
What is now emerging, after thirty years of turmoil, and without the repeal of a single ordinance, rule, or regulation, is a
system of five or so major national, if not transcontinental,
railroads. That is almost exactly what a long-dead ICC com-
missioner, Joseph Eastman, proposed almost sixty years ago

when it first became apparent that cars and trucks were nibbling away at the railroad's monopoly on land transportation. Other industries, airlines and trucking, for instance, have been "deregulated" with the major result of forcing their workers' wages down. And with respect to the telephone, we used an antitrust suit with results that no one can foresee as yet, but that almost certainly will not be what anyone—Bell System executive, antitrust lawyer, or disinterested outsider—would have foreseen, planned for, or aimed at.

Is there a better method? The answer is probably no. An old idea, a *sunset law* under which regulatory statutes expire every so often and have to be reenacted, say, every thirty years, is most unlikely to work. Every regulation creates its own constituencies. Regulation has to be undermined de facto; de jure it is likely to continue long after the reality of regulated monopoly has disappeared whether through the emergence of cars and trucks, through that of charter planes, through Citicorp's becoming in effect a truly "national" bank, or through discounters' offering long-distance telephone service at cut rates. Indeed, the one probable result of sunset laws is to tighten regulation just when economic and technological reality abolishes the natural monopoly. The only consolation may be that liquidating an obsolescent government monopoly is likely to be even messier, costlier, less predictable. (Witness the vicissitudes of the U.S. Post Office, beset on one side by electronic mail and on the other by private express services. Or examine the Japanese National Railroads, which are not allowed to do anything at all by their political and trade-union bosses, but which have already lost all their freight traffic and are now rapidly losing their passenger traffic as well, while unsubsidized private railroads paralleling the tracks of the national system run full trains to the same destinations, charge half the fare the national system charges, and make money into the bargain!)

≫ Antitrust Moralism

Antitrust, too, was an American contribution to the art of government, but a far more debatable one. It may come as a surprise to laymen to learn that most American economists have never had much to say for the antitrust laws. They consider such laws morality rather than economics. One reason is that economists, by and large, are not terribly frightened by nongovernmental, that is, business, monopolies. Ever since a German economist, Robert Liefmann, published his comprehensive study of business monopolies (*Die Kartelle*) in 1905, economists have known that business (that is, nongovernmental) monopolies are short-lived. All they do, as a rule, is provide an umbrella of high prices under which competitors then grow fast and risklessly. Thus, Rockefeller's Standard Oil Trust held an umbrella of high prices over the newcomers—Texaco, Gulf, Shell—eighty years ago. And the Bell System held an umbrella of high long-distance rates over such discounters as MCI and Sprint. The only exceptions are what Joseph Schumpeter (1883–1950) called *intelligent monopolies,* that is, monopolies that maintain their leadership position by cutting their own prices before competition does, and faster than competition can do it, and that themselves make their products obsolete before the competition does. Schumpeter's example was the Bell Telephone System—and that was, of course, the foundation for Bell's strength until it ran into the inflation of the late 1960s and 1970s. Another example would be IBM today. Intelligent monopolies may indeed last a long time, but of course the intelligent monopoly uses its economic power to benefit the consumer rather than to extort from him.

There is an even more important reason, however, for the jaundiced view most American economists take of antitrust: They see no results. Or rather they see only wrong results which are almost the opposite of what antitrust promises. In terms of concentration of economic power, the American economy, despite antitrust, differs very little—and certainly not in statistically significant magnitudes—from any other economy in a similar stage of development, even though most of these others have had no antitrust laws and have certainly not enforced those they have had. Indeed, it is pretty obvious that concentration is determined by technology and market forces rather than by law and is pretty much the same in the same industries across all boundaries. But as a result of antitrust, economic concentration and combination in this country have taken peculiar forms, and not necessarily the most benign ones. Antitrust has enormously encouraged mergers. For under the antitrust laws, units within the same legal entity are considered one business and are basically exempt from antitrust with respect to their dealing with one another. In other countries, however, there is the group rather than the merger. In the group, the individual units maintain their independence and identity though tied to each other through stock holdings (usually minority holdings, by the way). Antitrust would, however, consider the group, composed as it is of independent legal entities, a clear violation; as a result, antitrust has greatly favored the disappearance of autonomous, self-governing, and smaller enterprises in favor of the behemoth. And then because antitrust frowns on concentrations of economic power in the same markets, it has virtually forced American companies to grow by forming "conglomerates" without organic or business unity (for example, ITT's telephone equipment businesses' adding to themselves a bakery and an insurance company). Few economists would consider the merger preferable to the group, or the conglomerate preferable to either.

This will not, of course, impress antitrusters in the least. That economic concentration in this country, despite its antitrust laws, is no lower than among the heathen proves only two things: the antitrust laws have to be enforced much more strictly, and the evil is even more powerful, more wicked, and more devious than anyone could imagine. To economists, laws like antitrust are hygiene. To the true antitrust believer, they are morality. And morality, at least in the United States, always has a great deal more appeal than something so pedestrian as hygiene. Most American economists would agree that even repealing the antitrust laws in their entirety, let alone their monopoly provisions, would not cause great harm to the American economy. The offenses that need to be forbidden— price fixing, discriminatory pricing, discriminatory rebates— are adequately covered by common law, after all, and are adequately dealt with in countries that are totally innocent of antitrust legislation. Still, antitrust is sacred. A proposal to repeal the bans on "concentration" and "monopoly" would have about as much chance of success as a proposal to close all law schools for the next thirty years.

≫ The Social Costs of Antitrust

But still, the AT&T suit has shown that some reforms should at least be seriously considered. The first one might be to introduce into antitrust the overwhelming consensus among American economists about what is "analysis" and what is "policy." "All economists," an oft-quoted saying goes, "agree that the only purpose of economic activity and its touchstone is the consumer. Anyone who believes that the purpose is anything else (employment, for example) is not an economist." Not quite true, but it will do.

For the great majority of American economists, and of economists anywhere, this however applies only to *economic analysis* and not to *economic policy*. But for a tiny minority— George Stigler in Chicago and his disciples—it applies to both. To some considerable extent their influence has been wholesome. Stigler's insistence that in economic analysis nothing else be considered but strictly economic factors is a badly needed antidote to the sloppiness that prevails in arguments about economic policy. It is indeed highly desirable, as Stigler has demanded for years, that policymakers start out with the knowledge of the purely economic facts so that they face up to the costs of any deviation therefrom in the policy they then choose.

But his disciples go much further. They demand that no deviation from the pure economic analysis be followed in *decid-*

ing on economic policy. And Stigler's disciples control antitrust. To consider anything else—impact on foreign policy or on defense, social consequences, anything—is impure if not prostitution. For the antitrust economist, the benefit to an abstract consumer is the only consideration. The Chicago economists, for instance, refused to accept as relevant the argument that a Bell System breakup would inevitably mean higher rates for the poor and lower rates for business; the only thing they allowed was the total impact on all consumers, that is, the total national telephone bill. For, as the group argues, any concession, any deviation is the first step down the slippery slope. It is "playing politics with the law." To the great majority of American economists, this is virtue carried to the point of madness.

For antitrust *is* politics. The Reagan administration declared in the winter of 1984, in connection with an antitrust ban on a proposed merger between two very large steel companies, that "it does not allow politics to enter antitrust; it is entirely a matter of the law." This is sanctimonious twaddle, and disingenuous to boot. A major antitrust suit is, of necessity, a highly political matter—and the way it is settled even more so. The suit against AT&T, for instance, would hardly have been brought had inflation not eroded the company's support to the point that it became politically vulnerable. And the whole point of the steel-merger decision was political: whether it is politically preferable to allow major steel companies to merge rather than to impose import restrictions on steel from Europe and thereby to risk a trade war with the Common Market. And, indeed, no sooner had the White House officially declared that it had nothing to do with the steel-merger case than antitrust reversed itself and allowed the merger. It is also simply not true, as the antitrust economists maintain, that there exists no reasonably rigorous and objective theory to consider extra-economic factors in an economic-policy decision. That theory has been in existence for fifty years now, in the welfare economics of Arthur Cecil Pigou. What *welfare economics* does is determine, with considerable precision, the economic costs of trade-offs from the purely economic, purely consumer-focused result of economic analysis. How much would it mean in additional costs if, for example, long-distance rates were maintained at a higher than strictly economic level to provide subsidies for minimum local service? How much would it cost in economic terms to make this or that social or political concession? What, in other words, are the *economic* costs of a given policy? Policy, by definition, can never be just one thing—that is, social or economic or military—it always has many dimensions. Who loses, who benefits, and by how much?

But the antitrust economists are quite right: The answers to these questions are not really to be found in the law any more than are the settlement terms for an antitrust decree. What is therefore needed (and, by the way, most judges would agree) is to divorce analysis from policy in major antitrust suits as we routinely do in so many other areas. Legal and economic analysis should govern until a company or an industry is found in violation. But then a panel of high-level experts—maybe one nominated by the prosecution, one nominated by the defense, one a public member (or a panel appointed by the Council of Economic Advisors)—would work on the trade-offs, the welfare economics. The panel should probably be limited in its considerations to a fairly small number of issues: major social impacts; major economic impacts such as those on productivity, capital formation, and employment; the impact on America's competitive position in the world economy and on America's technological leadership; the impact on national security. In the AT&T case, such a panel would surely have recommended continuing financial support of the Bell Labs by the operating companies. And it might also have forced us to face the problem of defense communications. The panel should advise rather than arbitrate, the judge making the final decision. But the judge needs advice; nothing in a judge's background or career qualifies him in these matters. They are also matters that can only be mismanaged if handled in adversary proceedings.

Of course any such reform, or anything even remotely like

it, is in the future. But it may not be a very distant future. If the Bell breakup works out and if ten years hence the United States still has telecommunications leadership, well and good. But if, as is quite likely, the ten years after the antitrust liquidation of AT&T's "natural monopoly" bring more gadgets but otherwise only increased costs, damaged technological leadership, and compromised national security, we may then be ready to reconsider.

[1984]

35

Social Needs and Business Opportunities

In the early years of this century, two Americans, independently and, in all probability, without knowing of each other, were among the first businessmen to initiate major community reforms. Andrew Carnegie preached and financed the free public library. Julius Rosenwald fathered the county farm agent system and adopted the infant 4-H Clubs. Carnegie was already retired from business as one of the world's richest men. Rosenwald, who had recently bought a near-bankrupt mail-order firm called Sears, Roebuck and Company, was only beginning to build both his business and his fortune. Both men were radical innovators.

The monuments that earlier businessmen had erected for themselves were cultural: museums, opera houses, universities. In Carnegie's and Rosenwald's own time leading American businessmen, A. Leland Stanford, Henry E. Huntington, J. P. Morgan, Henry C. Frick, and a little later, Andrew Mellon, still followed this tradition. Carnegie and Rosenwald instead built communities and citizens—their performance, their competence, and their productivity.

But there the similarity ends. The two held basically different philosophies. Carnegie shouted his from the housetops: The sole purpose of being rich is to give away money. God, Carnegie asserted, wants us to do well so that we can do good. Rosenwald, modest, publicity shy, unassuming, never preached, but his deeds spoke louder than his words. "You have to be able to do good to do well" was Julius Rosenwald's credo, a far more radical one than that of the anarchist steelmaster from Pittsburgh. Carnegie believed in the social responsibility of wealth. Rosenwald believed in the social responsibility of business.

Rosenwald saw the need to develop the competence, productivity, and income of the still desperately poor and backward American farmer. To accomplish this it was necessary to make available the enormous fund of scientific farming knowledge and farming skills that had been amassed in decades of systematic study of agronomy and farm marketing, but that, in 1900 or 1910, were still largely theoretical and inaccessible to all but a tiny minority of more affluent agriculturalists. Although his motives were partially philanthropic, he also saw that Sears, Roebuck's prosperity was linked to the prosperity of its main customer, the farmer, which in turn depended on his productivity. The county farm agent—and Sears, Roebuck for almost a decade single-handedly supported this innovation of Rosenwald's until the U.S. government finally took it over—and the 4-H Clubs were clearly philanthropy. But they were also Sears, Roebuck's corporate advertising, public relations, and above all market and customer development. Their success partially explains how the near-bankrupt Sears, Roebuck became within ten years the country's first truly national retailer and one of its most profitable and fastest-growing enterprises.

After World War II, another American businessman developed yet another approach to social responsibility. William C. Norris, the founder (in 1957) and, until his retirement in

1986, chairman of Control Data Corporation, saw the solution of social problems and the satisfaction of social needs as opportunities for profitable business. He too was a philanthropist motivated by concern for his fellowman. He picked his projects (skill training and employment in the inner-city ghetto, rehabilitation and training of prisoners, teaching problem learners) by social need rather than by market demand. But he directed his investment and his corporation's human resources where information handling and data processing, his company's expertise, could create a business that, while solving a problem, would become self-sustaining and profitable.

Like Carnegie's philanthropy and Rosenwald's community development, Norris's investments in social needs aimed at creating human capital in the form of individuals capable of performance and of a healthy community able to help itself. But Norris's social enterprises also aimed at creating economic capital. Carnegie's public libraries were strictly philanthropies, though they did create opportunities for individual self-development. Rosenwald's community projects were not business ventures. However much they benefited Sears, Roebuck, they did so indirectly. They were good business, farsighted investments in market development, but not themselves business. Norris's good works or excursions into social problem solving were capital investments in new profit-making businesses, in a stricter sense. He was an entrepreneur.

In its view of social responsibility much of American business and the American public still follow Carnegie. They accept, as he did, that wealth and economic power entail responsibility for the community. The rich man as social reformer, Carnegie's innovation, established a uniquely American institution: the foundation. One after the other of the superrich, from Rockefeller to Ford, followed Carnegie's example. And Carnegie also set the tone for what is now known as the social responsibility of business, a phrase that has become exceedingly popular.

Julius Rosenwald has had far fewer followers. The best

known is probably Rosenwald's own successor as head of Sears, Roebuck, General Robert E. Wood. Even greater perhaps was the impact of James Couzens, cofounder of the Ford Motor Company, for ten years Henry Ford's partner as the company's financial and administrative head, then mayor of Detroit and finally, from 1922 to 1936, U.S. senator from Michigan and, though nominally a Republican, one of the intellectual fathers of the New Deal. Couzens introduced skill training into American industry as a social responsibility of business. A few years later, in 1913, he established, over Henry Ford's strenuous objections, the famous five-dollar-a-day wage—both out of deep compassion for the suffering of an exploited work force and as a highly successful and indeed immediately profitable cure for high rates of absenteeism and turnover that threatened Ford's competitive position.

In our own time J. Irwin Miller of the Cummins Engine Company in Columbus, Indiana, has systematically used corporate funds to create a healthy community that, at the same time, is a direct though intangible investment in a healthy environment for his company. Miller specifically aimed at endowing his small industrial town with the quality of life that would attract to it the managerial and technical people on whom a big high-technology business depends.

The thesis of this essay is that in the years to come the most needed and effective approach to corporate social responsibilities will be that exemplified by William Norris and Control Data Corporation. Only if business learns how to convert the major social challenges facing developed societies today into novel and profitable business opportunities can we hope to surmount these challenges in the future. Government, the agency looked to in recent decades to solve these problems, cannot be depended on. The demands on government are increasingly outrunning the resources it can realistically hope to raise through taxes. Social needs can be solved only if their solution in itself creates new capital, profits, that can then be tapped to initiate the solution for new social needs.

Fundamental changes in technology and society have changed the nature of social needs. Today we are very conscious of *technological change.* Few people realize that what actually is changing are not technologies but the very concept of technology. For three hundred years technology has had for its ultimate model the mechanical phenomena inside a star such as the sun. This development reached its climax with a technology that replicates the mechanical processes inside the sun, that is, with nuclear fission and fusion. Now the dynamics of technology are switching to what might be called an organic model, organized around information rather than around mechanical energy.

Fossil-fuel energy has been a mature, if not declining, industry since 1950, well *before* OPEC and the energy crisis. In all developed countries the ratio of energy usage to gross domestic product has been falling steadily and rapidly since then. Even in sectors that until then still showed an incremental energy growth—private automobiles; aviation, both civilian and military; and residential lighting, heating, and air conditioning—energy consumption per unit of output has been declining since well before 1973 and is almost certain to continue to do so, almost irrespective of cost.

Biological processes progress in terms of information content. The specific energy of biological systems is information. Mechanical systems are organized by the laws of physics; they express forces. Biological systems obey the laws of physics, of course. But they are not organized by forces but by information (for example, the genetic code).

As a consequence, the shift from the mechanical to the biological model calls for a shift in the resource that constitutes capital. Before the mechanical age, animal energy, that is physical exertion, constituted capital. Skill was of course highly prized. But there was so little market for it that it had to be organized as a monopoly, with access strictly controlled through apprenticeship programs and guild regulations. Skill beyond a minimum was simply not employable; there was no market for it. And knowledge was pure luxury.

In the age of the mechanical model, in the last three hundred years, human skill increasingly became the productive resource—one of the greatest advances in human history. This development reached its culmination in this century when mass production converted the laborer into the semiskilled worker. But in an age in which information is becoming the organizing energy the capital resource is knowledge.

This shift in the meaning of technology that is now well underway represents a far more important change than any technological change, no matter how rapid or how spectacular, and deserves even more attention than it gets.

Demographic changes may be even more important. Fortunately the educational explosion of the last fifty years in all developed countries coincided with the shift in technology. In the developed countries now about half of all young people undergo formal schooling beyond secondary school, developing the human resources needed to make the new technology operational, productive, and beneficial. In turn the new technology creates the employment opportunities for the new work force of the developed countries. Which is chicken and which is egg no one, I daresay, could determine.

These changes create major discontinuities and problems. First, in the developed countries there is the transition problem for a labor force trained to operate in the age of the mechanical model and left stranded in the shift to the technology of the biological model. And the remnants of what today we would call preindustrial society—for example, those in the inner-city ghettos or Chicano immigrants fleeing the destitution of over-populated Mexico—who are prepared only to use physical strength as the resource they are getting paid for, are problems in today's developed countries.

Second, between the developed and the poorest countries there is a new and dangerous discontinuity. Up to three hundred years ago there were no "poor countries." There were rich people in every country—not very many—and there were vast hordes of poor people in every country. One hundred dred years later, that is, by 1700, when the new technology of the mechanical model first began to make a difference, the world began to split into rich countries and poor countries. By 1900 average per capita income in the then-developed countries was as much as three times as high as per capita income in the developing countries. By now the gap has widened to an unprecedented and probably unsustainable ten to one, or worse. Today the poorest proletarian in developed countries has a higher standard of living than all but a minute minority of the rich in the poorest countries. The class conflict of earlier times has become a north-south cleavage, if not a source of racial conflict. There is another discrepancy between *developed countries,* that is, countries with a high standard of formal learning, and thus with access to the opportunities of the biological model, and countries that at best can begin to form human skill capital. One-third of humanity, in the developed countries, is ready to exploit the opportunities of the biological model, while two-thirds, in the developing countries, are just entering the stage in which their human resources are prepared for the opportunities of the mechanical model.

Just as the technology of the mechanical model requires a skill base, which is slowly and painfully being built in some of the developing countries, so does the technology of the biological model require a broad knowledge base. This, we now know, cannot be improvised but requires a long period of hard work and above all a capital investment far beyond the means of any but already highly developed countries. Thus for the foreseeable future the world will remain divided into societies with the knowledge base to convert the new technology into major economic and social opportunities and those without the broad base of schooled people on which the technology of the biological model rests and with a surplus of people equipped only for the technologies of the mechanical model.

It is the conjunction of the shifts in technology and demographics that creates the social needs business will have to learn to transform into opportunities.

Developed countries are facing a situation for which there is no parallel in recent economic history. We will have growing labor shortages and at the same time growing unemployment. A large and growing share of the new entrants into the labor force will have sat in school too long to be available for traditional manual, blue-collar work. By 1982 the proportion of Americans who entered the civilian labor force with only an elementary school education was down to about 3 percent. The proportion entering with only a high school education was down to about 50 percent. And the trend is most unlikely to be reversed.

This means that the basic employment problem of the United States and of every other developed country is to create challenging, satisfying, and well-paid jobs for people with so much schooling that they are qualified only for putting knowledge to work. It also means that demand for capital formation in the developed countries will go up rapidly. In particular, jobs for which capital requirements were traditionally lowest, that is in clerical and service areas, will be transformed. Whatever the office of the future will look like, it will be capital-intensive, with capital investment per worker going from a meager $3,000 at present to something like $20,000 or $30,000 within ten years or so. Knowledge jobs, on the average, require a multiple of the capital that manual jobs, on the average, require. They require a high and growing investment in schooling before the individual can begin to contribute, and, increasingly, substantial investment in continuing or refresher education. In other words they require an investment in human resources at least matching that in physical capital.

At the same time there will be redundancies of workers in traditional blue-collar employment. In developed countries traditional blue-collar manual labor will simply not be economical. This is in part because work based on information, whether this be called automation or data processing, will have so much greater value added per unit of effort. Whatever processes can be automated—that is, shifted to an information base—must be automated. Otherwise industry cannot compete, especially with the very large and abundant low-cost labor resources of the Third World. It is almost certain that by the year 2010, that is, within twenty-five years, the proportion of the labor force in the developed countries that is engaged in traditional blue-collar work in manufacturing will be down to what it is now in our most highly scientific and most capital-intensive industry, modern agriculture. Manufacturing blue-collar labor accounts for almost one-fifth of the labor force in all developed countries. But the proportion employed in modern agriculture is about one out of every twenty or less.

For the transition period, the next twenty-five years, there will be highly visible and highly concentrated populations of traditional blue-collar workers who are being made redundant and now have nothing to offer except skill, or, more often, semiskills. That there will at the same time be shortages in certain places of manual, blue-collar workers, because so many entrants into the labor force will have too much education to be interested in blue-collar jobs, will not help these redundant workers. They will not be where the shortages are and will, usually, not have the skills the available jobs demand.

The blue-collar workers who are being made redundant by the shift of manufacturing from work requiring brawn and skill to knowledge-intensive work are typically found in high-wage jobs in the mass-production industries. For the last fifty years these groups have been among the favored groups in industrial society, the groups that have gained the most in economic and social position with the least increase in their actual capacity to perform. They are likely to be older people; younger people move before an industry decays. They are highly concentrated in a very small number of metropolitan areas and thus both visible and politically potent. Eight hundred thousand automobile workers, for instance, are concentrated mostly in twenty counties in the Midwest, from Milwaukee to Dayton and Cleveland, and in only four states. And they tend to be unionized and to act collectively rather than as individuals.

Paradoxically, the labor shortages will be as real as the redundancies. What is needed to bring the two together? Is it training? Is it organized placement? Is it moving industries in need of traditional labor into the areas where the redundancies will occur? Above all, there is need to anticipate redundancies and to organize the systematic placement of individuals in new jobs.

The gap between labor shortages in manufacturing and unemployment in manufacturing may coexist even within the same geographic area. But it will be particularly sharp between different sections of the same country, between different industries and between different wage levels. Unless we succeed in bridging this gap, we will be in grave danger. Instead of promoting the new information-based industries and their employment, which fit the needs and qualifications of the young population, economic policy will focus on maintaining yesterday's employment. We will, in other words, be sorely tempted to follow the example of Great Britain and sacrifice tomorrow on the altar of yesterday—to no avail, of course.

Government cannot tackle this problem, let alone solve it. It is a problem for the entrepreneur who sees in the available labor surplus an opportunity. Government can provide money; the best examples are probably the retraining grants of West Germany, which now amount to 2 percent of West German GNP but, according to some German estimates (for example, those of the West German *Arbeitsministerium*), save as much as four times the amount in unemployment and welfare benefits. But the actual training, to be effective, has to be focused on a specific job the individual can be assured of getting once he reaches the required skill level. It has to be individual rather than general, and it has to be integrated with placement. Government, we have learned in sixty years of work on "distressed industries" and "distressed areas," going back to Lloyd George's first post–World War I cabinet in Great Britain, cannot do either. By its very nature government focuses on large groups rather than on *this* person with *his* or *her* specific skills, background, and needs.

Also the new jobs are likely to be in small and local rather than in big, national business. Since about 1960, unprecedented growth in the American labor force and employment has occurred. The great majority of all new jobs (between two-thirds and three-quarters) has been created in the private sector, not in large, let alone giant, companies, but in businesses employing twenty employees or fewer. During this period employment in the Fortune 500 companies actually declined by 5 percent. And since 1970 the former rapid increase in government employment, federal, state, and local, has leveled off in all developed countries.

Finding workers about to become redundant, identifying their strengths, finding new jobs for them, and retraining them as needed (and often the new skills needed are social rather than technical) are tasks to be done locally and for this reason are business opportunities. But unless redundancy is seen systematically as an opportunity, and above all by existing businesses with the knowledge and capital to act, we will suffer an ever-worsening problem that threatens the future of any developed economy and especially of the American economy.

Several other severe social problem areas, which offer business opportunities, are of particular interest. Within every developed country, and particularly in the United States, there is the problem of the preindustrial population, which in an American context means primarily racial minorities and, above all, the blacks. Only a minority of blacks by now have not been able to acquire the competence needed to become productive in an economy in which brawn is not adequate to provide the kind of living developed societies consider standard. Yet few of the many attempts to educate these groups have lived up to expectations. Part of this failure is due to the fact that training and education succeed only where there is a vision of the future. It is the lack of vision, grounded in decades, if not centuries, of frustration, failure, and discrimination, that prevents education and training from being converted into confidence and motivation.

But we also know that these people work well if the opportunity is provided for them. Until the job is there, there is, however, no motivation for training, no belief that it will lead to a permanent change, and a conviction that this effort too will fail. There is thus a major task of putting human resources to work and developing their competence. Opportunities exist in all kinds of services, if only because the supply of people willing and able to do the work will fall far below the demand, whether in hospitals, in maintenance, or in repair and services of all kinds.

One company that has turned this social problem into an opportunity is based in Denmark. It operates in some fifty countries of the world, mostly developed ones. It systematically finds, trains, and employs preindustrial people for maintenance of office buildings and plants, at good incomes, with a minimum of turnover, and with only one problem: It cannot find enough people to satisfy the demand. It does not "train" people. It employs them, making high demands on performance that then create self-respect and workmanship. It provides career opportunities for advancement within the competence of the individual. This company, which now has sales well in excess of a half billion dollars, started with one small crew less than twenty years ago. The opportunities are there—but is the vision?

Then there is the unprecedented problem of the earthquake fault between the developed countries, with their large supply of highly educated people and shortages of people qualified and prepared for traditional manual work, and the Third World countries in which, in the next fifteen years, unprecedentedly large numbers of young people will reach adulthood prepared and qualified only for traditional blue-collar manual work. These young blue-collar workers will find employment opportunities only if labor-intensive stages of production are moved to where the labor supply is, that is, to the developing countries. Production sharing is the economic integration ahead of us. If it cannot be developed as a successful business opportunity, we face both fast-decreasing standards of living in the developed countries, where traditional manufacturing work cannot be performed both because there is an absolute shortage of labor and because the price of manual labor will become totally noncompetitive, and social catastrophe on a massive scale in the Third World. No society, no matter what its political or social system, whether capitalist or communist, can hope to survive the strains of 40 or 50 percent unemployment among young, able-bodied people prepared for work, and willing to do work, and familiar, if only through television and radio, with the way the rich countries of the world live.

Why shouldn't government do these tasks and tackle these problems? Governments have had to concern themselves with social problems since time immemorial. There were the reforms of the Gracchi in Republican Rome in the second century B.C. and the Poor Laws of Elizabethan England. But as part of a systematic political theory the idea that the solution of social problems is permanently a task of government and one for which no other social institution is fitted dates back only two hundred years. It is a child of the Enlightenment of the eighteenth century; it presupposes a modern civil service and a modern fiscal system. It was first expressed and practiced in the most enlightened of the enlightened despotisms and, so to speak, their development lab, the Hapsburg Grandduchy of Florence where, between 1760 and 1790, the first countrywide hospital system, the first countrywide public health planning, and—first in Europe—a countrywide system of free compulsory schooling were established.

The nineteenth century saw the blossoming of this new idea. From the British Factory Acts of 1844 to Bismarck's social security legislation in the 1880s, one social problem after the other was tackled by governments—and solved triumphantly.

The twentieth century and especially the last fifty years saw this idea elevated to an article of the faith, to the point where a great many people consider it practically immoral and certainly futile for a social need to be tackled any way other than by a government program, and where a substantial majority, only a few years ago, in the heady Kennedy and Johnson years, was convinced that *any* social problem would almost immediately yield to attack by a government program. But the years since then have brought increasing disenchantment. There is now no developed country, whether free enterprise or communist, in which people still expect government programs to succeed.

One reason is surely that government is doing far too many things. By itself a social program accomplishes nothing except the expenditure of money. To have any impact at all such a program requires above all the hard work and dedication of a small number of first-rate people. First-rate people are always in short supply. There may be enough for a very few social programs at any one time (though the two most successful entrepreneurs of social programs with whom I have discussed this, the late Arthur Altmeyer, the father of America's Social Security program, and the late David Lilienthal, the builder of the Tennessee Valley Authority [TVA], both said— and independently—that in their experience there were *at most* enough first-rate people available at any one time in any one country to launch *one* major social program). But under the Johnson administration the United States in four short years tried to launch a half dozen—in addition to fighting a major overseas war!

One might also say that government is congenitally unsuited to the time dimensions of social programs. Government needs immediate results, especially in a democracy where every other year is an election year. The growth curve of social programs is the *hyperbola*: very small, almost imperceptible results for long hard years, followed, if the program is successful, by years of exponential growth. It took eighty years before America's program of agricultural education and research began to revolutionize American farming and farm productivity. It took twenty years before every American at work was covered by Social Security. Would the American electorate have waited twenty, let alone eighty, years before seeing major results from President Johnson's War on Poverty? And yet we know that learning has a long lead time before it shows massive results. Individuals, not classes, learn, and there has to be built up, one by one, a large stock of individuals who have learned, who serve as examples, as leaders, who give encouragement.

Paradoxically, government that finds it hard to start small and to be patient finds it even harder to abandon. Every program immediately creates its own constituency, if only the people who are employed by it. It is easy, all too easy, for modern government to give. It is all but impossible for it to take away. The rule for failures is therefore not to bury them but to redouble the budget and to divert to them the able people who might, if employed on more promising opportunities, produce results.

Furthermore, it is all but impossible for government to experiment. Everything it now does has to be nationwide from the start, and everything has to be finite. But that, in anything new, is a guarantee of failure. It is no coincidence that practically all successful New Deal programs had been pilot tested as small-scale experiments in states and cities over the preceding twenty years—in Wisconsin, New York State, New York City, or by one of the Chicago reform administrations. The two total New Deal failures, the National Recovery Administration (NRA) and the Works Progress Administration (WPA), were also the only genuine inventions without prior experiment at the state or local level.

Surely William Norris was right when he spoke of his company's social business enterprises as research and development. Long lead times, willingness to experiment, and to abandon in case of nonresults are precisely the characteristics of research and development work. But R & D is, we now know, not done well by government, for a variety of well-studied reasons. It is done best in autonomous institutions, whether university laboratory, individual hospital, or business laboratory, although the provider or source of the funds might well be government.

Equally important as an explanation for the inability of government to tackle successfully the kind of social problems we face is that they are *hard* problems. A hard problem is one in which there are so many constituencies that it is difficult, if not impossible, to set specific goals and targets. It is perhaps here that the social problems of the mid-twentieth century differ most fundamentally from those of the eighteenth and nineteenth centuries. But the problems we face in the decades ahead will be even harder than those we now handle so poorly. Each of them has powerful constituencies with radically different, indeed mutually exclusive, goals and values, which practically guarantee that government could not succeed in solving them.

"Reindustrializing America," for instance, means to the labor union preserving traditional blue-collar jobs in traditional industries in central cities or at least slowing the shrinkage of traditional jobs. However, if *reindustrializing* America means restoring the country's capacity to increase the output of manufactured goods and to compete internationally, it unambiguously means the fastest possible automation of traditional processes and in all probability a shift to new and decentralized locations. It means liquidating Big Steel in Pittsburgh and Chicago and shifting to minimills near customers. The first definition is politically acceptable for a short time. But it can lead only to failure, as the British and the Polish examples show. But can any *government* program embrace the second definition? Even the Japanese, who reportedly invest in winners and starve losers (at least according to a currently popular American myth), are finding that it cannot be done politically. Indeed the Japanese have found that they cannot give up support of a retail distribution system that everyone in Japan knows to be obsolete and frightfully expensive but the only social security for a fairly small group of older people.

Nongovernmental institutions, whether businesses or institutions of the rapidly growing nonprofit third sector, can, however, direct themselves to a single objective. They can break down hard problems into several easy problems, each capable of solution or, at least, of alleviation. And because nongovernmental institutions can and do compete with each other, they can develop alternate approaches. They can experiment.

The increasing inability of government to tackle effectively the social needs of contemporary society creates a major opportunity for nongovernmental institutions and especially for the most flexible and most diverse of nongovernmental institutions: business. Increasingly, even countries organized on what are proclaimed to be socialist principles will have to "privatize." It will be necessary, in other words, to create conditions under which a task is outlined by government and the means to perform the task are provided for either by government (as for instance in the case of the rapidly growing private health-care insurance in Britain, which is reimbursed by the National Health Service) or by third-party payors, but in which a task is actually performed by nongovernmental institutions, especially business, locally and on a competitive basis.

A good example is the American communication system, in which increasingly the tasks exclusively done fifty years ago by the post office are now carried out by a host of agencies competing with one another and with the postal service. Quite clearly, garbage removal, health care, and many other services will become privatized in such a way that the service itself is grounded in public policy and law (if only through tax advantages), while the performance is the task of competitive private business enterprises.

The true mixed economy of the future will consist of three parts. There will be a *private sector* in which government limits itself to protection against fraud, extreme exploitation, collusion, unsafe working conditions, and deprivation of civil rights. There will be a true *public sector,* for defense (excluding procurement) and justice, in which government will both specify the job and do it. And there will be a *mixed sector,* the best example being the American hospital system, which is primarily a private system. Nonprofit community hospitals, church-affiliated hospitals, and proprietary-for-profit hospitals are increasingly organized in large and growing chains. All then compete for patients. Yet most of their income is public money, whether it comes directly from the government via the tax system or through compulsory private health insurance plans. Another well-known example is defense procurement.

In most discussions of the social responsibility of business it is assumed that making a profit is fundamentally incompatible with social responsibility or is at least irrelevant to it. Business is seen as the rich man who should, if only for the good of his soul, give alms to the less fortunate.

Most people who discuss social responsibility, including its opponents, would be exceedingly suspicious of any business that asserts, as does for instance William Norris, that it is the purpose of business to do well by doing good. To those hostile to business, who believe that profit is a "rip-off," this would appear the grossest hypocrisy. But even to those who are pro-business and who then, as did Andrew Carnegie, demand that business, the rich man, give alms and become a philanthropist, doing good in order to do well would not be acceptable. It would convert what is seen as virtue into self-interest. And for those who counsel business to stick to its last and to leave social problems and issues to the proper authorities, which in fact means to government (this is where Milton Friedman stands), the self-interest of business and the public good are seen as two quite separate spheres. But in the next decade it will become increasingly important to stress that business can discharge its social responsibilities only if it converts them into self-interest —that is, into business opportunities.

The *first* social responsibility of business in the next decade will be one not mentioned in the discussion of the social responsibilities of business today. It is the increasingly important responsibility for creating the capital that alone can finance tomorrow's jobs. The shift from the mechanical model of technology to the organic model will require substantial increase in capital investment per worker. The demand for capital formation will be as great as the demand was a hundred years ago when today's modern industries emerged; and there will be equal need for a surplus to pay for the R&D needed when technology, as well as the world economy and society, is rapidly changing.

We have been in a phase in which existing technologies were extended and modified with fairly low marginal costs, as a result of which there was a fairly low need for capital formation. Now we are well past that stage. To be sure, old industries are still declining or are being restructured, but more important, new industries are exploding: information, communication, biochemistry, bioengineering, and genetic medicine, for example. And with them emerge other new industries, such as the continuing education of already well-educated adults, which may well be the major growth industry of the next ten years and which increasingly is in the hands of entrepreneurs.

The early growth stages make the greatest demands on capital formation. But what does *capital formation* actually mean, especially in a modern society in which the traditional incentives to personal savings have largely been eliminated? Savings rates in all countries tend to go down with two factors: one, an increase in the proportion of the population past retirement age, who as a rule do not tend to save but who primarily consume; and two, the degree to which Social Security takes care of the risks and contingencies for which individuals traditionally save. One example is the United States, where savings rates have gone down in direct proportion to both the aging of the population and the extension of social services to cover such risks as retirement, illness, and unemployment. Another is Japan. In the last ten years the savings rate in Japan has been going down steadily, although it is still high.

Furthermore we now have conclusive proof that rising income levels for wage-earning families do not materially increase the savings rate. We know that new consumer needs, rather than investment, take over. As a result, in a modern economy the main source of capital formation is *business profits.* Indeed we now know that the term *profit* is a misunderstanding. There are only costs—costs of the past and costs of the future; the costs of economic, social, and technical change; and the costs of tomorrow's jobs. Present revenues must cover both, and both costs are likely to go up sharply in the next twenty years.

The first social responsibility of business thus is to make enough profit to cover the costs of the future. If this social responsibility is not met, no other social responsibility can be met. Decaying businesses in a decaying economy are unlikely to be good neighbors, good employers, or socially responsible in any way. When the demand for capital grows rapidly, surplus business revenues available for noneconomic purposes, especially for philanthropy, cannot possibly go up. They are almost certain to shrink.

This argument will not satisfy those who believe that today's businessman should become the successor to yesterday's prince, a delusion to which businessmen unfortunately are themselves only too susceptible. But princes were able to be benefactors because they first took it away, and, of course, mostly from the poor.

There are also those, again especially among businessmen, who feel that to convert problems into business opportunities is prosaic and not particularly romantic. They see business as the dragon slayer and themselves as St. Georges on white chargers.

But the proper social responsibility of business is to tame the dragon—that is, to turn a social problem into economic opportunity and economic benefit, into productive capacity, into human competence, into well-paid jobs, and into wealth.

[1984]

AFTERWORD

Social Innovation— Management's New Dimension

Are we overemphasizing science and technology as this century's change agents? *Social innovations*—few of them owing anything to science or technology—may have had even profounder impacts on society and economy, and indeed profound impacts even on science and technology themselves. And management is increasingly becoming the agent of social innovation.

Here are five examples—five among many:

the research lab;
Eurodollar and commercial paper;
mass and mass movement;
the farm agent; and
management itself as an organized function and discipline.

≫ *The Research Lab*

The research lab as we now know it dates back to 1905. It was conceived and built for the General Electric Company in Schenectady, New York, by one of the earliest "research managers," the German-American physicist Charles Proteus Steinmetz. Steinmetz had two clear objectives from the start: to organize science and scientific work for purposeful technological invention and to build continuous self-renewal through innovation into that new social phenomenon—the big corporation.

Steinmetz took two of the features of his new lab from nineteenth-century predecessors. From the German engineer, Hefner-Alteneck, he took the idea of setting up within a company a separate group of scientifically and technically trained people to devote themselves exclusively to scientific and technical work—something Hefner-Alteneck had pioneered in 1872 in the Siemens Company in Berlin five years after he had joined it as the first college-trained engineer to be hired anywhere by an industrial company. From Thomas Alva Edison, Steinmetz took the *research project*: the systematic organization of research, beginning with a clear definition of the expected end result and identification of the steps in the process and of their sequence.

But Steinmetz then added three features of his own. First, his researchers were to work in teams. Hefner-Alteneck's "designers"—the term *researcher* came much later—had worked the way scientists worked in the nineteenth-century university, each in his own lab with a helper or two who ran errands for the "boss," looked up things for him, or, at most, carried out experiments the boss had specified. In Steinmetz's lab there were seniors and juniors rather than bosses and helpers. They worked as colleagues, each making his own contribution to a common effort. Steinmetz's teams thus required a research director to assign researchers to projects and projects to researchers.

Second, Steinmetz brought together on the same team people of diverse skills and disciplines—engineers, physicists, mathematicians, chemists, even biologists. This was brand-new and heretical. Indeed, it violated the most sacred principle of nineteenth-century scientific organization: the principle of maximum specialization. But the first Nobel Prize awarded to a scientist in industrial research was awarded in 1932 to a chemist, Irving Langmuir, who worked in Steinmetz's electrotechnical lab.

Finally, Steinmetz's lab radically redefined the relationship between science and technology in research. In setting the goals of his project, Steinmetz identified the new theoretical science needed to accomplish the desired technological results and then organized the appropriate "pure" research to obtain the needed new knowledge. Steinmetz himself was originally a theoretical physicist; on a recent U.S. postage stamp he is being honored for his "contributions to electrical theory." But every one of his "contributions" was the result of research he had planned and specified as part of a project to design and to develop a new product line, for example, fractional horsepower motors. Technology, traditional wisdom held and still widely holds, is "applied science." In Steinmetz's lab science—including the purest of "pure research"—is *technology-driven,* that is, a means to a technological end.

Ten years after Steinmetz completed the General Electric lab, the famed Bell Labs were established on the same pattern. A little later du Pont followed suit, and then IBM. In developing what eventually became nylon, du Pont worked out a good deal of the pure science for polymer chemistry. In the 1930s when IBM started to develop what eventually became the computer, it included from the beginning research in switching theory, solid-state physics, and computer logic in its engineering project.

Steinmetz's innovation also led to the "lab without walls," which is America's specific, and major, contribution to very large scientific and technological programs. The first of these, conceived and managed by President Franklin D. Roosevelt's former law partner, Basil O'Connor, was the National Foundation for Infantile Paralysis (March of Dimes), which tackled polio in the early 1930s. This project continued for more than twenty-five years and brought together in a planned, step-by-step effort a large number of scientists from half a dozen disciplines, in a dozen different locations across the country, each working on his own project but within a central strategy and under overall direction. This then established the pattern for the great World War II projects: the RADAR lab, the Lincoln Laboratory and, most massive of them all, the Manhattan Project for atomic energy. Similarly, NASA organized a "research lab without walls" when this country decided, after Sputnik, to put a man on the moon. Steinmetz's technology-driven science is still highly controversial, is indeed anathema to many academic scientists. Still, it is the organization we immediately reach for whenever a new scientific problem emerges, for example, when AIDS suddenly became a major medical problem in 1984–85.

≫ Eurodollar and Commercial Paper

In fewer than twenty years, the financial systems of the world have changed more perhaps than in the preceding two hundred. The change agents were two social innovations: the Eurodollar and the use of commercial paper as a new form of "commercial loan." The first created a new world economy, dominated by the "symbol" economy of capital flows, exchange rates, and credits. The second triggered the "financial revolution" in the United States. It has replaced the old, and seemingly perennial, segmentation of financial institutions into insurance companies, savings banks, commercial banks, stock brokers, and so on, by "financial supermarkets," each focused on whatever financial services the market needs rather than on specific financial products. And this financial revolution is now spreading worldwide.

Neither the Eurodollar nor commercial paper was designed as "revolutionary." The Eurodollar was invented by the Soviet Union's State Bank when General Eisenhower was elected president of the United States in 1952, in the middle of the Korean War. The Russians feared that the new president would embargo their dollar deposits in American banks to force them to stop supporting the North Koreans. They thus hurriedly withdrew these deposits from American banks. Yet they wanted to keep their money in American dollars. The solution they found was the *Eurodollar*: a deposit denominated in U.S. currency but kept in a bank outside the United States. And this then created, within twenty years, a new supranational money and capital market. It is outside and beyond the control of national central banks, and indeed totally unregulated. Yet in its totality—and there are now Euroyen and Euro-Swiss-francs and Euromark in addition to Eurodollars— it is larger in both deposits and turnover than the deposits and turnover of the banking and credit systems of all major trading nations taken together. Indeed, without this innovation on the part of the overseas executives of the Soviet State Bank—every one undoubtedly a good Communist—capitalism might not have survived. It made possible the enormous expansion of world trade, which has been the engine of economic growth and prosperity in the developed free enterprise countries these last thirty years.

At about the same time, perhaps a little later, two American financial institutions—one a brokerage house, Goldman Sachs, the other a finance company, General Electric Credit Corporation (founded to provide credit to the buyers of General Electric's electrical machinery)—hit on the idea of using an old but totally obscure financial instrument, the "commercial paper," as a new form of *commercial loan,* that is, as a substitute for bank credit. Neither institution is allowed under American financial regulations to make commercial loans— only banks are. But *commercial paper,* essentially simply a promise to pay a certain amount at a certain date, is not considered a loan in American law but a security, and this, in turn, banks are not permitted to issue. Economically, however, there is not the slightest difference between the two—something which nobody had, however, seen earlier. By exploiting this legal technicality these two firms, and dozens of others following them in short order, managed to outflank the seemingly impregnable lending monopoly of the commercial banks, especially as credit based on commercial paper can be provided at substantially lower interest rates than banks can lend money against customers' deposits. The banks at first dismissed commercial paper as a mere gimmick. But within fifteen years it had abolished most, if not all, of the demarcation lines and barriers between all kinds of credits and investments in the American economy to the point that, today, practically every financial institution and every financial instrument competes with every other institution and every other financial instrument.

For almost two hundred years economists have considered the financial and credit system to be the central core of an economy, and its most important feature. In every country it is hedged in by laws, rules, and regulations, all designed to preserve the system and to prevent any changes in it. And nowhere was the financial system more highly structured and more carefully guarded than in the United States. Commercial paper—little but a change in a term and almost insignificant as an innovation—has broken through all safeguards of law, regulation, and custom and has subverted the American financial system. We still rank the country's banks. But although New York's Citibank is surely the country's largest bank—and altogether the country's largest "financial institution"—the "number-two bank" is probably not a bank at all, but General Electric Credit Corporation. And Walter Wriston, the long-time chairman of Citibank, points out that Citibank's biggest competitor in banking and finance is not a financial institution at all but Sears, Roebuck, the country's largest department store chain, which now gives more consumer credit than any credit institution.

≫ Mass and Mass Movement

A third social innovation of this century are mass and mass movements. The *mass* is a collective. It has a behavior of its own and an identity of its own. It is not irrational; on the contrary, it is highly predictable. But its dynamics are what in an individual we would call "the subconscious."

The essence of the *mass movement* is concentration. Its individual "molecules," the individuals who comprise it, are what a chemist calls highly organized and highly charged. They all point in the same direction, all carry the same charge. In the nuclear physicist's terms, the mass is a *critical mass,* that is, the smallest fraction big enough to alter the nature and behavior of the whole.

The mass was first invented—for it was an invention and not just a discovery—in the closing years of the nineteenth century when, exploiting the then brand-new literacy, two Americans, Joseph Pulitzer and William Randolph Hearst, created the first mass medium, the cheap, mass-circulation newspaper. Until then a newspaper was meant to be "written by gentlemen for gentlemen," as the masthead of one of the London newspapers proudly proclaimed for many years. Pulitzer's and Hearst's "yellow press" by contrast was sneered at as "being written by pimps for guttersnipes." But it created a mass readership and a mass following.

These two men and their newspapers then created and led the first modern political mass movement, the campaign to force the United States into the Spanish-American War of 1898. The tactics that these two men developed have since become standard for all mass movements. They did not even try to win over the majority as earlier American movements—the abolitionists or the Free Soilers, for instance—had done. On the contrary, they tried to organize a minority of true believers: they probably never attracted more than 10 percent of the electorate. But they organized this following as a disciplined "shock troop" around the single cause of fighting Spain. They urged their readers in every issue to clip out and mail a postcard to their congressman demanding that America declare war on Spain. And they made a candidate's willingness to commit himself on the war issue the *sole* criterion for endorsing or opposing him regardless of his position on any other issue. Thus, their small minority had the "swing vote" and could claim control of the political future of the candidates. In the end it imposed its will on the great majority, even though almost every opinion maker in the country was opposed.

A mass movement is powerful precisely because the majority has a diversity of interests all over the lot and is thus lukewarm in regard to all of them and zealous in respect to none. The single cause gives the mass movement its discipline and its willingness to follow a leader. It thus makes it stand out and appear much bigger than it really is. It enables a single cause to dominate the news and, indeed, largely to determine what is news. And because it makes its support of parties and candidates totally dependent on their willingness or unwillingness to commit themselves to the single cause, it may cast the deciding vote.

The first to apply what Pulitzer and Hearst had invented to a permanent "crusade" was the temperance movement. For almost a century such temperance groups as the Anti-Saloon League and the Women's Christian Temperance Union had struggled and campaigned without much success. Around 1900 their support was probably at its lowest level since the Civil War. And then they adopted the new tactics of the mass movement. The Women's Christian Temperance Union even hired several of Pulitzer's and Hearst's editors. The "true believers" in Prohibition never numbered more than 5 or 10 percent of the electorate. But in less than twenty years they had Prohibition written into the Constitution.

Since then, single causes—the environment, automobile safety, nuclear disarmament, gay rights, the Moral Majority— have become commonplace. But we are only now beginning to realize how profoundly the single-cause mass movement has changed the politics of all democratic countries.

And outside of the United States the social innovation of the mass has had even greater impacts. The great tyrannies of this century—Lenin's and Stalin's Bolsheviks, Mussolini's Fascism, Hitler's Nazism, even Maoism—are all applications of the mass movement, the highly disciplined single-cause minority of true believers, to the ultimate political goal of gaining and holding power.

Surely no discovery or invention of this century has had

greater impact than the social innovation of mass and mass movement. Yet none is less understood.

Indeed, in respect to the mass we are today pretty much where we were in respect to the psychodynamics of the individual a hundred years ago. Of course we knew of the "passions." But they were something one could only explain away as part of "animal nature." They lay outside the *rational,* that is, outside prediction, analysis, and understanding. All one could do was to suppress them. And then, beginning a hundred years ago, Freud showed that the passions have their reasons, that indeed, in Pascal's famous phrase, "the heart has its reasons of which Reason knows nothing." Freud showed that the subconscious is as strictly rational as the conscious, that it has its own logic and its own mechanisms. And although not all psychologists today—indeed, not even the majority—accept the specific causative factors of Freudian psychoanalysis, all accept Freud's psychodynamics of the individual.

But so far we still lack a Sigmund Freud of the mass.

≫ *The Farm Agent*

The single, most important *economic* event of this century is surely the almost exponential rise in farm production and farm productivity worldwide (except, of course, in the *Soviet Union*). It was brought about primarily through a social innovation of the early years of this century: the farm agent.

Karl Marx, a hundred years ago, had good reason for his dismissal of the "peasant" as hopelessly ignorant and hopelessly unproductive. Indeed, practically every nineteenth-century observer shared Marx's contempt. By 1880, serious, systematic scientific work on agricultural methods and agricultural technology had been going on for two hundred years. Even the systematic training of farmers and agronomists in an "agricultural university" had been started one hundred years earlier. Yet only a very small number of large landowners were paying any attention. The vast majority of farmers—practically all American farmers, for instance—did not, in 1880, farm any differently, farm any better, or produce any more than their ancestors had done for centuries. And twenty years later, around 1900, things still had not changed.

And then, suddenly, around the time of World War I— maybe a little later—things changed drastically. The change began in the United States. By now it has spread everywhere; indeed, the surge in farm production and farm productivity has become most pronounced in Third World countries such as India.

What happened was not that farmers suddenly changed their spots. What happened was a social innovation that put the new agricultural knowledge within farmers' reach. Julius Rosenwald, the chief executive of a mail-order company, Sears, Rocbuck, himself a Chicago clothing merchant and the purest of "city slickers," invented the farm agent (and for ten years paid farm agents out of his own pocket until the U.S. government took over the Farm Extension Service). He did not do this out of philanthropy alone, but primarily to create purchasing power among his company's customers, the American farmers. The farm agent provided what had hitherto been lacking: a conduit from the steadily increasing pool of agricultural knowledge and information to the practitioners on the farm. And within a few short years the "ignorant, reactionary, tradition-steeped peasant" of Marx's time had become the "farm technologist" of the "scientific revolution on the farm."

≫ Management

My last example of a social innovation is management. "Managers," of course, have been around a long time. The term itself is, however, of twentieth-century coinage. And it is only in this century, and largely within the last fifty years, that management has emerged as a generic function of society, as a distinct kind of work, and as a discipline. A century ago most major tasks, including the economic task we call business, were done mainly in and by the family or by family-run enterprises such as the artisan's small workshop. By now all of them have become organized in institutions: government agency and university, hospital, business enterprise, Red Cross, labor union, and so on. And all of them have to be managed. *Management* is thus the specific function of today's "society of organizations." It is the specific practice that converts a mob into an effective, purposeful, and productive group.

Management and organization have become global rather than Western or capitalist. The Japanese introduced management as an organized discipline in the early 1950s, and it became the foundation for their spectacular economic and social successes. Management is a very hot topic in the Soviet Union. And one of the first moves of the Chinese after the retreat from Maoism was to set up an Enterprise Management Agency in the prime minister's office and import an American-style management school.

The essence of modern organization is to make individual strengths and knowledge productive and to make individual weaknesses irrelevant. In traditional organizations—the ones that built the pyramids and the Gothic cathedrals, or in the armies of the eighteenth and nineteenth centuries—everybody did exactly the same unskilled jobs in which brute strength was the main contribution. Such knowledge as existed was concentrated at the top and in very few heads.

In modern organizations everybody has specialized and fairly advanced knowledge and skill. In the modern organization there are the metallurgist and the Red Cross disaster specialist, the trainer and the tool designer, the fund raiser and the physical therapist, the budget analyst and the computer programmer, all doing their work, all contributing their knowledge, but all working toward a joint end. The little each knows matters; the infinity each doesn't know, does not.

The two cultures today may not be those of the humanist and the scientist as C. P. Snow, the English physicist turned novelist, proclaimed thirty years ago. They may be the cultures of what might be called the *literati* and the *managers*: The one sees reality as ideas and symbols; the other sees reality as performance and people.

Management and organization are still quite primitive. As is common in a rapidly evolving discipline—as was true, for instance, in medicine until fairly recently—the gap between the leading practitioners and the great majority is enormously wide and is closing but slowly. Far too few, even of the most accomplished of today's managers in all organizations, realize that management is defined by responsibility and not by power. Far too few fight the debilitating disease of bureaucracy: the belief that big budgets and a huge staff are accomplishments rather than incompetence.

Still, the impact has been enormous. Management and its emergence have, for instance, rendered equally obsolete both social theories that dominated the nineteenth century and its political rhetoric: the Jeffersonian creed that sees society moving toward a crystalline structure of independent small owners —the yeoman on his forty acres, the artisan in his workshop, the shopkeeper who owns his own store, the independent professional—and the Marxist theorem of a society inexorably turning into an amorphous gas of equally impoverished, equally disenfranchised proletarians. Instead, organization has created an employee society. In the employee society, blue-collar workers are a steadily shrinking minority. Knowledge workers are the new and growing majority—both the main cost and the main resource of all developed societies. And although knowledge workers are employees, they are not proletarians but, through their pension funds, the only capitalists and, collectively, the owners of the means of production.

It is management which in large measure accounts for this century's most extraordinary social phenomenon: the educational explosion. The more highly schooled people are, the more dependent they then become on organizations. Practically all people with schooling beyond high school, in all developed countries—in the United States the figure is 90 percent plus—will spend all their working lives as employees of managed organizations and could not make their living without them. Neither could their teachers.

≫ *Conclusion*

If this were a history of social innovation in the twentieth century, I would have to cite and to discuss scores of additional examples. But this is not the purpose of this essay. The purpose is not even to show the importance of social innovation. It is, above all, to show that social innovation in the twentieth century has largely become the task of the manager.

This was not always the case; on the contrary, it is quite new.

The act that, so to speak, ushered in the nineteenth century was an innovation: the American Constitution. Constitutions were, of course, nothing new; they go back to ancient Greece. But the American Constitution was different: It first provided expressly a process for its own change. Every earlier constitution had been presumed unchangeable and an "eternal verity." And then the Americans created in the Supreme Court a mechanism to adapt the Constitution to new conditions and demands. These two innovations explain why the American Constitution has survived where all earlier ones perished after a short life of total frustration.

A hundred years later, Prince Bismarck in Germany created, without any precedent, the social innovations we now call *Social Security*—health insurance, old-age pensions, and workmen's compensation insurance against industrial accidents, which were followed a little later by unemployment compensation. Bismarck knew exactly what he was trying to do: defuse a "class war" that threatened to tear asunder the very fabric of society. And he succeeded. Within fifteen years, socialism in Western and Northern Europe had ceased to be "revolutionary" and had become "revisionist."

Outside of the West, the nineteenth century produced the tremendous social innovations of the Meiji Restoration in Japan, which enabled the least Western and most isolated of all contemporary countries both to become a thoroughly "modern" state and nation and to maintain its social and cultural identity.

The nineteenth century was thus a period of very great social innovation. But, with only a few exceptions, social innovations in the nineteenth century were made by governments. *Invention,* that is, technical discovery, the nineteenth century left to the private sector. Social innovation was governmental and a political act.

Somehow, in this century, government seems to have lost its ability to do effective social innovation. It could still do it in America's New Deal in the 1930s, although the only New Deal innovations that worked were things that had been designed and thoroughly tested earlier, often before World War I, in the large-scale "pilot experiments" conducted by individual states such as Wisconsin, New York, and California. Since then, however, we have had very few governmental innovations in any developed country that have produced the results for which they were designed—very few indeed that have produced any results except massive costs.

Instead, social innovation has been taken over by the private, nongovernmental sector. From being a political act it has become a "managerial task." We still have little methodology for it, though we now do possess a "discipline of innovation." Few social innovators in management yet know what they intend to accomplish the way the American Founding Fathers, Bismarck, and the statesmen of Meiji did—though the examples of Rosenwald's farm agent would indicate that it can be done. Still, social innovation has clearly become management's new dimension.

[1986]

Acknowledgments

Thirty-five of the articles and essays in this volume have already been published. Twenty-five of the twenty-six short pieces have appeared on the editorial page of *The Wall Street Journal* (Chapters 2–11, 14–17, 19–20, 22–26, 29–32). The twenty-sixth of the short pieces (Chapter 18) originally appeared in *The Chronicle of Higher Education.* Of the longer pieces, two (Chapters 28 and 34) appeared in *The Public Interest,* one each, respectively, in *Inc.* magazine (Interview), *Foreign Affairs* (Chapter 1), *Forbes* (Chapter 12), *Harvard Business Review* (Chapter 13), *Connections,* the magazine of the Claremont Graduate School (Chapter 27), and *Esquire* (Chapter 33). Chapter 35 was originally presented as a paper at a symposium sponsored by the American Academy of Arts and Sciences in Minneapolis, Minnesota, in the summer of 1982 and then published in *Public-Private Partnership,* edited for the American Academy of Arts and Sciences by Harvey Brooks, Lance Liebman, Corrine S. Schelling (Cambridge, Mass.: Ballinger Publishing Co., 1984). Chapter 21, "Management: The Problems of

Success," was presented in an abridged version at the Fiftieth Anniversary Meeting of the American Academy of Management in Chicago, Illinois, in August 1986 but has not been previously published. The Afterword, finally, was written especially for this volume and has not been published or presented earlier.

In preparing the articles and essays for publication in this volume I have changed some of the titles and shortened lengthy introductions. And throughout the volume I have replaced "this year" or "last year" with the appropriate calendar year, such as 1984 or 1983. Otherwise I have not tampered with the original text. The reader can thus decide whether the author's predictions and conclusions have stood the test of time.

This volume and I owe an enormous debt to Truman M. Talley of Truman Talley Books/E. P. Dutton. Several years ago Mr. Talley edited and published an earlier volume of my articles and essays (*The Changing World of the Executive,* New York: Truman Talley Books/Times Books, 1982). He then suggested that I focus subsequent articles and essays on the frontiers of management, that is, on those issues and areas where today's decisions are shaping tomorrow. The pieces themselves were of course written for specific occasions and for specific publications. But thanks to Mr. Talley, all along I had an underlying theme and a unifying focus. He then devoted a great deal of time and effort selecting and organizing the book's structure and sequence, overseeing its physical appearance, and guiding it throughout the publication process. I can only hope that the finished product lives up to his high expectations. And thanks are also owing to Trent Duffy, managing editor, and Julia McGown, production editor, of E. P. Dutton, who supervised the transformation of a messy manuscript into a beautiful book and did so in record time.

INDEX